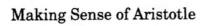

Making Sense of Aristotle

MAKING SENSE OF ARISTOTLE

Essays in Poetics

Edited by

Øivind Andersen

and

Jon Haarberg

Duckworth

This impression 2003
First published in 2001 by
Gerald Duckworth & Co. Ltd.
90-93 Cowcross Street, London EC1M 6BF
Tel: 020 7490 7300
Fax: 020 7490 0080
inquiries@duckworth-publishers.co.uk
www.ducknet.co.uk

A catalogue record for this book is available
from the British Library

ISBN 0 7156 3131 4

Printed in Great Britain by
Antony Rowe Ltd, Eastbourne

Contents

List of Contributors   vii

Making Sense of Aristotle's *Poetics*
  Øivind Andersen and Jon Haarberg   1
Aristotle and the Pleasures of Tragedy
  Malcolm Heath   7
Dramatic and Epic Time: 'Magnitude' and 'Length' in
  Aristotle's *Poetics*
  Elizabeth Belfiore   25
Aristotle on Comedy, Aristophanes and Some New Evidence
  from Herculaneum
  Richard Janko   51
Mimesis in Aristotle's Ethics
  Hallvard Fossheim   73
Aristotelian Mimesis and Human Understanding
  Stephen Halliwell   87
Roman Tragedy and the Teaching of Aristotle's *Poetics*
  Elaine Fantham   109
On the Rise of Genre-specific Poetics in the Sixteenth Century
  Daniel Javitch   127
Poetic Marvels: Aristotelian Wonder in Renaissance Poetics
  and Poetry
  Kirsti Minsaas   145
Aristotle, Rapin, Brecht
  M.S. Silk   173
The Afterlife of the *Poetics*
  Terence Cave   197

Select Bibliography   215
Index Locorum   219
General Index   225

Contributors

Øivind Andersen, Professor of Classics at the University of Oslo, is the author of *Die Diomedesgestalt in der Ilias* (1978) and *Im Garten der Rhetorik* (2001).

Elizabeth Belfiore is Professor of Classics at the University of Minnesota. She is the author of *Tragic Pleasures: Aristotle on Plot and Emotion* (1992) and *Murder among Friends: Violation of Philia in Greek Tragedy* (2000).

Elaine Fantham, Giger Professor of Latin emerita of Princeton University, is the author of *Roman Literary Culture* (1996) and commentaries on works of Ovid, Seneca and Lucan. She is currently working on a study of Cicero's *de Oratore*.

Terence Cave is Professor of French Literature, St John's College, Oxford. Among his major publications are *The Cornucopian Text: Problems of Writing in the French Renaissance* (1979), *Recognitions: A Study in Poetics* (1988), and an edition of George Eliot's *Daniel Deronda* (1995).

Hallvard Fossheim is Research Fellow in Philosophy at the University of Oslo. His Norwegian language publications include studies on Socrates, Plato and Aristotle.

Jon Haarberg is Associate Professor of Comparative Literature at the University of Oslo. His books include *Nature and Language* (with Ralf Norrman, 1980) and *Parody and the Praise of Folly* (1998).

Stephen Halliwell is Professor of Greek in the University of St Andrews. His publications include *Aristotle's Poetics* (1986/1998), *The Poetics of Aristotle: Translation and Commentary* (1987) and the new Loeb translation of the *Poetics* (1995).

Malcolm Heath is Professor of Greek at the University of Leeds. He is the editor of the Penguin Classics *Aristotle: Poetics* (1996), and his works include *The Poetics of Greek Tragedy* (1987) and *Unity in Greek Poetics* (1989).

Richard Janko, Professor of Greek in the University of London, is the author of *Aristotle on Comedy* (1984) and of *Aristotle: Poetics I* (1987).

Daniel Javitch is Professor of Comparative Literature at New York University, and the author of *Proclaiming a Classic: the Canonization of Orlando Furioso* (1991). Italian thinking about poetic genres in the sixteenth century will be the subject of his next book.

Kirsti Minsaas is Research Fellow in English Literature at the University of Oslo. Her chief publication is *Woe or Wonder: The Structure of Tragic Experience in Shakespeare's* Hamlet *and* Othello (1999).

M.S. Silk is Professor of Greek Language and Literature in the University of London at King's College. His works include *Nietzsche on Tragedy* (with J.P. Stern, 1981) and *Tragedy and the Tragic* (1996).

Making Sense of Aristotle's *Poetics*

Øivind Andersen and Jon Haarberg

Editing a book like this, we are, willy-nilly, confronted by the disquieting question of scholarly progress. Do we advance in our efforts trying to make sense of Aristotle? Can we, as Montaigne wondered, 'see any progress or advance towards serenity?'[1] Or is this book just another attempt at aligning an authoritative 2,300-year-old Greek treatise on poetics with our own concerns, with the critical preoccupations of the present? It might seem un-Aristotelian to answer both questions in the affirmative, but do we have a choice?

Scholarly interest in the *Poetics* appears to have grown steadily during the course of the twentieth century. Some eighty years ago, the distinguished Aristotelian Sir David Ross ranked the *Poetics* as 'the most living' of Aristotle's works.[2] Whatever he may have meant by 'living' – that the *Poetics* was widely read, that it seemed relevant compared to other Aristotelian works, that it simply made a difference – it is beyond dispute that this tiny fragment of the great *Corpus Aristotelicum* continued to exert its influence on the ways in which we relate to literature as readers and teachers, scholars and critics. Omert Schrier's printed bibliography, covering the period 900-1996, clearly shows that the number of publications specifically devoted to the *Poetics* since the 1920s has been increasing markedly, decade by decade. Generalising Ross's statement, Schrier claims that the *Poetics* is 'the only piece of technical writing from Antiquity that still plays a role in scholarly discourse'.[3] What his bibliography does not document, however, are the thousands of critical papers employing *mimesis*, *anagnorisis* and *katharsis* as household words, students' essays examining plot structures according to the criteria of probability and necessity, everyday conversations about the effect of tragedy and comedy, and so on. The history of the reception of the *Poetics* in the West is as overwhelming as it is complex, which may perhaps explain why no one has yet ventured to give a full account of it.[4]

Admittedly, it is difficult not to assume that scholarship makes progress, that we have a better understanding of the *Poetics* today than eighty years ago. At least if we broaden our field of vision and consider

1

the question again in a 500-year perspective it seems patently obvious that considerable progress has been made: Georgio Valla, who in 1498 published a version of the *Poetics* in Latin – the first ever printed version, irrespective of language – definitely made mistakes, partly, however, due to a corrupt text: in the well-known definition of tragedy, for example (ch. 6), his manuscript read *mathêmatôn* (lessons) instead of *pathêmatôn* (emotions); no wonder he ran into difficulties. Only one generation later, Alessandro Pazzi, who himself edited the text in 1536, was in a position to label Valla's work as 'smelly', apparently with perfect justice.[5] Yet another generation later, in 1570, Lodovico Castelvetro published his commentary, famous for its doctrine of the three unities, which obviously made sense to the French classicists of the seventeenth century. Nevertheless, his reading cannot be termed other than un-Aristotelian – some will definitely not hesitate to denounce it altogether. The Aristotelian text does not say what Castelvetro wants it to say: place is not an issue in the *Poetics*, and the unity of action could not possibly be subordinated to the other two.[6] It seems obvious today that the sixteenth-century commentators generally were biased by their rhetorical training and the unchallenged status of Horace's *Ars poetica*, that their interpreations often lacked coherence and, consequently, should be considered inferior to those which do not. Thus it should be fair to assume that twentieth-century interpretations of Aristotle's enigmatic text are better, i.e. closer to what was presumably the author's intention, than those of the sixteenth century. It would most probably be easier to convince Castelvetro of the superiority of, for example, Halliwell's interpretation(s) than *vice versa*. But what if we move on to our own century, for instance to Gerald Else's interpretation of 1957? Is his reading of Aristotelian *katharsis*, for example, still tenable? Is Else right? Partly right? Or may we now safely set him aside, relegating his giant essay to the reception history of the *Poetics*? Although it was welcomed as an important step forward, Else's structural theory no longer seems to appeal as once it did. Serious objections have been raised[7] and the hegemony is now definitely lost to later ethical interpretations. Various questions arise: For how long will this new position be held by the great majority of scholars? Who will be able to convince us about something else and presumably better? Do we need new and yet undiscovered evidence to make further scholarly advances? Is it just a question of changing the focus? Or is it simply a question of a changing world?

There are numerous reasons why we have not been able to terminate the discussion. First, there is the philological challenge: Problems regarding the genesis and survival of the text may seem quite decisive. No one in his/her right mind would dispute that Kassel's text of 1965 is closer to the original than the sixteenth-century versions,[8] but, in principle, we still face the same problems as did Georgio Valla, Alessandro Pazzi and Lodovico Castelvetro.

Second, there is the specifically hermeneutical challenge: the fragmented and lapidary style of the *Poetics* in 1996 enticed George Steiner to wager that 'the young man who took the notes at Aristotle's lecture was sitting very near the door on a very noisy day'.[9] The very brevity of the text has made it peculiarly open to colonisation. Throughout history, scholars as well as critics have taken an interest in Aristotle's *Poetics* most of all in order to satisfy their *own* needs rather than those of the disputed text. The great Scaliger, in his *Poetices libri VII* from 1561, constitutes a brilliant example: His theory of tragedy is demonstrably a version of Diomedes the Grammarian's; what he borrows from Aristotle is his authority as the 'imperator' of philosophy.[10] One may wonder: was Scaliger an unscrupulous forger, or was he just absorbed by his own preoccupations and concerns? How do we know for certain which concerns are ours and which are Aristotle's? With the conviction that different interpretative communities inevitably create different meanings, we have lost faith in one, final meaning. Thus the borderline between readings and misreadings, 'Aristotelian' and 'un-Aristotelian' interpretations, becomes blurred, and the concept of scholarly progress no longer seems to make sense. Montaigne, who was Scaliger's younger contemporary, may be counted among the disillusioned at this point: 'There is no end to our inquiries: our end is in the next world.'[11] Meanwhile, the historicist enterprise has been and still is searching for new metaphors: the voice of the dead, can it be anything other than our own? Our privileged point of view, as the most recent, may be seen to be the most prejudiced as long as the interpretation of texts is inseparable from the history of their reception. 'Wie es eigentlich gewesen', and what they originally meant, is simply indeterminable. In this perspective, what we can hope for is some sort of a Gadamerian dialogue, from *our* position very close to the door, on another, still noisier day.

The question of scholarly progress, will, no doubt, acquire different answers from the ten authors of this volume. The categories introduced by Terence Cave in his closing remarks suggest that however different their approaches may be, the contributors here generally seem to acquiesce in some sort of conviction that it is worth while to struggle on with sense-making efforts, not only of the orginal text, but with all those previous efforts now deemed to belong to the reception history. Even if we are perfectly aware that we are 'negotiating' with the text, we still believe in progress: we believe that it is possible to argue for better interpretations. Looking back to Georgio Valla, we *know* it should be possible. This volume contains new, and to some extent, provoking,

Aristotelian negotiations. We are prepared to wager that at least some of the insights mean progress in our efforts to make sense of Aristotle.

*

The contributions to the present book originate in papers given at a symposium in Oslo in May 2000, organised by the editors. The international symposium marked the end of a three-year long project at the Faculty of Arts, University of Oslo, addressing 'The interpretation and reception of Aristotle's *Poetics*'. A series of papers and presentations were given on a monthly basis during the years 1998-2000 by faculty members of various departments and by visitors from abroad, on aspects ranging from the relationship between poetics and rhetoric in Aristotle through Magister Mathias Lincopensis' *Poetria* to Aristotelian poetics and the movies. In addition to several contributors to the present volume, who visited the seminar as well as the international symposium, we should like to thank the following: Birger Bergh (Lund), Arnfinn Bø-Rygg (Oslo), Eyjolfur Emilsson (Oslo), Lone Klem (Oslo), Jørgen Langdalen (Oslo), Mats Malm (Gothenburg), Arne Melberg (Oslo), Tor Martin Møller (Oslo), Jackie Pigeaud (Nantes), Trond Kruke Salberg (Oslo), Omert Schrier (Amsterdam), Isolde Stark (Halle-Wittenberg), and Truls Winther (Bergen).

The project as a whole was made possible by a grant from a programme to promote classical studies in Norway (*Antikkprogrammet*) established by the Norwegian Research Council for the years 1996-2001. We should like to take this opportunity to thank the Norwegian Research Council for its generous support. Finally, thanks go to Deborah Blake at Duckworth for her expert and expedient work with the publication and to Eirik Welo who prepared the indices.

Notes

1. Michel de Montaigne, *The Complete Essays*, trans. M.A. Screech (London, 1991), 1211 ('On experience', III.13).
2. David Ross, *Aristotle* (London, 1995 [1923]), 286.
3. Omert J. Schrier (comp.), *The Poetics of Aristotle and the Tractatus Coislinianus: A Bibliography from about 900 till 1996* (Leiden, 1998), 1.
4. Cf. Stephen Halliwell, *Aristotle's Poetics* (London, 1998 [1986]), ch. 10, 'Influence and status: the *Nachleben* of the *Poetics*', 286-323; and 'Epilogue: the *Poetics* and its interpreters', *Essays on Aristotle's Poetics*, ed. Amélie Oksenberg Rorty (Princeton, 1992), 409-24.
5. Cf. E.N. Tigerstedt, 'Observations on the reception of the Aristotelian *Poetics* in the Latin West', *Studies in the Renaissance* 15 (1968), 14-20.
6. Cf. Bernard Weinberg, 'Castelvetro's theory of the *Poetics*', *Critics and Criticism: Ancient and Modern*, ed. R.S. Crane (Chicago, 1952), 349-71.
7. Summarised by Halliwell in *Aristotle's Poetics*, 356.

8. R. Kassel (ed.), *Aristotelis de arte poetica liber* (Oxford, 1965).

9. George Steiner, 'Tragedy, pure and simple', *Tragedy and the Tragic: Greek Theatre and Beyond*, ed. M.S. Silk (Oxford, 1996), 545.

10. Cf. Paul R. Sellin, 'Sources of Julius Caesar Scaliger's *Poetices libri septem* as a guide to Renaissance poetics', *Acta Scaligeriana: Actes du Colloque International organisé pour le cinquième de la naissance de Jules-César Scaliger*, ed. J. Cubelier de Beynac et M. Magnien (Agen, 1986), 75-84, and Luc Deitz, "*Aristoteles imperator noster* ...'"? J.C. Scaliger and Aristotle on poetic theory', *International Journal of the Classical Tradition* 2 (1995), 54-67.

11. Montaigne, loc. cit.

Aristotle and the Pleasures
of Tragedy

Malcolm Heath

Tragedy causes us distress and gives us pleasure. That pleasure is felt
not in spite of, but in some sense because of the distress that we
undergo: we *enjoy* the experience of tragic distress. That is a paradox,
and has long been recognised as a central problem in the theory of
tragedy. In this chapter I shall attempt to outline an Aristotelian
resolution of the paradox.

In speaking of 'an Aristotelian resolution' I choose my words with
care. The resolution I shall propose is not one that I myself would
accept: on the substantive issue of the tragic paradox, I am agnostic.
But I am not even going to claim that *Aristotle* accepted this resolution.
Since his extant works do not (in my view) contain an explicit analysis
of the paradoxical pleasure of tragedy, we cannot be sure that he ever
thought the issue through to a conclusion or (if he did) what conclusion
he reached. So my claim is a more cautious one: that the proposed
resolution is *Aristotelian*, in the sense that it is consistent with the rest
of his theory of tragedy and with his broader philosophical outlook. It is
quite possible that Aristotle himself did not draw the inferences that I
shall be concerned with; but it may still shed light on his theory of
tragedy if we can show that those inferences are there to be drawn. In
discovering what kind of resolution of the tragic paradox is *possible*
within an Aristotelian framework, we will be achieving a fuller understanding of Aristotle's general theory of tragedy and its implications.

That Aristotle's theory of tragedy really does commit him to the
tragic paradox seems clear. One of the key concepts in the *Poetics* is the
'characteristic pleasure' (*oikeia hêdonê*) of tragedy, which he identifies
as the pleasure which comes 'from pity and fear through imitation'
(1453b10-13); and in the *Rhetoric* pity and fear are defined as species of
distress (*lupê*, 1382a21, 1385b13). The paradoxical nature of such a
pleasure was a familiar notion in Greek thinking about poetry: Gorgias,
for example, had spoken of poetry producing in its audience a 'yearning
that is fond of grief' (*pothos philopenthês*, fr. 11.10). Since Aristotle
makes no attempt to dissociate himself from that tradition, it is reason-

able to suppose that he accepted the *prima facie* implication of paradox in the notion of a pleasure that comes *from* pity and fear.

It is true that the idea that pleasure might be associated with distressing emotions is not foreign to Aristotle. Anger is an emotion that involves distress, but the angry man anticipates vengeance, and that is pleasurable in two respects: the belief that one is going to achieve some aim is pleasant, and so is the imagery which arises when one dwells on the thought of vengeance (*Rhet.* 1378a30-b10, cf. 1370b10-15, 30-2). Similarly, pleasure can accompany grief and lamentation: the absence of a loved one causes distress, but there is pleasure in the imagery that arises from one's memory of him or her (*Rhet.* 1370b25-9). However, no comparable analysis is offered for pity or fear. Moreover, these cases cannot provide us with a model for resolving the tragic paradox. In anger and grief, the pleasure is part of the general structure of the emotion, and is felt under normal circumstances; but the characteristic pleasure of tragedy arises under special circumstances: it is 'the pleasure which comes from pity and fear ... *by means of imitation*'.

That qualification is obviously crucial. If one were to witness the events of *Oedipus* in real life, one would not feel pleasure; so if tragic emotion is to be experienced as pleasurable, it must be mediated by imitation. But this does not take us all the way to a solution. To say that in other circumstances we could not find the experience pleasurable does not explain why in these circumstances we do. It does not tell us what it is about the experience of emotion in tragedy that *makes* it pleasurable. This problem cannot be addressed simply by asking what it is in tragedy that gives us pleasure. For the total experience of tragedy is a complex one, and is pleasurable in a variety of ways. We cannot assume that all of these pleasures bear on the tragic paradox: there is a logical distinction between deriving pleasure from an object that excites distressing emotions, and deriving pleasure from the distressing emotions which that object excites. In the first part of this chapter I shall discuss a number of the pleasures which, in Aristotle's analysis, we derive from tragedy, and argue that they fail to provide a full analysis of the characteristic pleasure of tragedy.[1] In the second part of the chapter the discussion of cultivated leisure in the last book of the *Politics* will provide a context in which my proposal can be aired and briefly defended against some objections.

1. The pleasures of tragedy

(a) Pleasures of text and performance

Various pleasures arise from qualities that tragedy possesses as verbal text and as staged performance. In the definition of tragedy Aristotle describes its language as 'made pleasurable' (1449b25), which he glosses as 'that which possesses rhythm and melody' (1449b28-9); according to 1448b20-1 rhythm and melody are both natural, and therefore pleasurable, for human beings. In 1450b16-17 it is noted that song is the most important of tragedy's pleasurable embellishments, and staging too is attractive; music and (probably: the text is disputable) staging are mentioned together as sources of intense pleasure at 1462a16.

The pleasures which these things give us are genuine pleasures of tragedy, but they do not account for tragedy's characteristic pleasure. When Aristotle identifies the characteristic pleasure as 'that which comes from pity and fear ... *by means of imitation*', he is arguing that tragedy should evoke pity and fear *not* through the visual effect of a staged performance, but by means of the plot (1453b1-14).[2] Indeed, he is willing to claim that it should be possible for a tragic plot to excite pity and fear (and therefore, presumably, the characteristic pleasure) in abstraction not only from performance, but even from a particular performable text – for example, through a plot-summary (1453b3-6).[3] For Aristotle, what makes tragedy an imitation is not the fact that people appear on stage in costume speaking verse and singing, but the fact that it tells a story. A tragedy is in essence an imitation of an action (1449b24), and it is because it has a plot that a tragedy imitates action (1450a3-4). To derive pleasure by means of imitation is therefore to derive it through the plot.[4]

(b) Cognitive pleasure

In chapter 4 of the *Poetics* Aristotle considers the anthropological roots of poetry, and notes that it is natural to human beings to take pleasure in imitation, as well as in rhythm and song (the pleasures of text and performance that we have just considered).[5] Aristotle explains the pleasure which we take in imitations as such by reference to the process of reasoning and inference that we have to go through in order to reach a conclusion of the form 'this is so-and-so'.[6] Understanding an imitation (recognising it as an imitation of whatever the object imitated may be) involves us in a process of learning; and learning is universally pleasant to humans – for 'all human beings by nature desire knowledge' (*Met.* 980a22; cf. *Rhet.* 1371b4-10, 1410b10-11).

Aristotle notes that we can derive pleasure from an imitation even without this process of recognition (1448b17-19). If I look at a picture of something I am not familiar with I may get pleasure from it as an object (for example, from its execution or colour), but I will not get the cognitive pleasure that attends the recognition that this is so-and-so. If these non-imitative pleasures of visual imitation are analogous to the

9

verbal, musical and visual pleasures of tragedy, then the cognitive pleasure in tragedy will be that which we gain from our grasp of the plot. This is not as trivial as it may sound. In Aristotle's theory of tragedy, a proper grasp of the plot involves recognition of its conformity to certain relatively sophisticated structural and ethical criteria. For example, we have not grasped the plot if we do not see how the events are causally dependent one on another (which involves understanding the events in terms of universals).

So the cognitive pleasure is a pleasure which comes through imitation; and Aristotle observes, it explains how we can take pleasure in imitations of objects that are, in themselves, distressing, such as corpses (1448b10-12).[7] This is a paradox similar in some respects to that of the characteristic pleasure, but not identical; as noted earlier, there is a distinction between deriving pleasure from something that causes distress and deriving pleasure from the distress it causes ('from pity and fear'). And the cognitive pleasure fails in a number of ways to provide a full analysis of the characteristic pleasure of tragedy.

First, it is not characteristic. Cognitive pleasure arises from all kinds of poetry, and indeed from all kinds of imitation. We cannot plausibly seek an explanation of the distinctive power of tragedy in features which tragedy shares with poetry of every kind, and poetry with a much broader class of human activities. Secondly, this pleasure is purely cognitive. This is not to deny that Aristotelian emotions have a cognitive dimension. Fear, for example, involves an expectation of harm, and so necessarily presupposes beliefs of a certain kind about the world. But the cognitive pleasure of chapter 4 is emotionally neutral; it could not otherwise be a universal pleasure of imitation. We get it from pictures of nice things and from pictures of nasty things alike. By contrast, the characteristic pleasure of tragedy, which comes from pity and fear, can *only* be derived from imitations of events that are pitiable and terrible. Thirdly, the cognitive pleasure of chapter 4 fails to solve the paradox of tragedy. The observation that we can derive cognitive pleasure from pictures of unpleasant objects despite their unpleasantness leaves intact the natural assumption that we would derive *more* pleasure from a picture of a pleasant object.[8] If the characteristic pleasure of tragedy were the cognitive pleasure of chapter 4, our taste for tragedy would be inexplicable: why seek this pleasure from imitations of distressing events which cause us pain, when imitations of happy events would give us the cognitive pleasure unmixed with pain?[9]

Elizabeth Belfiore has offered a sophisticated attempt to bridge the gap between the characteristic pleasure and the cognitive pleasure of chapter 4. On her interpretation 'pity and fear, though painful and not in themselves productive of pleasure, are nevertheless essential to the production of the *oikeia hêdonê*, 'proper pleasure', of tragedy':[10]

Because we shudder and weep at the tragedy ... we realise that it is an imitation of a pitiable and fearful event ... This pleasurable recognition requires us to focus on those features of the imitation which make it similar to the original, that is, on what is pitiable and fearful. In this way, painful pity and fear and pleasurable learning ... reinforce one another, with a physically disturbing involuntary response resulting in a pleasurable intellectual activity which in turn heightens our awareness of what is pitiable and fearful.

I do not believe, however, that this theory meets the stated objections. It is still not a theory of tragedy's characteristic pleasure; the specified pleasure is a cognitive one common to all imitations, and what is characteristic to tragedy is simply the mechanism of reinforcement. Furthermore, Belfiore herself notes that the theory does not explain the paradoxical taste for tragedy, given that a similar process of reciprocal reinforcement could be set up using pleasurable emotions, which would dispense with the pain; therefore (she concludes) the 'mediation of recognition' cannot be 'the sole contribution' which 'pity and fear make to tragic pleasure'. She responds to this objection thus:

Tragedy ... deals with the most serious and important aspects of human life: change, mortality, the constant threat of pain and death. It concerns events that arouse pity and fear. Thus, the tragic emotions are essentially connected with the object imitated by tragedy, the *spoudaia praxis* ... Aristotle does explicitly state that perception or contemplation of an object most worthy of attention (*spoudaiotaton*) affords most pleasure (*EN* 10.4.1174b20-3). For this reason, recognition of a fearful or pitiable object affords more pleasure than recognition of a comic object.

The observation that the seriousness or worthiness of the object enhances the pleasure of perception or contemplation is acute, and must indeed find a place within an Aristotelian theory of tragic pleasures. But it does not answer to the present problem, since the difficulty for Belfiore's thesis is not posed by comedy, but by inferior kinds of tragedy. There is no evidence that Aristotle thought the tragic action serious because it is concerned with death and suffering; it is serious because of the elevated moral and social status of the people it involves. Tragedy is the imitation of a 'serious' action (*spoudaia praxis* 1449b24) because it is an imitation of 'serious' people (*spoudaioi*; cf. 1448a2, 26-7, 1449b10). An imitation of such people that failed to arouse pity and fear would still be a serious action in Aristotle's sense, but Aristotle would

11

argue that it was defective as a tragedy and that its appeal was intrinsically inferior to that of proper tragedy (1453a33-4). I cannot see any grounds for such a conclusion so far as the cognitive pleasure is concerned. So the cognitive pleasure fails to account for the characteristic pleasure of tragedy.

(c) Katharsis

We know from the definition of tragedy in the *Poetics* that tragedy works a *katharsis* of pity and fear (1449b27-8); and however obscure the notion of *katharsis* may be, it is at any rate clear from the *Politics* that it is pleasurable (1342a16). There is, moreover, a *prima facie* case in favour of identifying the pleasure of *katharsis* with the characteristic pleasure of tragedy: clearly, the pleasure of a *katharsis* of pity and fear satisfies the condition of coming 'from pity and fear', and it could be argued that it is (unlike the cognitive pleasure) distinctive to tragedy.[11] However, I do not think that this identification can be correct. Because of the complex and elusive nature of the problems posed by the concept of *katharsis*, I cannot offer more than a brief, and inevitably somewhat dogmatic, treatment here.[12]

I begin with a simple premise: the characteristic pleasure of tragedy must be available to all members of an audience, and especially to the better members. Consider the final chapter of the *Poetics*, where Aristotle argues in defence of tragedy against critics who regarded it as rather vulgar. That defence would surely be compromised if tragedy's characteristic pleasure were only or especially available to inferior audiences. In fact, there is evidence that it is inferior audiences that are least attached to the characteristic pleasure of tragedy: in chapter 13, it is the *weakness* of audiences that explains their preference for inferior tragedies with 'comic' plots (1453a30-9).[13] A second premise: if *katharsis* is in any sense therapeutic, it will not apply to all members of an audience (or not to all equally), and it will not apply (or will apply least) to the best members of an audience. For the best members of the audience will (by definition) be least in need of therapy.[14] A third premise: *katharsis* must be therapeutic in some sense: in the *Politics* Aristotle links *katharsis* with healing (*iatreia* 1342a10-11) and with relief (*kouphizesthai* 1342a11-15), a word from the same semantic field.[15] So: *katharsis* puts right something that is wrong with us; but the best members of the audience will have least need to be put right; but the characteristic pleasure of tragedy must be most available to the best members of the audience. So the pleasure of *katharsis* is not tragedy's characteristic pleasure, even though it is a pleasure of tragedy.

2. The characteristic pleasure of tragedy

(a) Leisure in Politics 8

We have examined a variety of pleasures of tragedy which fail to provide a resolution of the paradox which attends the characteristic pleasure. Our investigation must now move into a more speculative phase. I shall begin by making a detour through Aristotle's discussion of the role of 'music' in education in book 8 of the *Politics*. What he says there about the nature of cultivated leisure will prove heuristically useful in our enquiry.

In the first stage of this discussion, in chapter 3 (1337b27-1338a30), Aristotle concludes that music is to be included in education with a view to the correct use of leisure (variously designated in this context *skholê*, *hê en diagôgêi skholê*, *hê en skholêi diagôgê*, or simply *diagôgê*). This section is marked off in ring-form by the opening and concluding references to the ancients as having held this view (1337b29-32, 1338a13-30); the intervening argument clarifies the antithesis between this view and the view attributed to most moderns, that music is for the sake of pleasure (1337b28-9). That initial formulation needs to be made more precise, since Aristotle of course does not deny that leisure includes pleasure. So he makes a further distinction, between leisure and amusement (*paidia*). Leisure and amusement are both pleasant, but the two stand in a different relationship to pleasure, and also to labour. If you are not at leisure, then you are labouring after some end that you have not yet achieved; so in amusement, pleasure provides rest (*anapausis*) and recovery (*pharmakeias kharin*) after the labours of non-leisure (1337b35-1338a1). Amusement serves a purpose beyond itself (preparing you for further labour), but is trivial in itself. By contrast, leisure is intrinsically serious: it serves no purpose beyond itself, since if you are at leisure then you have achieved the end. But the end is well-being (*eudaimonia*), and everyone agrees that this involves pleasure (1338a1-6). So in leisure, pleasure constitutes part of the end at which human life aims.[16]

Aristotle returns to musical education in chapter 5 (1339a14-b10). Here he is particularly interested in the question of why children are taught skills in musical performance: whatever function one assigns to musical education, there seems to be no reason for learning to perform oneself, as distinct from learning to appreciate the performances of others. Having introduced the question he leaves it to one side until chapter 6, and for our present purposes we do not need to go into his answer to this question. But we should pay some attention to the rest of chapter 5. For now he has *three* possible functions of musical education in mind: to the two functions mentioned in the previous passage

13

(amusement and relaxation; leisure) he adds the formation of moral character.

It is not, of course, the amusement or leisure of the children who are being educated that is in question here. Education is not for children's amusement: on the contrary, education is unpleasant. But nor can it be for leisure, since leisure has to do with the end, which the child – being immature – cannot yet have attained. So the idea is that children are educated in music with a view to their amusement or leisure as adults. It is this that poses a problem about education in performance skills: the children are not going to be called upon to perform themselves when they are adults. But, as Aristotle points out, the same problem arises if the function of musical education is the formation of moral character, since this process turns on the cultivation of correct appreciation and judgement, not on performance skills (1339a41-b4).

Returning to the theme of amusement and leisure (1339b15-31), Aristotle notes that pleasures that are suitable to leisure are also able to provide relaxation and amusement. This provides an argument for the inclusion of music in education; for while people rarely achieve the end, they more often relax and amuse themselves. Relaxation and amusement, Aristotle adds, are sought not only for the sake of something beyond itself, but also because of the pleasure (*oukh hoson epi pleon alla kai dia tên hêdonên*). This point is rather obscure, but the following lines (1339b31-42), themselves extremely cryptic, seem to offer an explanation.[17] Amusement resembles leisure in two respects: first, both are pleasant; secondly, neither is chosen with a view to the future (leisure, being the end, is not chosen for the sake of something else at all, while amusement is chosen because of past labours). Thus, although amusement is not the end it is easily confused with it. People may assume that because an amusement is pleasant, and because the end involves pleasure, the amusement is part of the end. But that does not follow: 'for perhaps the end also involves a certain pleasure – but not just any chance pleasure' (1339b32-3). Hence proper leisure activities are not things that just happen to be treated as ends in themselves: they must be *worthy* of being treated as ends in themselves.

In what, then, does that worthiness reside? What is it that makes something intrinsically serious, and an appropriate leisure activity? Aristotle goes on (1339b42-1340b19) to raise the possibility of a function of music 'more valuable' than its role in amusement, and here he reintroduces the third function, moral education. He argues that musical education does have this function, and on the basis of this discussion he proceeds in 1340b20ff. to solve the problem held over from 1339b10-11, as to why children should be taught to perform. Some (for example, Carnes Lord) have argued that this third function of musical education – the formation of moral character – applies to adults as well as children, and that it is in this continuing morally educative effect that we are to locate the intrinsic seriousness which distinguishes music as leisure from music as amusement. On this view, music is a proper element of adult leisure because, and to the extent that, it changes moral character for the better.[18] But this conclusion cannot be correct.

First, leisure is the end; but the end (that is, well-being) does not consist in acquiring virtue, but in being virtuous (*energeia kat' aretên*). That is to say, for Aristotle it is not the formation of character that is the end, but rather the exercise of formed character. This is, in fact, another way of formulating a point we have already made in another context: on Lord's view, the more fully developed one's moral character is, the less one will stand to profit from music in leisure; but if leisure is the end, its value should be most available to the best individuals.

Secondly, Lord seems to have misconstrued Aristotle's argument about music's effect on character. The conclusion at 1340b13 proves that the question with which Aristotle is concerned in this section is, in the end, the use of music in the education of children. It is true that in the course of the argument he refers to music's effect on adults: he does so to provide evidence that imitation has the power to affect the soul. But the effect on adults which he cites is not educational.[19] He refers to an audience's sympathetic response during a musical performance (1340a12-13), and this is a transient and occasional effect; it is not equivalent to a change in the disposition of an unformed character. Aristotle's argument is that if imitation has an occasional effect on an adult character, it will tend (because of the associated pleasure) to have an enduring effect on the dispositions of the as yet unformed character of a child.

Finally, Lord's interpretation presupposes that the discussion of leisure is incomplete at the point at which the morally educative function of music is reintroduced (1339b42).[20] But in fact the distinction between leisure and amusement is clear from what has already been said. Our enjoyment of music as amusement arises from need – the need to recover from past labours, or to prepare for future ones. But our enjoyment of music in leisure is not subject to need:[21] it is simply the taking pleasure in an appropriate object of pleasure that is the natural expression of a correctly formed character. The worthiness of an activity to be treated as an end in itself (and thus the difference between genuine leisure and amusements misconstrued as leisure) will consist precisely in the appropriateness of the object of pleasure, as judged by someone who – having a properly formed character – will judge such things correctly. So leisure is something which is engaged in as an end in itself, and which is worthy to be treated as an end in itself. Amusement is a pleasure sought for some further end, or sought for its own

15

sake but not worthy, in the judgement of a mature and virtuous agent, to be sought for its own sake.

(b) Leisure and tragedy

How does this advance us? Tragedy, for Aristotle, is something to be taken seriously; I have already referred to his defence of tragedy in the last chapter of the *Poetics*. It follows that tragedy must be seen not just as an amusement, but as an appropriate component of leisure in the sense in which Aristotle uses this term in the *Politics*. That is, tragedy must be an appropriate component of the well-being that is the end of human existence.[22] This means that the proper response to tragedy must likewise be construed as the natural expression of a properly formed character. But what precisely is the appropriate object in which the possessor of such a character takes pleasure when responding to tragedy?

Certainly, the imitation is an appropriate object of pleasure both as a performable text and as an object on which the audience's cognitive skills are exercised. But we have seen already that these pleasures do not provide a sufficient account of the characteristic pleasure of tragedy, so this gets us no further. It is also true that what is imitated in a tragedy (the action) is likely to contain appropriate objects of pleasure, for example, a good man behaving well; and, as Belfiore observes, this element also enhances the pleasure. However, good men in tragedy tend to suffer, so that taken as a whole the tragic action is not an appropriate object of pleasure, but rather of pity and fear and therefore of distress. So this line of approach simply brings us back to the tragic paradox.

The only remaining option seems to be that the appropriate object of pleasure is the response of pity and fear itself. If pity and fear are an appropriate response to the tragic action, then they are as such a proper source of pleasure. After all, in Aristotle's view, actualisation in accordance with excellence (or – to use a more homely though perhaps misleading expression – virtuous activity: *energeia kat' aretên*) is in itself pleasurable to anyone who possesses the excellence in question (*EN* 1099a7-20, *EE* 1249a18-21).[23] My suggestion is, then, that pity and fear are an appropriate response to a tragic action that is pitiable and fearful; because they are an appropriate response, they are an expression of moral excellence; as such, they are pleasurable to those who possess moral excellence; so the characteristic pleasure of tragedy, which comes from pity and fear by means of imitation, is the pleasure which the virtuous take in this exercise of their virtue.

This theory has several attractions. First, the exercise of virtue constitutes well-being (*EN* 1177a9-11), and we have already observed the intimate connection which Aristotle perceives between well-being and leisure (*Pol.* 1338a4-6). It seems highly appropriate, therefore, that the pleasure which makes tragedy a suitable component of the virtuous man's leisure should be the pleasure which attends the expression of virtuous character required for the proper response to tragedy. Secondly, the theory conspicuously satisfies the condition laid down earlier, that the characteristic pleasure should be most available to the best members of the audience. By definition, they will be the most virtuous and will take the most pleasure in their virtue. Thirdly, the characteristic pleasure on this view is complementary to the cognitive pleasure of chapter 4. The tragic audience apprehends the action of which the play is an imitation, and in doing so derives the cognitive pleasure that underlies our experience of all imitations as such. If the action is apprehended correctly (as involving, for example, undeserved destructive or painful harm), then the cognitive presuppositions of the tragic emotions are in place; and in actually feeling those emotions the virtuous audience will also derive the pleasure which attends the expression of a virtuous character. The tragic audience thus enjoys a pleasurable exercise both of its intellectual and its ethical excellences.

But there are also some obvious objections to the theory. First, it seems to imply that all appropriate emotional responses are pleasurable, and that they are pleasurable under normal conditions. But pity and fear are sources of distress, and (as we observed at the outset) they are not a source of pleasure under normal conditions, but only when mediated by imitation. However, the implication that something may involve pain and distress and yet because it is an exercise of virtue still in some sense be pleasurable to a virtuous agent is not unique to my interpretation of the characteristic pleasure of tragedy; it appears elsewhere in Aristotle's ethics. Aristotle confronts a related problem in his discussion of courage (*EN* 1117a29-b22). Courage ought to be pleasant to the courageous, but its exercise tends to be painful: it may even get you killed. In his discussion of this problem Aristotle draws attention to the effect of the circumstances in which the virtue is exercised, which in the case of courage tend to make the pleasure 'disappear' (*aphanizesthai*). This argument is consistent with his general thesis that external goods are necessary to well-being (*EN* 1099a31-3, 1153b14-21). This consideration has a bearing also on the problem of tragic pleasure. Under normal conditions the circumstances under which we experience pity and fear are (by definition) painful, and make the pleasure disappear; but the circumstances under which we experience pity and fear in response to tragedy include the fact that it is an imitation, and our awareness of the unreality of the situation to which we are responding will limit the interference between pain and pleasure.[24] Hence the fact that in tragedy pity and fear come *through imitation* is in fact crucial to my account of its characteristic pleasure.

Secondly, it might be argued that this theory is vulnerable to the same objection which I used against the identification of tragedy's characteristic pleasure with the cognitive pleasure. One can exercise virtue by taking satisfaction in deserved good fortune, as well as by being distressed by undeserved bad fortune. An imitation of an action in which good people enjoyed sustained good fortune would cause us no distress, but would evoke moral satisfaction – and that satisfaction, since it would be an appropriate response to the action in question, would be pleasurable. So a tragedy in which good characters did not suffer would give pleasure without distress; but it would, by Aristotle's criteria, be an inferior tragedy. A solution to this problem is suggested by the way in which Aristotle associates the inferiority of such a tragedy with the inferiority of those members of the audience who prefer it, and in particular with their weakness (*Poet.* 1453a34). Presumably, the reason why tragedy appeals only to a stronger audience is precisely that it is distressing; because it requires endurance of pain, the response it demands requires a greater exercise of virtue, and is for that reason more satisfying to the virtuous. The distress which the characteristic pleasure involves is therefore integral, on my interpretation, to the preferential regard in which a superior audience will hold it.[25]

Finally, some might find the proposed theory so eccentric and absurd as to make it seem doubtful whether it can charitably be attributed to anyone at all. But this objection, at least, is easy to counter: similar theories can be documented in the history of criticism. Without my attempting any systematic search, the following instances come to hand:

(i) Among Italian Renaissance critics, Castelvetro in his commentary on the *Poetics* distinguished between the direct pleasure afforded by plots in which the fortunes of the virtuous turn from bad to good, and the indirect or oblique pleasure afforded by plots with the reverse movement. Plots of the latter type are directly a source of displeasure, but the recognition that this displeasure is evidence of a good character appeals to our self-love, and gives rise to an indirect pleasure.[26]

(ii) A number of eighteenth-century critics adopted a similar theory, of whom Hugh Blair will serve as an example:[27]

By the wise and gracious constitution of our nature, the exercise of all the social passions is attended with pleasure ... At the same time, the immediate pleasure which always goes along with the operation of the benevolent and sympathetic affections, derives an addition from the approbation of our own minds. We are pleased with ourselves, for feeling as we ought, and for entering, with proper sorrow, into the concerns of the afflicted. In Tragedy, besides, other adventitious circumstances concur to diminish the painful part of Sympathy, and to increase the satisfaction attending it. We are, in some measure, relieved by thinking that the cause of our distress is feigned, not real; and we are also gratified by the charms of Poetry, the propriety of Sentiment and Language, and the beauty of Action.

(iii) A comparable approach has been proposed more recently in an article by Susan L. Feagin, apparently without knowledge of these precedents:[28]

> Whence the pleasure? It is, I suggest, a meta-response, arising from our awareness of, and in response to, the fact that we do have unpleasant direct responses to unpleasant events as they occur in the performing and literary arts. We find ourselves to be the kind of people who respond negatively to villainy, treachery and injustice. This discovery, or reminder, is something which, quite justly, yields satisfaction.

So my interpretation would place Aristotle within a respectable tradition. I do not claim to find such theories plausible myself, but that is irrelevant. My aim in this paper has not been to propose a resolution of the paradox of tragic pleasure acceptable to myself (or to my readers), but to propose one acceptable within the framework of an Aristotelian theory of tragedy.

3. Conclusion

In the first part of this chapter I surveyed various pleasures that tragedy affords (the verbal, musical and visual pleasures of tragedy as performed, or performable, text; the cognitive pleasure; the pleasure of *katharsis*), and concluded that none of them provide a sufficient analysis of the characteristic pleasure that generates the tragic paradox. In the second part I have argued that this pleasure should be appropriate not merely to amusement, but also and more importantly to the leisure of those human beings who have attained the end of human existence. This end is, or includes, the exercise of virtuous character; responding with pity and fear to pitiable and fearful objects is an exercise of a virtuous character; and this means that it is also pleasurable to the virtuous. It seems plausible to infer, therefore, that this pleasure is the characteristic pleasure of tragedy.

If this reconstruction is correct, then tragedy's moral seriousness is independent of any morally educative function that might be attributed to it. This is not to exclude the possibility that tragedy may have an educative use; but any such use would in an important sense be incidental. Tragedy, like music, may have a role in helping the un-formed towards the achievement of moral excellence. But since that which is directed towards the end is subordinate to the end itself, the true value of tragedy will lie rather in the place it has within the leisured activities of one who has achieved moral excellence. Tragedy is morally serious, not so much because it is formative of virtuous charac-ter, as because it is expressive of virtuous character. It is an occasion for the leisured exercise of virtuous character once formed – and that is pleasurable.[29]

Notes

1. I build here on the discussion in M. Heath (tr.), *Aristotle: Poetics* (Har-mondsworth, 1996), xxxv-xliii. For another approach to the classification of tragic pleasures see S. Halliwell, *Aristotle's Poetics* (London, 1986), 62-81. Y.L. Too, *The Idea of Ancient Literary Criticism* (Oxford, 1999), 100-3 rejects the multiplicity of pleasures in Halliwell's analysis. I am not convinced that there is any substantive difference between the identification of different pleasures and the identification of different *sources* of pleasure (which Too concedes). Though I speak here of a multiplicity of pleasures, my project could equally well be described as an attempt to develop an analysis of the multiple sources of a unitary tragic pleasure that will make it possible to explain its distinctiveness.

2. The structure of the argument is as follows: pity and fear should arise from the plot; to derive them from staging is less appropriate; to derive a sense of 'the monstrous' from staging is quite untragic; for the characteristic pleasure of tragedy is that which comes from pity and fear (i.e. not from the monstrous) by means of imitation (i.e. not through staging). Thus into a context primarily concerned with the means of exciting emotion (plot, not staging) Aristotle has inserted parenthetically a comment on which emotions should be excited (pity and fear, not the monstrous); and 'by means of imitation' articulates the concluding return to the paragraph's primary concern. The phrase therefore does not serve primarily to define the nature of tragedy's characteristic pleas-ure, but to specify the means by which the emotions which give rise to it may properly be excited.

3. In a similar passage at 1462a11-12 the abstraction is only from perform-ance, not from the verbal text, which is allowed to have its effect through reading. But although in the present passage Aristotle only makes 'without seeing' explicit, the logic of his argument implies that the plot will have its effect 'without reading' also. However, Aristotle is not committed to the extreme (and surely absurd) view that the verbal and visual realisation of the plot is unim-portant and cannot or should not enhance the characteristic pleasure. His point is that achieving emotional effects verbally or visually is not a proper substitute for good plot construction – to which topic this passage is a preface (cf. 1453b14-15).

4. Characters and thought are also objects of imitation (1450a10-11), from which pleasure can be derived: but not the characteristic pleasure of tragedy (cf. 1450a29-b4).

5. I take it that the 'two causes' of 1448b4-5 are the natural human propen-sities to enjoy (i) imitation (1448b5-20), and (ii) melody and rhythm

(1448b20-2). Since poetry is imitation in rhythmical language, with or without melody, both elements are needed to complete Aristotle's anthropological grounding of poetry. For a different view see (e.g.) Halliwell (n. 1), 70-1.

6. I discuss this passage briefly in M. Heath, 'The universality of poetry in Aristotle's *Poetics*', *CQ* 41 (1991), 389-402, at 399.

7. At *PA* 645a7-17 Aristotle observes that pictures of unattractive objects give pleasure because along with the picture we observe the art which formed it. This, I take it, implies recognition not simply of *what* is portrayed but also of *why* it has been portrayed in the way it has (the parallel is with a philosopher taking pleasure in understanding why a natural organism is formed as it is). Since the artists themselves may achieve success in imitation by habit, instinct or trial and error (1447a19-20, 1451a24, 1454a10-11), i.e. without an understanding of the reasons for what they are doing, it seems unlikely that such an understanding is achieved by all, or even most, observers. So Aristotle is here describing a pleasure of more restricted accessibility than that of *Poetics* 4 (contrast 1448b14-15 'not just for philosophers but for others too in the same way, despite their limited capacity for it' with 645a10 'for those who can discern the causes', although this is strictly outside the artistic analogy). The *Poetics* is designed to help us gain access to this kind of understanding of poetry. See Heath (n. 1), x-xii.

8. Cf. *Pol.* 1340a23-8, discussed by E. Belfiore, 'Pleasure, tragedy and Aristotelian psychology', *CQ* 35 (1985), 349-61, at 353-4.

9. For further criticism of the idea that 'the peculiar pleasure of tragedy is a cognitive pleasure' see Jonathan Lear, '*Katharsis*', *Phronesis* 33 (1988), 297-326, at 307-14. Halliwell (n. 1), 69-77, interprets the cognitive pleasure as the genus of which the characteristic pleasure is a species. This would meet my first two points, but does not explain Aristotle's preference for a species in which the concomitant emotion is painful. Furthermore, although Aristotelian emotions presuppose cognitions, it is not clear that cognitions entail emotions. I may recognise (e.g.) that Oedipus has suffered undeserved destructive and painful harm, and that this is pitiful; but if I am callous, this causes me no distress; what I feel is therefore not pity, and I cannot experience the pleasure that comes from pity through imitation.

10. Belfiore (n. 8), 349; the following quotations are from p. 360.

11. But this last claim is not, perhaps, beyond dispute: what of *katharsis* in comedy? See R. Janko, *Aristotle on Comedy* (London 1984), 143-4; Halliwell (n. 1), 274-5.

12. I have no great confidence in any particular account of *katharsis*, including that given in Heath (n. 1), xxxvii-xlii. I have slightly more confidence in the constraints on any acceptable account of *katharsis* which I use as premises here.

13. Cf. Lear (n. 9), 305-6.

14. It is sometimes argued (e.g. Lear (n. 9), 300-1) that the availability of cathartic pleasure to all is guaranteed by an explicit statement in *Pol.* 1342a11-15 that '*katharsis* and pleasurable relief' occurs for 'all'. But in context this 'all' seems to mean not 'everyone', but 'all of them', referring to the previously enumerated categories: 'those prone to pity or fear, or, in general, any other emotion, and to others to the extent that each is susceptible to such things.' This implies that *katharsis* applies in varying degrees to a limited (though perhaps very large) constituency.

21

15. Caution is needed here. Medicine, for Aristotle, is allopathic (cf. Lear (n. 9), 301; Halliwell (n. 1), 193 n. 37), so Aristotle cannot have thought that *katharsis* was like homeopathic healing (cf. E. Belfiore, *Tragic Pleasures: Aristotle on Plot and Emotion* (Princeton 1992), 260-90 for a critique of homeopathic interpretations). Rather, he describes a homeopathic process, and thought that it produced 'as it were' healing.

16. See also *Pol.* 1333a30-b5; *EN* 1176b27-a11, 1177b4-5.

17. On this difficult passage cf. Carnes Lord, *Education and Culture in the Political Thought of Aristotle* (Ithaca 1982), 79-80. Lord's detailed exegesis is often very helpful, although I shall dissent from his overall interpretation in one crucial respect.

18. Lord (n. 17), 82-5.

19. Cf. R. Kraut, *Aristotle Politics Books VII and VIII* (Oxford 1997), 204-6.

20. Lord (n. 17), 83.

21. For the opposition between leisure and necessity see also *Met.* 981b19-20, 982b23.

22. At this point I come close to Too (n. 1), 94: 'Literature is leisure, and is thus self-justifying ... I suggest that where the *Politics* deals with literary art in the context of education, the *Poetics* deals with the citizen's post-pedagogic experience of literature, such that literature is to be seen as a form of leisure (now *diagoge*). As Leon Golden argues, it thus concerns the activity of the mature, free, and educated citizen ...' (the reference is to L. Golden, 'Aristotle and the audience for tragedy', *Mnemosyne* 29 (1976), 351-9). However, the *Poetics* recognises that tragic audiences do not in practice consist solely of the best kind of spectator; and I suspect that the differentiation of the tragic audience (Too 106) provides the opening for a therapeutic interpretation of *katharsis* (contrast Too 110 and many others), as already suggested by W.J. Verdenius, '*Katharsis tôn pathêmatôn*', in *Autour d'Aristote: Recueil d'Études offert à A. Mansion* (Louvain, 1955), 367-73.

23. Emotions are not, of course, virtues (*EN* 1105b28-1106a6), nor is feeling an emotion a virtuous *action* (since it is not prohaeretic); nevertheless, when a virtuous person feels an emotion appropriately this is an *energeia* in which his or her virtuous character is expressed. Outside the theatre, an emotional response is not enough to express virtue: some corresponding action is required. But in the theatre there is no appropriate action that the emotionally responsive spectator is failing to perform. So the absence of any additional action does not mean that spectator's response is in any way defective: in that context, the emotional response is the only appropriate *energeia*, and therefore suffices to express virtue.

24. See further Belfiore (n. 8), 355-9. Also relevant, perhaps, is *Rhet.* 1370b1-7: unpleasant objects may give pleasure in recollection, 'and the reason for this is that the absence of what is bad is also pleasant'. Note, too, that the virtuous activity of other people is easier to discern than one's own (*EN* 1169b33-5): is this in part because of the circumstantial distractions that attend one's own activities under normal conditions?

25. The discussion of courage may again be relevant: 'It is for facing what is painful ... that men are called brave. Hence also courage involves pain, and is justly praised; for it is harder to face what is painful than to abstain from what is pleasant' (*EN* 1117a32-5).

26. Lodovico Castelvetro, *Poetica d'Aristotele vulgarizzata e sposta* (1576),

ed. W. Romani (Rome, 1978-9), I 365 (on 1452b38), 391 (on 1453b10); a translation of the latter passage is available in A.H. Gilbert (ed.), *Literary Criticism:
Plato to Dryden* (New York, 1946). Baxter Hathaway, *The Age of Criticism: The
Late Renaissance in Italy* (Ithaca, 1962), 257, provides a further parallel from
Lorenzo Giacomini ('Sopra la purgazione della tragedia', 1586): 'Since feeling
compassion is an act of virtue and since every action that is in accordance with
virtue or resembles virtue is by its nature joyful the compassion of tragedy can
also in this way bring delight.'

27. Hugh Blair, *Lectures on Rhetoric and Belle-Lettres* (ed. 1, London, 1783),
II 494-6. See also Joseph Trapp, *Praelectiones Poeticae* (ed. 3, London, 1736), II
271-6; Richard Hurd, *Q. Horatii Flacci Epistolae ad Pisones et Augustum*
(London, 1753; ed. 5, 3 vols, London, 1776), on *AP* 103: 'Putting all these things
together, the conclusion is, That though the impressions of the theatre are, in
their immediate effect, painful to us, yet they must, on the whole, afford us
extreme pleasure, and that in proportion to the degree of the first painful
impression. For not only our attention is roused, but our moral instincts are
gratified; we reflect with joy that they are so, and we reflect too that the sorrows
which call them forth, and give this exercise to our humanity, are but fictitious.
We are occupied, in a word, by a great event; we are melted into tears by a
distressful one; the heart is relieved by this burst of sorrow; is cheered and
animated by the finest moral feelings; exults in the consciousness of its own
sensibility; and finds, in conclusion that the whole is but illusion.'

28. Susan L. Feagin, 'The pleasures of tragedy', *APQ* 20 (1983), 95-104. at
98. This paper is criticised by M. Packer, *JAAC* 47 (1989), 212-19, who however
fails to realise that for Feagin pleasure is taken not in the pain as such, but in
the implications of the fact that we are pained; moreover, counter-examples
involving meta-responses such as remorse are clearly irrelevant to a theory
based on meta-responses which approve and endorse a direct response.

29. An early version of this paper was given at Ohio State University and
Wellesley College in September 1990; I am grateful to both audiences, and to
Stephen Halliwell and Elizabeth Belfiore, for their helpful comments. The
discussion at the Oslo symposium in May 2000 was also enjoyable and illuminating.

Dramatic and Epic Time: 'Magnitude' and 'Length' in Aristotle's *Poetics*

Elizabeth Belfiore

1. Introduction

The idea of magnitude (*megethos*) figures prominently in Aristotle's aesthetic theory, according to which 'beauty consists in magnitude as well as order' (*Poet.* 7.1450b37: passage 5 in the Appendix to this chapter).[1] Tragedy is defined as an 'imitation of an action that is serious, complete and possesses magnitude' (6.1449b24-5: passage 3); and an important difference between tragedy and epic is that the latter has greater magnitude (24.1459b22-3: passage 11). In spite of its importance, magnitude and the related concept of length (*mêkos*) received relatively little attention in twentieth-century scholarly literature. Most books and commentaries provide little detailed analysis, and Omert Schrier's bibliography lists only three items devoted to the subject.[2] This neglect is partly due to the fact that Aristotle's views on magnitude and length present notorious difficulties.

One major problem is that Aristotle's statements are neither easy to interpret nor obviously consistent with one another.[3] The superior length of epic is sometimes said to be an advantage this genre has over tragedy (24.1459b17-31: passage 11). In other passages, however, epic's greater length is cited as a disadvantage (for example, 26.1462a18-b11: passage 12). Another problem concerns the meaning(s) of the terms. According to D.W. Lucas, 'the meaning of *mêkos* ... is one of the major problems of the *P[oetics]*'. He writes that the term 'has three possible meanings: (1) physical length of the written work, the number of feet of papyrus or the number of lines in the epic or tragedy; (2) ... the time required for the performance of a play or epic ... (3) the length of time of the action'.[4] Scholars also dispute about whether *megethos*, instead of or in addition to having a quantitative sense, also has qualitative connotations, meaning 'grandeur'.[5] Some support for all of these views can be found in the *Poetics*. Passage 12 (26.1462b1-3) states that a tragedy with as many verses as the *Iliad* would be inferior. The prescription that one epic should be equal to the number of tragedies presented at one hearing (24.1459b21-2: passage 11), clearly refers to performance time. Nevertheless, Aristotle states that the 'limit of length which is determined by theatrical performances and perception is not relevant to the art of poetry' (7.1451a6-7: passage 6). In still another passage, the statement that tragedy 'tries as far as possible to keep within one revolution of the sun' (5.1449b12-13: passage 2), might be interpreted as a reference to length of time of the action imitated, since Greek tragedies did not require an entire day to perform. Finally, 'magnitude' in the definition of tragedy (passage 3) could be taken to mean 'grandeur' because it has no obviously quantitative sense in this passage, where it occurs in conjunction with the term *spoudaias* ('noble' or 'serious'). To add to the difficulties, these questions of meaning are inextricably bound up with many other problems of interpretation. For example, what is the relationship between performance and the art of poetry (7.1451a6-7: passage 6)? And to what period of time does 'one revolution of the sun' refer (5.1449b12-13: passage 2)?

It may not be possible, with the limited information we have, to solve all these problems. The text of the *Poetics* does, however, provide some important clues. In the first place, Aristotle's usage of *megethos* does not differ significantly from his usage of *mêkos*. In fact, the two terms are often substituted for one another. For example, in chapter 7 (passages 4, 5 and 6) Aristotle generally uses *megethos* and cognates,[6] but at 1451a5 he writes of the *mêkos* of plots, and at 1451a6 he mentions the 'limit of *mêkous*'. The 'limit of *megethous*' given at 1451a11-15 is referred to as 'the limit of *mêkous*' in chapter 24 (1459b18: passage 11, cf. 1459b17: '*mêkos* of composition'). The term *megethos* is also used in this passage (1459b23). The frequent textual association of *megethos* with *mêkos* supports the view that both terms refer to length or extent. Indeed, every occurrence of the terms can be interpreted in this way, without recourse to an additional sense of 'grandeur'. E. Bignami notes that although a large size may contribute to grandeur, size in itself gives beauty, according to Aristotle (see 1450b37: passage 5). As Alfred Gudeman argues, not only does translating *megethos* at 1449a19 (passage 1) as 'grandeur' make *apesemnunthê* in 1449a21 tautologous, there is also no reason why 'small plots' cannot also be *semnoi*.[7] Furthermore, where a concept corresponding to the English term 'grandeur' is obviously in question, Aristotle uses other, less ambiguous terms: *apesemnunthê* (1449a21), *megaloprepeia* (1459b29: passage 11).

Aristotle also gives important information in clearly indicating that both magnitude and length are measured by time. After stating that 'beauty consists in magnitude as well as order', he writes that a very small animal is not beautiful because 'observation becomes confused as it comes close to having no perceptible duration in time' (7.1450b36-9 passage 5). In 4.1449b12-14 (passage 2), epic is said to differ from tragedy in length, for tragedy tries to 'keep within one revolution of the sun', while epic is 'without a limit in time'. In *Poetics* 26, tragedy is said to attain its end in shorter length than epic, because 'what is more concentrated is more pleasant than what is watered down by being extended in time' (*pollôi kekramenon tôi khronôi*: 1462a18-1462b2: passage 12).[8] The view that *megethos* and *mêkos* both refer to extent, measured by time, makes good sense in connection with Aristotle's views on tragic and epic plots. The tragic plot is a change or movement (*metabolê*: 11.1452a23, a31; *metabasis*: 18.1455b29) between the two end points of good and bad fortune, and therefore, like all change, is measured by means of time (*Physics* 4.220b15-32).

Close attention to Aristotle's views about time, then, can help us to understand his concept of poetic magnitude. According to David Bolotin, Aristotle holds that the time of one movement is always relative to and measured by the time of another movement.[9] Specifically, the time of the movement of the tragic plot, its magnitude, is measured by the times of two other movements. First, the time during which the action imitated is supposed to occur is measured by the time of both the literal and the metaphorical day that was held, in Greek thought, to govern ephemeral, changing, mortal affairs. The plot is also measured by the time required for the actors to perform the events and for the audience to perceive them as they are enacted. Tragedy, in turn, is the standard against which epic time and change are measured. Tragedy has a determinate *horos* ('boundary' or 'limit') of magnitude because it imitates events as taking place successively (*ephexês gignomenôn*: *Poet.* 7.1451a13: passage 6). Epic, on the other hand is 'without a limit in time' (*aoristos tôi khronôi*: 5.1449b14: passage 2), in large part because its narrative capabilities allow it to imitate events as happening either successively or simultaneously (24.1459b22-8: passage 11).

Careful analysis of Aristotle's statements about magnitude and length supports this interpretation. Section 2 argues that the puzzling phrase, 'one revolution of the sun', refers to the time of the action imitated, and resonates with traditional Greek connotations of the day and the sun. Section 3 draws on the philosopher's views about time, change and magnitude in the *Physics* to illuminate his concept of the 'limit of magnitude' in tragedy. Finally, section 4 shows how Aristotle's ideas about the 'limit of length' in epic are dependent on his theories about magnitude in tragedy.

2. 'One revolution of the sun'

A notoriously controversial passage associates tragic time with the sun: 'They [sc. tragedy and epic] also differ in length, since tragedy tries as far as possible to keep within one revolution of the sun, or to vary from this by only a little [*hupo mian periodon hêliou einai ê mikron exallattein*] whereas epic is without a limit in time, and differs in this respect' (5.1449b12-14: passage 2). This statement clearly indicates that one important distinction between epic and tragedy has to do with time, and that time in tragedy is more restricted than time in epic. Since the Renaissance, however, scholars have debated such questions as whether 'one revolution of the sun' refers to a twelve- or twenty-four hour period, whether performance time or time of the action imitated is in question, and what is meant by *mikron exallattein*.[10] Gerald Else has answered the last question by showing that *exallattein* does not mean 'exceed', but 'vary'.[11] However, the complete absence of further information about 'one revolution of the sun' makes it impossible to be certain about the meaning of the passage as a whole. Twentieth-century scholars reached consensus no more than did their predecessors.

A few accept the interpretation of Else, who follows Gustav Teichmüller in holding that the primary reference is to performance time.[12] Else points out, correctly, that the time scheme of actions represented in a play cannot be measured in the same way as that of real-life events. We cannot, in most cases, determine that the events in a play are supposed to last thirty-six or nine or seventy hours, so that elaborate calculations of action time measured in precise hours, like those of Wilhelm Felsch, are seriously misguided.[13] In any case, as Else notes, the action in some Greek plays is represented as taking place over several days (214). However, Else's argument that 'one revolution of the sun' refers to performance time is not convincing. He states: 'Plays were not performed, and we can be sure that they were not normally read, at night; they did not "exist", and were not experienced, during those hours. The drama was a daytime affair in Greece' (216). Among its other problems, this theory fails to account for the fact that the performance of a tragedy lasted only an hour or two instead of a whole day. Teichmüller goes to great lengths to overcome this difficulty. He argues that *tragôdia* at 1449b9 does not mean 'tragedy' but refers instead to the whole tragic festival during which tragedies were performed.[14] He also claims that the festival began at noon and ended with evening (209), and that comedy and tragedy were performed at the same time in different theatres (195). As these desperate attempts show, performance time is certainly relevant to tragic length, but 'one revolution of the sun' cannot plausibly be taken as a direct reference to time of performance.

Most scholars hold that this phrase refers to the time during which the action imitated is supposed to take place.[15] It makes no difference that this cannot be measured in precise numbers of hours, because, as Oliver Taplin points out: 'Dramatists do not deal in "clock time" but in "dramatic time".'[16] That is, they are concerned with creating the appearance that events take place within a brief period of time and in a continuous sequence, but do not keep to a rigid temporal framework.[17] Indeed, Aristotle's qualification, 'vary by a little', indicates that no strict clock time is in question. As Samuel Johnson remarked, 'There is no reason why a mind thus wandering in ecstasy [at the theatre] should count the clock, or why an hour should not be a century in that calenture of the brains that can make the stage a field.'[18] With this understanding, 'one revolution of the sun' can be interpreted as a reference to the time during which the action imitated appears to occur.

There are also reasons for holding that the phrase *hupo mian periodon hêliou* refers more specifically to a period of daylight in 'dramatic time'. Many scholars, even though they reject the idea of a twelve- or twenty-four hour period of clock time, agree that in many Greek tragedies the action represented gives the appearance of taking place within a period of about a day.[19] Moreover, night scenes are seldom represented on stage.[20] The fact that the extant tragedies contain frequent references to the sun, supposed to be visible to the agents of the dramatic action, also supports this view.[21] For these reasons, Else argues correctly, following O.J. Todd, that the phrase *hupo mian periodon hêliou* is equivalent to *hêmera*, in the early Greek sense of 'daylight period' and that Aristotle uses it 'to emphasise that he means the visible course of the sun'.[22] A technical, astronomical sense of *periodos* to mean 'complete circuit' is not required in this context.[23]

The many important connotations of the day and the sun in Greek thought also make it plausible to interpret the phrase as a reference to the daylight period. Aristotle and other Greeks recognised the uniform circular motion of the celestial sphere as the highest standard by means of which to measure time, and they used the visible movements of the moon and sun to measure months and years.[24] The sun, as a measure of the daylight period, provided a standard that was both variable and brief. The period of daylight varies throughout the year, so that each day varies with respect to the next, and within a single day the quantity and quality of light varies from morning to noon to evening. These aspects of the literal day, as measured by the sun, contributed to making it a good metaphor for ephemeral human life. In tragedy, and in Greek thought generally, the sun and the day it measures are associated with the brevity and instability of human life.

Not only is the day a frequent metaphor for human life in Greek thought, the term *ephêmeros* (*epi* + *hêmera*: 'that which is on day', or 'that which has day upon it'[25]) is often used to refer to mortals. In an important article, Hermann Fränkel claims that in early Greek literature the term does not mean 'creature of one day, short-lived', but 'subject to the (changing) day, variable' (131). He argues that, when applied to humans, the word refers primarily to instability and expo-

29

sure to circumstances and events that change each day, to our subjection to alternating good and bad fortune: 'Applied to man in general, the term *ephêmeros* reflects the thesis that inconstancy is inherent in human nature.'[26] Fränkel cites a number of passages in tragedy in which the concept of the day is significant. In Euripides' *Heraclidae* (851) one day is sufficient to overthrow Eurystheus, proving that for mortals 'chance is ephemeral' (*ephêmeroi tukhai*: 866). In Sophocles' *Ajax* Athena states: 'A day lowers and raises again all human affairs' (131-2), and in *Oedipus Tyrannus* Teiresias tells Oedipus: 'This day will give you birth and destroy you' (438). According to a fragment of Euripides, 'one day brought down some things from on high and raised others upwards'.[27] Fränkel argues that tragedies sometimes confine the time of action to a single day in order to highlight the *ephêmeros* nature of humans.[28]

Fränkel's claims are challenged by Matthew Dickie, who agrees that *ephêmeros* is often used to refer to inconstancy of fortune, but argues that the term can mean 'by day', 'from day to day' or 'lasting for a day', and that none of these senses has priority. Dickie also takes issue with Fränkel's view that the term refers to the instability of the human personality.[29]

Although Fränkel and Dickie each grasp part of the truth, neither interpretation recognises that there is an essential connection between brevity and variability in the Greek experience and concept of the daylight period. Because this period is both brief and variable, *ephêmeros* is a suitable term for both the brevity and the variability of human life, suggesting that we are beings subject to the brevity and the variability of the day. In the passages from tragedy cited by Fränkel, the single day often connotes both brevity and instability.

This inclusive interpretation of *ephêmeros* makes particularly good sense of a statement of Antiphon's quoted by Fränkel: 'Living is like a day's watch [*phrourai ephêmerôi*], and the length of life is like one day, so to speak [*hôs epos eipein*], during which, having looked towards the light [*phôs*], we hand it over to others coming after' (DK 87B 50). Fränkel, who cites this passage as a rare instance in which *ephêmeros* refers to the brevity of human life, observes that Antiphon adds the qualification *hôs epos eipein* ('so to speak') because the comparison of human life to a day was so unusual in his time.[30] This seems unlikely, given that the comparison of a *time of* life to a *time of* day was a commonplace by Aristotle's time. In the *Poetics* (21.1457b22-5), Aristotle quotes the saying, attributed to Empedocles, that 'old age is the evening of life' or 'the sunset of life', for which Alfred Gudeman cites a number of parallels, including Aeschylus' *Agamemnon* 1123.[31] According to Empedocles, human life, like the period of daylight, is short and varies in quality from morning, to noon, to evening. In the Antiphon passage also, it is reasonable to interpret the concepts of the day and of *ephêmeros* in this way. The mention of 'light' (*phôs*) indicates that Antiphon's 'day' is the period of daylight, lasting from morning, to noon, to evening. It is plausible to hold that Antiphon, like Empedocles, takes these periods of the day to correspond to youth, maturity, and old age, respectively. Antiphon adds a qualification not because his comparison is unusual, but because 'one day' is too absolute: 'so to speak' means 'practically', 'almost',[32] that is, 'more or less'. Human life, then, according to Antiphon, is measured in quantity and quality by the light of the variable period of daylight, and may itself last a longer or shorter time than this light.

In the passage about the sun, Aristotle is making a point similar to that of Antiphon: the length of tragedy, that is, the time during which the action represented appears to occur, like the length of human life in Antiphon, keeps 'more or less' to the limit of 'one day'. A plausible interpretation of this passage is that Aristotle, like Antiphon, considers this day to be both brief and variable, instead of lasting for a strict twelve- or twenty-four hour clock time. According to this view, Aristotle conceives of the 'dramatic time' of the tragic day as the measure of the life of mortals, who are bounded by and subject to, first, the changes that may occur within a literal period of daylight, and, second, the metaphorical day of ephemeral human life. The literal and metaphorical day is the period required for the passage of a mortal, according to probability or necessity, between the end points of good and bad fortune. As the imitation of an action that moves between these end points, tragedy is concerned with the affairs of mortals, whose existence is bounded by time, and whose fortunes can change completely in a single day. The 'tragic day', more or less, then, is one measure of the plot's movement. Aristotle's other statements about magnitude and length in tragedy indicate that there are also other standards against which the length of tragedy is measured.

3. The 'limit of magnitude' in tragedy

Aristotle's ideas about the magnitude of one kind of movement, or change – that of the plot – can be better understood in light of his ideas, expressed in the *Physics*, about other kinds of changes. *Physics* 4.220b15-32 states that time, change and magnitude are measured by means of one another:

> Not only do we measure change [*kinêsin*] by time, we also measure time by change, because they are defined [*horizesthai*] by one another .... This is reasonable, for change accompanies magnitude, and time accompanies change .... And we also measure

magnitude by change and change by magnitude. We say that the
road is long if the journey is long, and that the journey is long if
the road is long. And we say that time is long if the change is long,
and that change is long if the time is also.

Aristotle also holds that we are aware of magnitude, change and time
by means of the same faculty (*Memory and Recollection* 450a9-10).
Because we are aware of time and change simultaneously (*hama*: *Phys.*
219a3-4), if we have no awareness of changes in our consciousness, we
have none of time (*Phys.* 218b21-3).[33] According to Aristotle, then, time,
change and magnitude define and determine one another, and are
perceived and measured by means of one another. These ideas about
the relationships among time, magnitude (or length or distance), and
change (or movement) have a very modern sound. It is recognised today
also that length of time must be measured by change: 'The accurate
mechanical measurement of time must be based upon some repetitive
movement that occurs with complete regularity.'[34]

Aristotle would also have agreed in some respects with the idea in
modern physics that time and movement are relative. According to
David Bolotin, Aristotle holds not just that time is measured by change,
but that the time of one change is always relative to and measured by
the time of another change.[35] He argues that this interpretation best
explains Aristotle's puzzling account of 'the before and after' in change:

> But we recognize time when we mark off [*horisômen*] change
> [*kinêsin*], marking it off by the before and the after. We say that
> time has passed when we have perception of the before and after
> in the change. We mark it off by supposing that these are different,
> and that there is something other in between. When we think that
> the extremes are other than the middle, and the mind says that
> the nows are two – that the one is before and the other after – then
> we also say that this is time .... For this is time: the number of
> change with respect to the before and the after (*Phys.* 219a22-b2)

Bolotin points out some of the difficulties in this passage: '[W]hat is
there in motion [that is, change] that can be called "the before and after"
other than the different places that the moving body passes through or
the different moments at which it passes through these places?' Neither
of these possibilities is satisfactory, according to Bolotin. If the 'before
and after' are places, it is hard to see why Aristotle calls them 'nows'.
On the other hand, they cannot be moments in time, because the before
and after in motion is mentioned in the definition of time given in the
passage quoted above (219b1-2), and is said, at 219a14-19, to be prior
to the before and after in time.[36] Instead, Bolotin suggests, 'the measure

is always a motion, and a different motion from the one whose time we seek' (53). For example, the time of my walking can only be measured in terms of the time of some other motion, for example, that of the sun: 'I start hiking just as the sun is rising and ... I then stop for lunch when it is overhead. The former of these coincidences between stages of the different motions can be seen to come before the latter one, and the interval between this before and after is perceived as time' (52). Aristotle, according to Bolotin, recognised the general principle 'that time appears only in the comparison of different motions' (53). Our perception of time also involves the comparison of the times of two different motions. According to Bolotin, because perception of an external motion 'is itself a kind of motion, a change in the state of my mind or soul', Aristotle holds 'that awareness of our own perceiving, and a comparison between this motion and the motion that we primarily perceive, is the basis for the full awareness of time' (54-5).

The principle that time, change, magnitude, and our perception of these things are defined and measured relative to one another can help to illuminate Aristotle's views about time and magnitude in tragedy. The passage about the sun (passage 2, discussed above, section 2), explicitly connects length with time. The philosopher's other statements about the length and magnitude of tragedy (passages 1 and 3-9) also support the view that these concepts are related to time and give further information about how tragic time is measured.

It has seldom been recognised that in merely stating that tragedy is an imitation of an action (*praxis*) possessing magnitude Aristotle implies that this action takes place over time. The definition of tragedy states: 'tragedy is an imitation of an action that is ... complete and possesses magnitude' (passage 3). In a brief but insightful remark, Aryeh Kosman interprets this to mean that tragedy imitates 'an action which is complete although taking place over time: *teleias megethos ekhousês*'.[37] This interpretation is supported by Aristotle's explanation in passage 4, which contains an explicit reference ('we have laid down') back to passage 3. Aristotle writes: 'We have laid down that tragedy is an imitation of a complete, i.e. whole, action, possessing a certain magnitude.' He goes on to define the kind of 'whole' that has a certain magnitude as something whose middle and end follow its beginning by necessity, nature, or 'in general' (*hôs epi to polu*), that is, according to probability or necessity.[38] We know from *Physics* 219a22-b2, quoted above, that if something has a beginning, middle and end that differ from one another, it must take place over time. An action with magnitude, then, is one that takes place over time.

The most detailed account of length and magnitude in tragedy is given in Chapter 7. Aristotle writes (passage 6):

But the limit which agrees with the actual nature of the matter is that invariably the greater the plot is (up to the point of simultaneous perspicuity) the more beautiful it is with respect to magnitude; or, to state a straightforward definition, 'the magnitude in which a series of events occurring successively in accordance with probability or necessity gives rise to a change from good fortune to bad fortune, or from bad fortune to good fortune', is a sufficient limit of magnitude.

The idea of time enters into this 'limit' or 'definition' in a number of ways. Passages 3 and 4, as was shown above, indicate that action, the object imitated by tragedy, takes place over time. Passage 6 states that the plot (that is, the imitation of action: 6.1450a3) itself has magnitude, and that it changes (*metaballein*), that is, moves, between good and bad fortune.[39] Because change is measured by time, and time by change (*Phys.* 220b15-32, quoted above), the tragic plot, as well as the action imitated, takes place over time. Furthermore, this change occurs according to probability or necessity, and must therefore have a beginning, middle and end (see passage 4). The magnitude of the tragic plot, then, is the magnitude, measured in time, of the change from beginning, to middle, to end.

Aristotle provides more specific information about what magnitude is appropriate to tragedy, and neither too large nor too small. For tragedy, the rule is 'the greater the plot is ... the more beautiful' (passage 6), provided it does not exceed the limit of magnitude appropriate to its genre.

In specifying that the two end points of the change are good and bad fortune, passage 6 indicates that the change must be a big one, between distant end points. This means that a plot without any change in fortune, or with a change from good to only slightly less good fortune would be a small one, no matter how many events it contained, and no matter how long it took to perform. Plots would also be too small if they failed to have a beginning, middle, and end. This implies that a plot must have at least three events, and that these events must be connected in a probable or necessary sequence. A play in which a statue happens by chance to fall and kill a man would have only one event, and hence no beginning, middle or end. However, the events in a plot in which a man murders Mitys, goes to Argos, and is killed when the statue of Mitys falls on him would have magnitude in that the events would at least appear to take place 'because of one another' (1452a1-11). This play would have a beginning (the murder), a middle (the journey to Argos) and an end (the fall of the statue), and these events could be linked, or appear to be linked, in a causal sequence. It appears likely, then, that the 'short plots' referred to in passage 1 lack magnitude in that they do not have a sequence, over time, of events moving, according to probability or necessity, between the end points of good and bad fortune.

On the other hand, a tragic plot can be too large. The requirement in passage 6 that the plot imitate events happening successively (*ephexês gignomenôn*) is in part a stricture against a tragic plot that has too great a magnitude for its genre. Epic, but not tragedy, can extend its magnitude by imitating events as happening at the same time rather than successively (passage 11, discussed below, section 4). In tragedy, episodic plots are inferior because they 'distort the successive aspect' of this genre (passage 7). Moreover, if there are too many episodes in a tragedy, the plot will be broken up into too many pieces, and no episode will have its appropriate magnitude (passage 9). Episodes that are too long can also spoil a tragedy: this genre must have short episodes (passage 8).

The limit of magnitude for tragedy, then, requires that the plot have a beginning, middle and end, that its events take place in succession, and that it move between good and bad fortune. It also puts constraints on the number and length of the episodes. In discussing this limit, Aristotle does not specify any absolute standard, in number of lines or episodes, in performance time, or time of the action imitated, but he does provide information about how the magnitude of tragedy can be measured. The times of all changes, or movements are relative to and measured by the times of other changes. In the case of tragedy, the time of the movement of the plot, its magnitude, is measured by the times of two other movements. The first, as was shown in section 2, is that of the tragic day, the time required for the movement of a mortal, according to probability or necessity, between the end points of good and bad fortune. The time within which mortal change is represented as occurring in tragedy is both a literal period of daylight, 'more or less', as measured by 'one revolution of the sun', and the metaphorical day of ephemeral human life. The magnitude of tragedy is also measured by the time it takes the audience to perceive it, whether it is performed on stage or only heard.[40] Because the tragic plot is imitation in the manner of enactment (3.1448a19-28; 6.1449b31-3), it must necessarily be measured by the time of the changes that take place during perception and performance. Passage 6 states that this kind of time, this 'limit of length which is determined by theatrical performance and perception is not relevant to the art of poetry' (1451a6-7). That is, it is not the same as the 'limit which agrees with the actual nature of the matter' (1451a9-10). Nevertheless, perception of performance is one way in which we can measure the limit that belongs to the art of poetry. If a plot is too short, performance will take place in too short a time for the change to be perceived adequately; it will be 'close to having no perceptible duration

35

in time' (1450b38-9). If the plot is too long, or too episodic, performance will be so lacking in probable or necessary sequence, or take place in so long a time that it will be hard to remember the whole plot all together. The appropriate magnitude of the plot is instead one that is measured in part by our ability to see and remember it as a whole. It must be easily seen at one view (*eusunopton*: 1451a4), and easy to remember (*eumnêmoneuton*: 1451a5; cf. 1459a33: *eusunoptos* and 1459b19: *sunorasthai*). The times of these two movements – that of the tragic day by means of which the time of the action represented is measured, and that of perception by means of which the time of performance is measured – are compatible, for a dramatic action that is supposed to occur within one day can be performed in a brief time so as to be easily seen and remembered as a whole.[41]

4. The 'limit of length' in epic

Aristotle's statements about length in epic (passages 2 and 8-12) are even more difficult to understand than are his statements about tragedy. For one thing, they are notoriously difficult to reconcile with one another. It is clear that tragedy is more limited than epic in its ability to extend the plot by means of episodes (passage 7), and that tragic episodes must be short and few, while those of epic can be longer and more numerous (passages 8, 10, 11). However, it is not easy to determine what Aristotle's views actually are about the relative advantages of epic's greater length. In passage 12, tragedy's shorter length is said to be an advantage because it gives this genre greater unity, and allows it to produce a more concentrated pleasure. On the other hand, epic's superior length is cited as an advantage in passage 11, where Aristotle writes: 'Epic has an important distinctive resource for extending its magnitude', and he calls this an 'advantage in achieving grandeur [*megaloprepeian*], variety of interest for the hearer and diversity of episodes'. Passage 6 also appears to claim that length is an advantage, stating that even in a tragic plot, bigger is better, so long as the whole can be seen together.

A related difficulty concerns the unity of epic. In passage 10, Homer is praised for composing a poem about 'one part' (*hen meros*) of the Trojan War, and using other parts as episodes, in contrast to other epic poets, who write about 'a single action of many parts' (*mian praxin polumerê*). This might appear to support Else's view that Aristotle has in mind 'a core approximating to the limit of length [for tragedy], which is then expanded more or less without limit by the addition of episodes'.[42] Else's interpretation might also seem to be supported by the claim that epic 'is about one action' (*peri mian praxin*: 8.1451a28, 23.1459a19). Other passages, however, appear to support Lucas's view that different passages have different emphases, and that it is impossible to draw a firm line between what Else calls a 'core', and subordinate episodes.[43] Passage 9 states that an epic plot structure, that of the *Iliad*, for example, is one that 'contains a multiplicity of stories [*polumuthon*]'. Aristotle indicates that more than one tragedy can be made from one epic at 23.1459b2-7 and 24.1459b20-2 (passage 11). He also states (26.1462b8-9: passage 12) that epic 'comprises a number of actions' and that even the *Iliad* and the *Odyssey* have 'many parts' (*polla merê*). It may also be significant that Aristotle uses the plural, *mesa* ('middles'), in characterising epic at 23.1459a20.[44] All of these apparent inconsistencies lead Roselyne Dupont-Roc and Jean Lallot to argue that epic is ruled by contradictory constraints: it must be long but also unified.[45] According to Stephen Halliwell, the difficulties arise from Aristotle's attempt to assimilate epic to the standards of tragedy.[46] And Malcolm Heath argues that Aristotle's statements about the inferiority of epic length in Chapter 26 result from his attempt to make a case against those who claim that tragedy is inferior.[47]

At least some of the difficulties in Aristotle's account can be solved if we note the fact that epic length is relative to that of tragedy. Indeed, epic time and length are doubly relative. Aristotle's statements appear inconsistent in large part because epic length and time are relative to those of tragedy, which are themselves relative to other times and lengths. Epic, unlike tragedy, is by nature 'without a limit in time' (*aoristos tôi khronôi*: passage 2), and for this reason is only 'an imitation of a single action to the greatest possible degree' (26.1462b10-11: passage 12). No epic can be as unified as a tragedy. Nevertheless, the more closely an epic approaches the ideal of imitation of a single action, the more nearly it approximates tragic time.[48]

Aristotle's ideas about the differences between time and length in tragedy and epic depend in large part on his ideas about the differences between the two genres with respect to their manner of imitation (*hôs*: 3.1448a19). Tragedy is said to use only the dramatic manner, imitating 'everyone as acting and doing' (1448a23), and in the definition of tragedy narrative is explicitly excluded (*ou di' apaggelias*: 6.1449b26). Epic, on the other hand, even though it can use direct discourse (when the narrator 'becomes something else': 3.1448a21), is a characteristically narrative form (*apaggelonta*: 1448a21; *diêgêsin*: 24.1459b26; *diêgêmatikês*: 23.1459a17), in which the poet speaks 'as the same person, without changing' (3.1448a22; 24.1460a7). As a consequence of this essential generic characteristic, epic is less clearly defined in respect to time than is tragedy.

As a dramatic genre, without narrative, tragedy is circumscribed by the conditions necessary for performance on stage. Aristotle writes: 'Since the imitation is performed by actors [*prattontes*] it follows first of all that the management of the spectacle [*opseôs kosmos*] must be a component part of tragedy' (6.1449b31-3). This statement is consistent with his claim that tragedy does not need to be performed in order to accomplish its proper effect (14.1453b3-10). Spectacle is a necessary part of tragedy whether or not it is actually performed, because a dramatic work from which narrative is excluded is only able to imitate the part of the story 'on stage involving the actors' (24.1459b24-6: passage 11). That is, tragedy can only imitate events as they occur in, the dramatic present, along a single, forward-moving time line. In this genre the sequence of events on stage is the same as that of the actions it imitates. Epic, on the other hand, is able to imitate 'many parts being carried on simultaneously' (*hama prattomena polla merê*: 1459b24-5; passage 11). The epic narrator is able to stop the forward movement of the time line of the plot, and go backwards or forwards along it to relate events out of the sequence in which they occur in the action imitated. Although the narrator can indicate that these events occur before other events (flashback, *analêpsis*), after them (anticipation, *prolêpsis*), or at the same time, Aristotle mentions only the last possibility.[49]

This important generic difference between tragedy and epic is mentioned in a number of passages. In defining the 'limit of magnitude' appropriate to tragedy, Aristotle states that this kind of imitation should represent 'events occurring successively' (*ephexês gignomenôn*: 7.1451a13: passage 6). Here and elsewhere, he uses the term 'successively' (*ephexês*) to refer to the single, forward-moving time line of dramatic imitation. He also criticises tragic poets who 'draw out the plot beyond its potential, and are often forced to distort the successive aspect' (*to ephexês*: 9.1451b38-1452a1: passage 7). When Aristotle turns to epic, and, in a clear reference back to Chapter 7, mentions the 'stated limit of length' (24.1459b18-20: passage 11), he omits the phrase about successive events, merely stating that one should be able to see together the beginning and the end. A distinction between events happening successively and events happening simultaneously is explicitly made at the beginning of Chapter 23, where Aristotle writes that history and epic can represent everything that happened at one time (*henos khronou*: 1459a23), or things happening 'in successive times' (*en tois ephexês khronois*: 1459a27-8).

Scholars have not always fully understood Aristotle's exclusion of the representation of simultaneous events from dramatic genres. For example, Ingram Bywater sees 'an indirect recognition of the Unity of Place', and Stephen Halliwell notes that Aristotle ignores the messenger speech in tragedy.[50] Aristotle, however, is merely taking into account the constraints inherent in the dramatic manner of imitation. As Else notes:

38

[T]he 'part on the stage' supplies an ineluctable point of reference for all other actions. Nor is it a matter of the stage *per se*: that is, it is not one of those external factors which Aristotle had rejected (7.51a6) as *pros tên aisthêsin* [determined by perception]. It is inherent in the *idea* of the drama as a continuous action going on in a certain place and enacted by a given set of people, whether the play is ever performed – or even written to be performed – or not .... So long as the dramatic setting and continuity of action are retained, they imperatively establish a single time-perspective.[51]

More recently, Manfred Pfister has helped to elucidate the distinction between dramatic and epic (or narrative) time.[52] He notes that in narrative texts, a 'mediating, fictional narrator' allows for an 'arbitrary rearrangement of time-and-space relationships ... especially in the chronology of the narrative' (5). Narrative is able to present 'a number of parallel phases of action' (202). In contrast, '[t]he absence of a mediating communication system in drama means that the story is presented according to the principle of succession' which 'precludes the use of flashbacks ... and restricts the possibility of scenically presenting simultaneous actions and events to those that are bound to one and the same locale' (201), for example, when an event off stage is represented by noises heard by the audience, or when a figure on stage gives a 'teichoscopic report' (279). The principle of succession also means that 'only in drama can presented time always be clearly defined' (246). According to Pfister, drama rarely subverts 'the expectation that situations presented in successive scenes follow the same successive pattern as fictional chronology'. When such a thing occurs, 'this is a dramatic deviation from the norm and must be clearly signalled' (277), for example, by means of the introduction of 'epic communication structures', such as the use of a narrator figure, or freezing the movements of the figures (278), or even by physically dividing the stage into several parts (279).

Ancient Greek tragedy made limited use of noises heard off-stage and of teichoscopic reports. Antonios Rengakos cites a number of passages in which these techniques are used, in arguing that Greek tragedy, contrary to Aristotle's claim, did represent simultaneous actions.[53] In Aeschylus' *Choephori* 869, Aegisthus gives a cry within the house as he is being murdered. In Euripides' *Heracles*, Lycos (750, 754), Amphitryon (887ff.) and Heracles (906-8) are heard crying out, and in *Orestes*, Helen (1296, 1301) and Hermione (1347) cry out from within. In Euripides' *Phoenissae* 118-93 the Pedagogue shows Antigone the leaders of the Argives from the walls of Thebes, and both remark on their movements (131, 145, 172, 180-1). A well-known example not cited by Rengakos is Aeschylus' *Agamemnon* 1343 and 1345, where the king cries out within as he is being struck.

Although these passages contain indications that two actions are occurring simultaneously, the tendency of Greek tragedy to adhere to the principle of succession is apparent even in these exceptional cases. The cries heard off stage are represented less as separate actions than as integral parts of the dramatisation of a single action, in which those on stage react to noises they hear. It is significant that not only in *Orestes*, as Rengakos notes,[54] but also in *Choephori*, *Heracles* and *Agamemnon*, the cries are followed by a messenger speech. Without this speech, those on stage and the audience do not really know what action has in fact occurred, whatever they may conjecture. After Agamemnon cries out, the Chorus asks: 'What is happening?' (871). The Servant then arrives to tell them that Aigisthos is dead (877). In *Orestes* 1360, the Chorus says that it knows some things, but others 'not clearly'. The Phrygian slave is needed to reveal what events have occurred. That cries off stage are not represented as dramatisations of separate actions but as signs that must be interpreted, as prophets interpret bird cries, is sometimes made explicit. At *Agamemnon* 1366-7, the Chorus asks whether by means of the signs (*tekmêrioisin*) from the cries they have heard they will prophesy (*manteusomestha*) that Agamemnon is dead, after which Clytemnestra acts as her own messenger, reporting what she has done (1372-98). At *Heracles* 911, the Chorus addresses the Messenger as a prophet (*mantin*), before asking him to tell how the children met their fate (917-21). In the Lycos passage in this play, the Chorus does not need a messenger because it reacts to his cries as though he is visibly present on stage, responding to him directly (754-5). This interchange is preceded by the Chorus' statement: 'Let us see [*skopômen*] what is happening inside the house' (747-8).

In the teichoscopy in *Phoenissae* the movements of the Argives are vividly presented to the audience at the same time that it sees the figures on stage who report it. Even in this case, however, the tendency of Greek tragedy to avoid simultaneity is apparent from a comparison with the two models for this passage. In the epic model, the teichoscopy in *Iliad* 3, the narrator states that the Greeks lay aside their arms (114), and then Helen and Priam observe Odysseus going among the ranks while his weapons lie on the ground (195-6). The teichoscopy, then, occurs at the same time as the events on the battlefield presented by means of narration.[55] In the dramatic model, Aeschylus' *Seven Against Thebes* 375-652, a messenger reports the movements and speeches of the Argive leaders to Eteocles and the Chorus. These reported movements in the dramatic past are brought vividly before the imagination of the audience by means of the historical presents throughout the speech.[56] Nevertheless, they are neither simultaneous with the events on stage nor seen by the audience. The *Phoenissae* passage resembles its epic model in reporting action that is present rather than past, but it resembles its dramatic model in presenting this action only by means of the reports of figures on stage. These figures, and not those off stage, are the ones 'acting and doing' (*Poet.* 3.1448a23).

Messenger speeches are no exception to the dramatic principle of succession. Although reports of past events in drama have two temporal levels – that of the report, in the dramatic present, and that of the reported event, in the dramatic past[57] – any act of reporting in the tragedy is itself a part of the imitation of successive events. For example, in the action imitated in Sophocles' *Oedipus Tyrannus*, Oedipus kills Laius, and then, at a later stage, searches for the murderer. In the stage action, however, Oedipus first searches for the murderer of Laius, and only later tells Jocasta about the murder. This latter sequence can be presented in two ways: (1) the search is followed, in inverted order, by the murder; (2) the search is followed, in successive order, by narration of the murder. The first way of presentation requires a mediating narrator. In the second manner of presentation, the dramatic, the actual *pathos*, the murder, takes place prior to the beginning of the play, and is part of the 'things that have happened before' (*propepragmena*: 18.1455b30). Oedipus' narration of the *pathos*, however, is enacted within the time-frame of the play itself. That Aristotle was aware of this distinction is evident from his statement in *EN* 1101a 32-3 that it makes a difference whether 'terrible events in tragedies happen before [*prouparkhein*], or are enacted [*prattesthai*]'.[58]

Epic, unlike tragedy, is not restricted to the representation of events in successive order. This genre, as the Homeric scholiasts were well aware, is able to use narration in 'inverted order' (*ex anastrophês*) to relate events prior to or subsequent to the main action.[59] For example, the way in which Odysseus acquired his scar (*Od.* 19.392-466) is narrated in inverted order in an account of the Nurse's recognition of the mature Odysseus by means of the scar. Aristotle does not appear to have a general concept of narration in 'inverted order', but he does note that epic is able to narrate simultaneous events: 'In epic, because it is narrative, it is possible to treat many parts being carried on simultaneously [*hama ... perainomena*]' (1459b26-7: passage 11). For many years, modern scholars appealed to 'Zielinski's law', in arguing that, contrary to Aristotle's claim, Homeric epic does not represent simultaneous events.[60] Aristotle's assessment of epic, however, has been vindicated by recent research. In 1995, Antonios Rengakos not only questioned the view that Homeric epic does not represent simultaneous events, but also claimed that according to Zielinski himself, the Homeric narrator represented simultaneous actions, although he did not use the later technique of the flashback.[61] Rengakos offered many examples from

Homeric epic in support of the ancient view that epic is characterised by the representation of simultaneous actions.[62] Following Rengakos, René Nünlist provided convincing evidence that the Homeric narrator on occasion goes backwards in narrated time.[63] Although Douglas Olson, writing before Rengakos' 1995 article, argued that 'Zielinski's conception of the poet's treatment of time is ... fundamentally correct', he nevertheless offered three examples of actions both conceived and narrated as occurring simultaneously.[64] In criticising Olson's defence of Zielinski, Rengakos argued in 1998 that these three passages are actually examples of flashbacks.[65] The work of all of these scholars shows that Homeric epic, just as Aristotle claimed, represents simultaneous actions.

We are now in a better position to understand Aristotle's views on time and magnitude in epic. Because the epic plot, like that of tragedy, has a beginning, middle and end (23.1459a17-20), and epic has the same function (*ergon*) and goal (*telos*) as tragedy (26.1462a18-1462b1; 1462b12-15), it is a reasonable inference that the epic, like the tragic plot, moves between the two distant end points of good and bad fortune. In tragedy, magnitude and time are limited by the need to imitate events as happening successively, and as measured by the time of the tragic day during which the events are represented as occurring, and by our perception of performance time on the stage. For this reason, tragedy has a definite limit of magnitude. This limit extends even to reported events. In contrast to epic, in which reported events may cover a span of years, messenger speeches in tragedy, as Irene de Jong notes, restrict the events reported to a period of hours or days.[66]

Epic, on the other hand, is 'without a limit in time' (passage 2) because it is not restricted to the representation of events enacted on the stage. The convention of a mediating narrator allows this genre to extend the magnitude of the plot with longer and more numerous episodes, including those that are represented as taking place at the same time as other events. For example, the story of Odysseus' homecoming is lengthened by many episodes occurring successively, including his departure from Ogygia, his journey to Scheria and his adventures with the Phaeacians there, his return to Ithaca and his meeting with Eumaius. These episodes contain action that is supposed to occur over many days, and they are narrated in many lines that require a long time to read or to hear. The *Odyssey* is also lengthened by other episodes, the story of Telemachus, for example, that take place at the same time as other episodes. Nevertheless, in the best epics, a clear distinction between plot and episode preserves the hearers' sense of the movement of the time line between good and bad fortune, while allowing them to appreciate the stretching out of this movement by means of episodes. The limit of magnitude for tragedy, however, remains the standard against which this genre 'without limit' is measured. Aristotle illustrates this idea for the *Odyssey*, writing that the story (*logos*) of this epic is not long (17.1455b17). A single tragedy could be made out of this epic plot (23.1459b2-3: passage 10), in which Odysseus returns home, is recognised, and punishes his enemies (17.1455b17-23).

Homer in fact constructs his epic so as to subordinate what Aristotle calls 'episodes' to what he refers to as the 'story'. Many of Odysseus' adventures (for example, the Ciconians, the Lotus-Eaters, the Cyclops, Aiolos, the Laistrygonians, Circe, the Underworld, the Sirens, Scylla and Charybdis, the Cattle of the Sun, Calypso) are narrated as episodes told by Odysseus within the episode of the Phaeacians. Odysseus' narration, moreover, is reported as taking place within a single night (Books 9-12), the passing of which is alluded to repeatedly (11.330-1, 375-9; 13.17-18). Odysseus tells these same adventures, as well as that of the Phaeacians, to Penelope in Book 23 (306-43), once again within a single night. In the latter passage, the narrator of the *Odyssey* calls attention to this fact even more explicitly than is the case in the Phaeacian episode, for Odysseus' story to Penelope is framed by the narration of Athena's deliberate lengthening of this night (23.241-6, 344-8). During the same night, Penelope narrates the story of the suitors (302-5). As a story within a story, Odysseus' adventures are clearly separated from the main story of his homecoming. As a story recounted during a long night in Phaeacia, or a timeless night in Ithaca, the adventures are marked off as taking place outside the time measured by the days during which the events of the main story are represented as taking place. In these ways, the *Odyssey* is a good example of Aristotle's principle: although epic is 'less unified' than tragedy, good epics nevertheless imitate a single action 'to the greatest possible degree' (passage 12), and they make skilful use of episodes to diversify the composition (passage 10).

5. Conclusion: the relativity of time and magnitude

I have argued that *megethos* and *mêkos* in the *Poetics* both refer to length, measured in time. Aristotle's apparently inconsistent remarks about these concepts can be more easily comprehended if we understand that magnitude and time are not absolute in themselves, but are relative to other times and magnitudes. Tragedy has a 'limit of magnitude' that is not the same as a specific number of verses, or as the time of performance measured by a waterclock, or as the time of a single day during which the action is represented as occurring. Nevertheless, all of these ways of measuring time are relevant. The magnitude of tragedy, an imitation of an action that moves between good and bad fortune and that is presented on stage by actors speaking verses, is measured by a time that is neither too long nor too short relative to our ability to perceive and remember. In turn, the time of the action imitated is measured relative to the 'tragic day', both literal and metaphorical. Epic is doubly relative, for this genre is in itself 'unlimited in time', and is instead measured by the more determinate time of tragedy, which it can only approximate. According to Aristotle, then, 'beauty consists in magnitude', not absolutely, but relative to the perception of ephemeral beings.[67]

Notes

1. For the *Poetics*, I adapt the translation of M. Heath, *Aristotle: Poetics* (Harmondsworth, 1996). The Greek text is that of R. Kassel, *Aristotelis De arte poetica liber* (Oxford, 1965). All other translations are my own. Passages frequently cited are listed by number in the Appendix to this chapter.

2. O.J. Schrier, *The Poetics of Aristotle and the Tractatus Coislinianus: A Bibliography from about 900 till 1996* (Leiden, 1998), s.v. *megethos*. In spite of its title, V. Goldschmidt, *Temps physique et temps tragique chez Aristote* (Paris, 1982) is disappointingly lacking in detailed analysis. Earlier discussions focused primarily on the meaning of 'one revolution of the sun' (1449b12-13).

3. M. Heath, *Unity in Greek Poetics* (Oxford, 1989), 43-4 provides a good, brief summary of some of the major difficulties.

4. D.W. Lucas, *Aristotle: Poetics* (Oxford, 1968), 93 on 1449b12-16.

5. See below, n. 7.

6. 1450b25, 1450b26, 1450b36, 1450b37, 1451a4, 1451a11, 1451a12, 1451a15.

7. E. Bignami, *La Poetica di Aristotele e il concetto dell' arte presso gli antichi. Studi filosofici* 7 (Florence, 1932), 199 n. 1, who also notes that the two terms are used interchangeably; A. Gudeman, *Aristoteles. Peri Poietikes* (Berlin, 1934), 139. Among scholars who argue that the term *megethos* can include some connotations of 'grandeur' are I. Bywater, *Aristotle on the Art of Poetry* (Oxford, 1909), 137-8; R. Dupont-Roc and J. Lallot, *Aristote. La Poétique* (Paris, 1980), 174; Lucas, op. cit., 84; R. Janko, *Aristotle's Poetics I* (Indianapolis, 1987), 78, 89, 213.

8. G.F. Else, *Aristotle's Poetics: The Argument* (Cambridge, MA, 1957), 215 n. 114 and 218 n. 125 notes that 'time' and 'length' are equivalents in passages 2 and 12.

9. D. Bolotin, 'Aristotle's discussion of time: an overview', *Ancient Philosophy* 17 (1997), 47-62, discussed below, section 3.

10. For discussions of the literature on the subject, from the Renaissance through the early twentieth century, see S.H. Butcher, *Aristotle's Theory of Poetry and Fine Art* (New York, 1911), 289-301; Gudeman, op. cit., 155-8; Else, op. cit., 210-17; B. Weinberg, *A History of Literary Criticism in the Italian Renaissance*, 2 vols (Chicago, 1961), esp. 69, 415, 453, 470, 508-10, 540-1, 547, 570-2, 587, 695-7; S. Halliwell, *Aristotle's Poetics* (London, 1986), 286-323.

11. Else, op. cit., 212.

12. Else, op. cit., 210-17; G. Teichmüller, *Aristotelische Forschungen I. Beiträge zur Erklärung der Poetik des Aristoteles* (Halle, 1867). Others who

argue in favour of performance time include L. Golden and O.B. Hardison, Jr., *Aristotle's Poetics: A Translation and Commentary for Students of Literature* (New Jersey, 1968), 110; Goldschmidt, op. cit., 221-2; R.T. Urban, 'All or nothing at all: another look at the unity of time in Aristotle', *Classical Journal* 61 (1966), 262-4.

13. Else, op. cit., 210, and 214 n. 110, citing W. Felsch, *Quibus artificiis adhibitis poetae tragici Graeci unitates illas et temporis et loci observaverint. Breslauer philologische Abhandlungen* 9 (1907).

14. Teichmüller, op. cit., 206.

15. For example: Bywater, 147-8; Butcher, 289-91; Gudeman, 156-7; Lucas, on 1449b12-16; Dupont-Roc and Lallot, 183-4; Janko, on 1449b12; Heath, op. cit. n. 3, 44.

16. O. Taplin, *The Stagecraft of Aeschylus* (Oxford, 1977), 291.

17. Taplin, op. cit., 290-4, who cites R.C. Flickinger, *The Greek Theater and Its Drama* (Chicago, 1918) and T.W. Goodell, *Athenian Tragedy: A Study in Popular Art* (New Haven, 1920). That Else was aware of this issue, although he did not realise its implications for his interpretation of 1449b12-16, is shown by his discussion of 'empty time': 292-5.

18. S. Johnson, 'Preface to Shakespeare' [1765]. In P. Cruttwell, ed., *Samuel Johnson. Selected Writings* (Harmondsworth, 1968), 275.

19. Noted by Flickinger, op. cit., 254-5; O.J. Todd, 'One circuit of the sun: a dilemma', *Transactions of the Royal Society of Canada* III 36 (1942), 120-3; Else, 214 n. 110; Janko on 1449b12. For examples see below, n. 28.

20. Gudeman, 157 and Else, 216 cite *Rhesus* as the only extant drama represented as taking place at night.

21. For example: Aes. *Ag.* 279, *Ch.* 983-6, *Supp.* 213; Soph. *Aj.* 856-8, *Ant.* 879-80; *El.* 17-19, *OT* 1424-9; Eur. *Alc.* 244, *IA* 1506-9, *Ba.* 918, *Ion* 82-5.

22. Else, 216 (citing Todd, op. cit.), and n. 118.

23. In arguing that the phrase means *entos mias hêmeras* ('within one day'), that is, one period of daylight, Alfred Gudeman (157) cites *Top.* 142b3: *hêmera estin hêliou phora huper gês* ('a day is the passage of the sun above the earth'). Francis Dunn, in correspondence, suggested to me that Aristotle chooses a semi-technical phrase in order to imply that the limitation is 'natural' or necessary.

24. *Phys.* 223b12-224a2, with *Phys.* 8.8-9 (e.g. 265b8-11). On celestial motion see also *Metaph.* 12. 8; *De Caelo* 2.8. Good recent discussions of the solar and lunar calendars used by the Athenians are those of F.M. Dunn, 'The uses of time in fifth-century Athens', *Ancient World* 29 (1998), 37-52 and 'The Council's solar calendar', *American Journal of Philology* 120 (1999), 369-80.

25. H. Fränkel, 'Man's 'ephemeros' nature according to Pindar and others', *TAPA* 77 (1946), 131.

26. Fränkel, op. cit. 132-5; quotation: 135. Convincing support for Fränkel's views, in connection with Hesiod's *Days*, has recently been provided by A. Lardinois, 'How the days fit the works in Hesiod's *Work and Days*', *American Journal of Philology* 119 (1998), 319-36, who might also have noted that human characters are said to vary according to the day on which they are born: *Op.* 788-9, 792-3.

27. Fränkel, op. cit., 135 n. 13 (*Heracl.*), 141 (*Aj.*, *OT*), 143 (Eur. frag. 420 Nauck). Translations are my own.

28. Fränkel, op. cit., 141 and n. 13, citing *OT* 438. Other examples are Soph.

Aj. 753-7 (Athena's wrath against Ajax lasts for one day); Eur. *Alc.* 20-1 (this is the day on which Alcestis is fated to die). Else, 214 n. 110 lists 11 plays (Aes. *Supp.*; Soph. *Aj., Trach., OT, El.*; Eur. *Alc., Hipp., Med., Ion, Phoen., Or.*) for which Felsch (op. cit., 3, 18-21, 44-7 claims explicit evidence that the action takes place in one day. Gudeman, op. cit., 157 cites 7 plays (Aes. *Pers., Ag.*; Soph. *Trach., OC*; Eur. *Sthenboia, Heracl., Andr.*) that depart from the rule of one day. The subjectivity of these kinds of assessments is indicated by the fact that Soph. *Trach.* appears on both lists. As noted above, precise indications of the time of day are not necessary to give the appearance of the passage of a period of about a day.

29. M.W. Dickie, 'On the meaning of *ephêmeros*', *Illinois Classical Studies* 1 (1976). Inconstancy: 8; quotations: 14.

30. Fränkel, 144. Dickie, 13-14 explains the qualification as an apology for the 'boldness of his comparison', but does not say why it is so 'bold' if the brevity of life was, as he holds, a common idea.

31. Gudeman, 359. The analogy is also implicit in the riddle of the Sphinx, mentioned, for example, in Soph. *OT* 393, 1524; Eur. *Phoen.* 48, 1731. On the sources for the riddle see L. Edmunds, *The Sphinx in the Oedipus Legend. Beiträge zur klassischen Philologie* 127 (Konigstein/Ts., 1981), esp. 18-21.

32. LSJ s.v. *epos* II.4.

33. On this idea, and for related passages in Aristotle's other works, see E. Hussey, *Aristotle: Physics Books 3 and 4* (Oxford, 1983) on 218b21.

34. T.K. Derry and T.I. Williams, *A Short History of Technology* (Oxford, 1960), 225. Cf. W. Markowitz, 'Time as systematized in modern scientific society', in *Encyclopaedia Britannica*, 15th ed., vol. 28 (1998), 668: 'The progress of any phenomenon that undergoes regular changes may be used to measure time.'

35. D. Bolotin, op. cit.

36. Bolotin, 49.

37. A. Kosman, 'Acting: *drama* as the *mimêsis* of *praxis*', in A.O. Rorty, ed., *Essays on Aristlotle's Poetics* (Princeton, 1992), 57.

38. On the concept of probability and necessity and this passage see E. Belfiore, *Tragic Pleasures: Aristotle on Plot and Emotion* (Princeton, 1992), 111-14.

39. In later chapters also, Aristotle uses both *metabolê* and *metabasis* to refer to the tragic change (10.1452a16, 11.1452a23; 18.1455b29). Hussey, op. cit., 55 notes that the difference between *kinêsis* and *metabolê* is not important, even in *Physics* 3 and 4, and that Aristotle sometimes uses the terms interchangeably. See also S. Waterlow, *Nature, Change, and Agency in Aristotle's Physics* (Oxford, 1982), 93-4, 96.

40. 14.1453b3-7 states that the effects of tragedy can be produced without the visual aspects, when someone 'hears' the plot of the Oedipus; cf. 1462a12 and 17: 'reading'.

41. Cf. Dupont-Roc and Lallot, op. cit., 183-4; Heath, op. cit. n. 3, 43-4.

42. Else, 604.

43. Lucas, op. cit., on 1462b7 (*legô de* ...).

44. Noted by Malcolm Heath, in discussion.

45. Dupont-Roc and Lallot, 412.

46. Halliwell, 256-61

47. Heath, op. cit. n. 3, 54-5.

48. Stephen Halliwell pointed out in the discussion that the issue of the relationship between epic and tragedy is confused by Aristotle's apparently inconsistent statements about the evolution of tragedy. At 4.1449a19, tragedy is said to develop from 'short plots'. However, at 5.1449b15-16, immediately after the statement that epic is 'without a limit in time', Aristotle writes: 'At first, the poets did this similarly in tragedies and in epics.' In any case, it is clear that tragedy in its mature stage differs from epic in having a definite limit in time.

49. The terms 'analepsis' and 'prolepsis' are those of G. Genette, *Discours du recit: essai de methode*, in *Figures III* (Paris, 1972).

50. Bywater, 314; Halliwell, 260, n. 12; cf. A. Rengakos, 'Zeit und Gleichzeitigkeit in den homerischen Epen', *Antike und Abendland* 41 (1995), 5.

51. Else, 609-10.

52. M. Pfister, *The Theory and Analysis of Drama*, trans. J. Halliday (Cambridge, 1988).

53. Rengakos, op. cit., 5-6.

54. Rengakos, 6 and n. 17.

55. Rengakos, 6 n. 17, and 19.

56. For example, 378, 381, 392, 385, 462, 487, 537, 579, 633, 639, 640.

57. Discussed by Pfister, op. cit., 207, 277. See also I.J.F. de Jong, *Narrators and Focalizers: The Presentation of the Story in the Iliad* (Amsterdam, 1987), 149, and *Narrative in Drama: The Art of the Euripidean Messenger Speech* (Leiden, 1991), esp. 1-62, on the 'dramatic' aspects of messenger speeches; M. Bal, *Narratology: Introduction to the Theory of Narrative*, trans. C. van Boheemen (Toronto, 1985), 142-9; S. Rimmon-Kenan, *Narrative Fiction: Contemporary Poetics* (London and New York, 1983), 51.

58. Cited by S. Halliwell, *The Poetics of Aristotle: Translation and Commentary* (London, 1987), 120. On the murder of Laius and other events 'outside the drama' see D.H. Roberts, 'Outside the drama: the limits of tragedy in Aristotle's *Poetics*', in Rorty, op. cit., especially 144, citing *Rhet*. 3.16.1417a12-16, and 148, citing *NE* 1101a32ff.

59. Heath, op. cit. n. 3, 115-18.

60. T. Zielinski, *Die Behandlung gleichzeitiger Ereignisse im antiken Epos*, *Philologus* Suppl. 8 (1899-1901), is frequently cited by commentators on the *Poetics*: e.g. Else; 610 n. 49; Lucas, 223. For recent discussions of Zielinski and his followers see A. Rengakos, op. cit. n. 50 and 'Zur Zeitstruktur der Odysee', *Wiener Studien* 111 (1998), S.D. Olson, *Blood and Iron: Stories and Storytelling in Homer's Odyssey* (Leiden, 1995), ch. 5, R. Nünlist, 'Der homerische Erzähler und das sogenannte Sukzessionsgesetz', *Museum Helveticum* 55 (1998), 2-8. I am indebted to Richard Janko for calling my attention to the important articles by Rengakos and Nünlist.

61. Rengakos, op. cit. n. 50, 9.

62. Among the examples cited by Rengakos, op. cit. n. 50, 17-19, are: *Il*. 6.112ff., *Il*. 10.53ff., *Il*. 6.490ff., the teichoscopy in *Il*. 3 (161ff.). Rengakos cites (6-8) Aristarchos (Aristonikos Scholion M 2 on *Il*. 10.299) as evidence that the ancients agreed with Aristotle.

63. Nünlist, op. cit., 5-7, citing *Il*. 14.428-41, *Il*. 15.458ff. and 484ff., *Il*. 13.183-209, *Il*. 13.650-60.

64. Olson, op. cit., 95; examples (108-13): *Od*. 17.462-3 and 492-4 (cf. J. Russo, 'Books 17-20', in J. Russo, M. Fernández-Galiano and A. Heubeck, *A*

Commentary on Homer's Odyssey, vol. 3, books 17-24 (Oxford, 1992), on 17.492-506); *Od.* 15.493-16.1-3; *Od.* 23.347-24.548.

65. Rengakos, 1998, op. cit. n. 60, 56-8.

66. Odysseus remains with Circe for a year: *Od.* 10.467-71. Tragedy: de Jong, *Narrative in Drama*, op. cit. n. 57, 173.

67. I am indebted to Malcolm Heath, André Lardinois, and Douglas Olson for helpful comments on earlier drafts of this chapter, and to the audience at the Oslo symposium for lively discussions of important issues and insightful suggestions about specific points.

Appendix. List of passages frequently cited
(translations adapted from M. Heath, *Aristotle: Poetics*)

(1) In addition, the magnitude increased from short plots; and in place of comic diction, as a consequence of a change from the satyric style, tragedy acquired dignity at a late stage. (4.1449a19-21)

(2) They [sc. tragedy and epic] also differ in length, since tragedy tries as far as possible to keep within one revolution of the sun, or to vary from this by only a little, whereas epic is without a limit in time, and differs in this respect. (5.1449b12-14)

(3) Tragedy is an imitation of an action that is serious, complete and possesses magnitude. (6.1449b24-5)

(4) We have laid down that tragedy is an imitation of a complete, i.e. whole, action, possessing a certain magnitude. (There is such a thing as a whole which possesses no magnitude.) A *whole* is that which has a beginning, a middle and an end. A *beginning* is that which itself does not follow necessarily from anything else, but some second thing naturally exists or occurs after it. Conversely, an *end* is that which does itself naturally follow from something else, either necessarily or in general, but there is nothing else after it. A *middle* is that which itself comes after something else, and some other thing comes after it. (7.1450b23-31)

(5) Any beautiful object, whether a living organism or any other entity composed of parts, must not only possess those parts in proper order, but its *magnitude* also should not be arbitrary; beauty consists in magnitude as well as order. For this reason no organism could be beautiful if it is excessively small (since observation becomes confused as it comes close to having no perceptible duration in time) or excessively large (since the observation is then not simultaneous, and the observers find that the sense of unity and wholeness is lost from their observation, e.g. if there were an animal a thousand miles long). So just as in the case of physical objects and living organisms, they should possess a certain magnitude, and this should be such as can readily be taken in at one view, so in the case of plots: they should have a certain length, and this should be such as can readily be held in memory. (7.1450b34-1451a6)

(6) The limit of length which is determined by theatrical performances and perception is not relevant to the art of poetry; if it were necessary to perform a hundred tragedies they would time the performances by the clock, as they say used to be done on other occasions. But the limit which agrees with the actual nature of the matter is that invariably the greater the plot is (up to the point of simultaneous perspicuity) the more beautiful it is with respect to magnitude; or, to state a straightforward definition, 'the magnitude in which a series of

events occurring successively in accordance with probability or necessity gives rise to a change from good fortune to bad fortune, or from bad fortune to good fortune', is a sufficient limit of magnitude. (7.1451a6-15)

(7) Of simple plots and actions, the episodic ones are the worst. By an *episodic* plot I mean one in which the episodes come after one another in a way that is neither probable nor necessary. Inferior poets compose plots of this kind of their own accord; good poets do so on account of the actors – in writing pieces for competitive display they draw out the plot beyond its potential, and are often forced to distort the successive aspect. (9.1451b33-1452a1)

(8) In plays the episodes are concise, but epic is lengthened by them. (17.1455b15-16)

(9) One should not compose a tragedy out of a body of material which would serve for an epic – by which I mean one that contains a multiplicity of stories (for example, if one were to use the whole plot of the *Iliad*). In epic, because of its length, every part is given the appropriate magnitude; but in plays the result is quite contrary to one's expectation. (18.1456a11-15)

(10) So (as we have already said) Homer's brilliance is evident in this respect as well, in comparison with other poets. He did not even try to treat the war as a whole, although it does have a beginning and an end. Had he done so, the plot would have been excessively large and difficult to take in at one view, it would have been over-complicated in its variety. Instead, he has taken one part and used many others as episodes (e.g. the catalogue of ships, and other episodes which he uses to diversify his composition). The other poets write about a single person, a single period of time, or a single action of many parts – e.g. the poet of the *Cypria* and the *Little Iliad*. This means that only one tragedy can be made out of the *Iliad* and *Odyssey*, or at most two .... (23.1459a30-b4)

(11) Epic is differentiated in the length of its plot-structure and in its verse-form. The stated limit of length is sufficient; one must be able to take in the beginning and the end in one view. This would be the case if the structures were shorter than those of the ancient epics, and matched the number of tragedies presented at one hearing. Epic has an important distinctive resource for extending its magnitude. In tragedy it is not possible to imitate many parts of the action being carried on simultaneously, but only the one on stage involving the actors. But in epic, because it is narrative, it is possible to treat many parts being carried on simultaneously by means of which, when they are appropriate to it, the bulk of the poem is augmented. So epic has this advantage in achieving grandeur, variety of interest for the hearer and diversity of episodes; similarity quickly palls, and may cause tragedies to fail. (24.1459b17-31)

(12) Also, [in tragedy] the end of imitation is attained in shorter length; what is more concentrated is more pleasant than what is watered down by being extended in time (I mean, for example, if one were to turn Sophocles' *Oedipus* into as many lines as the *Iliad* has). Also the epic poets' imitation is less unified (an indication of this is that more than one tragedy comes from any given imitation). So if they treat a unified plot, either the exposition is brief and appears curtailed, or else it adheres to the length of that verse-form and is diluted. (I mean, for example, if it comprises a number of actions. The *Iliad* and *Odyssey* have many parts of this kind, which possess magnitude in their own right; and yet the construction of these poems could not be improved upon, and they are an imitation of a single action to the greatest possible degree.) (26.1462a18-b11)

Aristotle on Comedy, Aristophanes and Some New Evidence from Herculaneum

Richard Janko

I

In this chapter I shall argue that scholarship on comedy has still not understood with sufficient clarity just how much there is to learn from the remains of Aristotle's pronouncements on that genre, whether we look at comedy in its ancient context or across various cultural and historical horizons. We have missed especially what we can learn from these sources about the workings of comedy and its effect on audiences, in Aristotelian terms its efficient and final causes. Modern theorists of humour frequently reinvent some of the spokes of Aristotle's wheel – if indeed they get as far as that. Others prefer to reject theory entirely, claiming that laughter, humour and comedy are often non-transparent and cannot be explained. I profoundly disagree, except in those cases where for historical or linguistic reasons we do not know enough to see the point of the joke: comedy is fundamentally attached to its society. However, the mechanisms both of jokes and of larger comic structures such as comic drama are no less analysable, even if multi-determined, than those of other structures, whether linguistic or non-verbal, provided that we do not expect the application of theory to be other than in some way reductive (nor, of course, should we expect the analysis to be funny). Theory is necessarily a description of numerous individual examples, which abstracts their common features: and much of the adverse reaction to Aristotle's pronouncements on comedy (and the urge to deny that he could have said some of them) comes from the same impulse which seeks to belittle the extant book of the *Poetics* because much of what is says about tragedy and epic seems both self-evident and reductive, i.e. theoretical. It is of course no less a theoretical position to say that we should not construct theories which seek to study, classify and explain the common features of different entities: but that position is open to the objection that we are unlikely to learn much about the objects of our study by any other means, and it can be refuted empirically if we do learn something valuable from a given theoretical approach!

Aristotle's *Poetics* lost its second book, which dealt with comedy and with catharsis, at some time in late antiquity.[1] Umberto Eco, in his novel *The Name of the Rose*, invented the story that the book on comedy was deliberately suppressed, because Jesus was supposed never to have laughed and a book on comedy by Aristotle would have been regarded by some clerics as especially dangerous.[2] The truth may be more prosaic: the *Poetics* was arranged as the last item in the collection of Aristotle's logical works; if the second book was ever transferred from roll to codex, which it may not have been, it would have been at the back of the volume, and the last few pages in a volume were those most liable to fall out as the binding weakened.[3] Only two or three copies of the *Poetics* survived from antiquity to be recopied in the Middle Ages; not one contained the second book, although the MS Riccardianus 46 (Kassel's B) ends with a *reclamans* ('Regarding lampoons and comedy ... '), which indicates that Book II had once followed.[4] Hence, whenever I cite the extant *Poetics* below, I shall call it *Poetics* I.

In my somewhat notorious *Aristotle on Comedy*, published in 1984, I argued that the second book did not perish entirely. According to my hypothesis, before the book-roll dealing with comedy and catharsis was lost, someone copied out short extracts from its sub-section on the theory of laughter, with some of the jokes which illustrate it, into the Prolegomena to Aristophanes, whence it appears in a number of medieval manuscripts; and someone else copied a brief, untitled, anonymous summary of the whole book, leaving out all the jokes, onto leaves bound into a volume of extracts from commentators on Aristotle's logic, composed in the sixth century AD. A copy of this summary, in a schematic format like a student's notes, survives in a manuscript of *c.* AD 925 once kept in the main library of the Grand Lavra on Mt Athos (where it had the call-number shelf 3 volume 36) but now in Paris, whence J.A. Cramer first published it in 1839.[5] This, of course, is the *Tractatus Coislinianus*, whose complex textual history explains, I think, much of the adverse reaction to *Aristotle on Comedy*. Malcolm Heath sums up the consensus with the words 'few scholars currently accept this view of the tractate's origins; fewer still believe that in its present, severely mangled form much reliance can be placed in it as a source for what Aristotle wrote'. The 'few' who have had the courage to accept in print my main point are, so far as I know, only six: Jonathan Barnes,[6] Jan Maarten Bremer (who also produced a version in Dutch),[7] Matteo Campagnolo, in an valuable monograph applying the *Tractatus*' theory to the fragments of Eubulus,[8] A. Sottomayor,[9] Fernando Báez (who produced a version in Spanish)[10] and (with grave reservations) Malcolm Heath.[11] Among the authors of the most instructive adverse responses

I would mention Leon Golden,[12] Diego Lanza,[13] Dana Sutton,[14] W.W. Fortenbaugh,[15] Geoffrey Arnott[16] and Dirk Schenkeveld[17] (who writes that he was at first convinced). The prize for length and detail in the critique goes to Heinz-Günther Nesselrath, in his study of Middle Comedy.[18] One must not neglect to mention Anna Maria Mesturini,[19] who argues that the definition of comedy in the *Tractatus* is so confused that it must be the work of a forger, and so all attempts to emend it to make sense must be wrong. It is certainly *petitio principii* to assert that, because a piece of Greek is corrupt, its author is an incompetent falsifier. To her and others' central objection to my work, that my own argument is circular, I can only reply that the circle involved is the well-known hermeneutic one: if we do not formulate, test and refine hypotheses about what the *Tractatus* is, we will never understand it or benefit from it. Its existence is, after all, a phenomenon in need of explanation.

In fact the critics pointed out genuine errors of fact, omission, argument, editorial technique and arrangement in my book. But most of their complaint is in fact an expression of frustration with the *Tractatus* itself: only thus can I explain why many of them repeat objections which had been raised either by Jacob Bernays in 1853 or in the 1920s to Lane Cooper's work,[20] and which I had already refuted from verbal parallels in the acknowledged writings of Aristotle. People have continued to complain, for instance, that the *Tractatus* defines the action represented by comedy as a *praxis geloia* rather than as a *praxis phaulê*, as if *spoudaia* cannot be opposed to both qualities: remember how in the *Frogs* Aristophanes' chorus says at lines 391-2 *polla men geloia m' eipein, polla de spoudaia*. Moreover, it would not be accurate, either in Aristotelian terms or in actuality, to define comic action as bad action or the action of bad characters, because some bad actions or actions done by bad characters can be very unfunny indeed. We recall that Aristotle defined *to geloion* as only a part of what is ugly: 'the laughable is a sort of error and ugliness that is not painful or destructive' (*Poet.* I 5.1449a32-7). I shall not rehearse these and similar arguments again, but I do think that disgust at having to work with so skeletal and corrupt an epitome, and timidity in the face of needing to emend its text so often, has prevented most critics from perceiving how much we can learn from it. In particular, the critics have been unwilling to appreciate the significance of the structure of the *Tractatus*, which has the peculiar characteristic that it discusses tragedy only in connection with catharsis, and otherwise discusses comedy according to categories which Aristotle uses in his extant works. Thus even Malcolm Heath, whose conclusions in his article of 1989 in fact resolve several major difficulties of which I had failed to give an adequate account, holds that this 'obscure and contentious little document', as he calls it, 'has suffered more distortion – and is less useful – in detail than Janko contends'.[21]

Ever since Bernays' article of 1853,[22] critics have also argued that parts of the *Tractatus* are too like Aristotle to be by him – these must be impostures, they suggest, invented in order to make up for the loss of *Poetics* II; yet they also argue that other parts are too *un*like Aristotle to be attributable to him. But they cannot have it both ways. I have never replied to any of these objections, except by pursuing my investigations in two different directions: first, by editing and translating *Poetics* I, and supplying a full commentary which aims to reveal the unity, consistency, and value of Aristotle's theory of literature; and secondly by continuing to unearth new evidence derived, notably, from the Herculaneum papyri of Philodemus' *On Poems*. Nor shall I rebut such objections here. Instead I shall concentrate on three larger aspects of the problem, which are essential to understanding the contribution which Aristotle's ideas can still make to the poetics of comedy, as well as to seeing how his words can and do lie behind the *Tractatus Coislinianus*. These aspects are (a) Aristotle's attitude to Old Comedy in general and Aristophanes in particular, (b) the nature of comic laughter, and (c) comic catharsis.

II

In order to appreciate the *Tractatus'* importance, it is essential to understand what has generally been denied, that Aristotle regarded Aristophanes as the best of the comic poets. Had he lived to see Menander, the *Poetics* itself would have had to draw the contrasts between comedy and tragedy in divergent terms, since Menander took over so much of his material and approach from Euripides. Instead, Aristotle put Aristophanes on the same level of achievement for comedy as Homer for epic and Sophocles for tragedy: 'in one respect Sophocles is the same sort of representational artist as Homer, in that both represent good people, but in another he is like Aristophanes, since both represent men in action' (*Poet.* I 3.1448a25-9). One of the commonest objections to this conclusion, voiced by Stephen Halliwell in particular,[23] has been that Aristotle could not have approved of Aristophanes, because he objected to the obscene language (*aischrologia*) and the personal attacks on individuals which are so common in Aristophanic comedies.

Let us first consider *aischrologia*. In the *Republic*, Plato had objected that comedy is not only mimetic (and hence bad) like tragedy and epic, but also bad *for us* because it habituates us to behaviour which we would be ashamed of in real life, and thereby nourishes emotional responses which would be better suppressed (X 606c). Such imitative genres are not to be allowed into the state. Aristotle's position is more nuanced. At *Politics* VII 17.1336a39-b23, Aristotle advises legislators to ban *aischrologia*, more than anything else, from the city, to protect the young; and this must include stories, paintings or statues of the same kind, except in certain religious rites to which the law also assigns 'licentious speech' (*tôthasmos*). Young people are also not to be spectators of lampoons or comedy until they are old enough to recline at table and to drink, and their education has rendered them immune to the harm that comes from such things. We shall see what Aristotle meant by this last clause when we consider comic catharsis. As Malcolm Heath pointed out in 1989,[24] the whole passage has been misunderstood. Aristotle does not intend to ban comedy and lampoon from the city, only from being seen by minors. Just like certain religious rites, they are to be available only to adults. There is to be a system of X-rating according to which only adults may attend, but not an outright ban such as Plato would prefer. Heath went on to deduce that, if comedy is a representation of *phauloteroi*, as Aristotle says it is in *Poetics* I 5.1449a32-3, 'one must (logically) represent them doing and saying morally inferior things; [b]y Aristotle's own poetical criteria, therefore, the contents of comedy must deviate from the ethical norms of polite social intercourse.'

This helps to explain the passage on which the misunderstanding about Aristophanes has rested, where Aristotle discusses the social graces. He defines wit as the mean between buffoonery (*bômolochia*), where the buffoon will go to any length to raise a laugh, and boorishness (*EN* IV 8.1128a3-16). He illustrates the point that there are some things suitable for a free man to say and hear by comparing the difference between 'old' and 'new' comedies: for the former, *aischrologia* was laughable, but for the latter, rather, innuendo (*hyponoia*), which is superior in respect to decency (1128a22-32). Heath again comes to the rescue of the *Tractatus* (without acknowledging that that is what he is doing), by pointing out that, in defining wit, Aristotle is discussing the kind of behaviour appropriate in everyday life, not that in comedy. As for his preferences in comedy, they may be quite different: what is a virtue in everyday life might be unsuited to comedy, where inferior characters are to be represented. Hence we cannot assume that Aristotle prefers the 'new' comedies.[25]

Heath does not point out that exactly this development is paralleled at the end of the *Tractatus* (§18), where comedy is divided into three types – old, which goes to excess in the laughable; new, which inclines towards earnestness (*to semnon*); and middle, which is mixed from both, and is, presumably, neither excessive in the laughable, nor deficient in it, but attains the golden mean. The contrast between *geloion* and *semnon* appears in a discussion of metaphors in *Rhetoric* III 3.1406b6-8 (some are unsuitable because of *to geloion*, others because of *to semnon agan kai tragikon*, i.e. they are 'excessively solemn and tragic'), in *Poetics* I 4.1449a20-1 as part of the evolution of tragedy which, from slight plots and ridiculous diction, 'became majestic late' (*opse apesem-nunthê*), and in a Herculaneum papyrus which we shall shortly consider. I believe that Aristotle preferred the middle type; and, as I argued at length in my book, he regarded most of Aristophanes' plays as 'middle' comedy. A number of late writers set the boundary between 'old' and 'middle' comedy within the 420s BC, considering Aristophanes, Eupolis and Cratinus as within 'middle' comedy; some deemed the last plays of Aristophanes the start of 'new' comedy. I showed this at length, with citations of eight different sources including grammarians, ancient lives and scholia;[26] but except for Nesselrath, who objects to the lateness of the sources and holds that they are deforming the Hellenistic tripartition,[27] my critics ignored this argument, and continued to single out the reference to 'new' comedy as a signal proof that the *Tractatus* does not descend from Aristotle.

What about the personal attacks? Surely these would render Aristophanes unpalatable? Certainly they would to Plato. At *Laws* XI 935e-936a, he is very clear about this:

> No composer of comedy, iambic or lyric verse shall be permitted to hold any citizen up to laughter, by word or gesture, with passion or otherwise; in case of disobedience the presidents of the festival shall give orders for the offender's expulsion from the state's territory within the course of the day, on pain of a fine of three minas to be paid to the deity in whose honour the festival is held. The persons to whom permission has already been granted by an earlier arrangement to compose personal satire shall be free to satirise each other dispassionately and in jest, but not in earnest or with angry feeling. (trans. A.E. Taylor)

Aristotle's view is more nuanced: in his discussion of wit at *EN* IV 8.1128a25-32, he wonders whether jokes (*skôptein*) should be restricted to what is not unfitting to a free-born person, or by the fact that they should not cause pain to their victims or even please them. There are some jokes a free-born man will not make, since a joke is a kind of abuse, and there are things that legislators forbid us to abuse; they ought perhaps to have forbidden us to joke about them too. But, he concludes, a well-bred man will be as it were a law to himself. Once again, note that these remarks concern everday life, not the theatre. At *Rhetoric* III 18.1419b3-9, Aristotle promises to talk about the kinds of the laughable in his *Poetics* (fr. II Kassel), and at once mentions *bômolochia* (buffoonery), contrasting it with *eirôneia*. These are two of the three types of comic character picked out by the *Tractatus* (§12). The *Tractatus* also makes the following claim (§§7-8): 'comedy differs from abuse (*loidoria*), since abuse rehearses without concealment the bad <qualities> which attach <to people>, but comedy needs what is now called innuendo. The joker aims to expose faults of mind and body.' The term for innuendo, *emphasis*, is not Aristotle's, although I am much obliged to Nesselrath[28] for showing that it is attested in this sense as early as Praxiphanes of Mytilene. But the concept is his, as we saw from *EN* IV 8.1128a25, where he remarks on the use of innuendo (*hyponoia*) in the 'new' comedies: we also have a fragment of Theophrastus which says that a joke is concealed criticism of an error, from which the hearer himself adds to the innuendo (*hyponoia*) what is lacking.[29] Innuendo in this sense could be used even by Cratinus, as we learn from a plot-summary of the *Dionysalexandros*, in which, we are told, the criticism of Pericles was presented by means of *emphasis*.[30] If Cratinus' abuse, normally considered the most ferocious in Old Comedy, could be described in this way, then so could much of Aristophanes'. Even in the *Knights*, Cleon is named once only (at line 976), and Jeffrey Henderson has well shown how personal insults tended to act as a mode of social (and political) control by the *demos* where actual illegality could not be proved.[31] It is worth remembering, as he shows, that the Solonian laws of slander were far less severe than those of present-day England, and far less deferential to the wish of politicians to sweep their malfeasances under the carpet. Hence I cannot accept that Aristophanes' bad language or personal insults are any barrier as to why Aristotle should not have regarded him as *the* comic poet.

My conclusion is supported by the first papyrus from Herculaneum which I shall discuss, *P. Herc.* 207; this contains the end of Philodemus, *On Poems* IV. Philodemus' papyri are extremely hard to read, as they are blackened by the eruption of Vesuvius and badly damaged during their opening; moreover, Philodemus names his opponents only on rare occasions. The first editor of *P. Herc.* 207, Theodor Gomperz,[32] had thought the object of Philodemus' polemic was Aristotle's *Poetics*. However, the second editor of the papyrus, F. Sbordone, argued[33] that the target work contained almost the same doctrines as the *Poetics*, but in different wording and with other material besides, including a discussion of the music of tragedy, and that Philodemus was therefore attacking not Aristotle's *Poetics* but his lost dialogue *On Poets*. I strengthened and developed his conclusions in producing a new edition of the papyrus, published in 1991, where I also showed that the *On Poets* presented the essentials of Aristotle's theory (*mimêsis* and catharsis), and was not limited to literary history.[34] Subsequently Cecilia Mangoni told me that she had read the name of Aristotle a few columns earlier in the papyrus (fr. 7d.8 Sbordone); although she died before she could publish her discovery, I have now confirmed her reading. The importance of this papyrus for my present discussion is that column IV, which is badly damaged, discusses Aristophanes in lines 5-13. Mario Capasso[35] and Jürgen Hammerstaedt[36] have both independently re-inspected this passage. Their work has led to a better restoration of it, with contributions by all three of us. The translation below, which follows a lacuna, is based on these sources and my own notes:

> He also adds the claim that 'Archilochus and Aristophanes have represented more human actions' (*anthrôpikôteras memimêsthai praxeis*); of these, Archilochus would contend that he did not even make representations, but Aristophanes <would contend that he represented characters> uglier than Pauson, who according to him (*sc. the opponent*) 'represented everything in a laughable manner' (*geloiôs*); in addition to the fact that comedies and lampoons are not epic or tragedy, which were the topic under discussion.

The opponent evidently cited Archilochus and Aristophanes, and compared the latter with the caricaturist Pauson, in order to illuminate a claim which is quoted in the preceding column III about playwrights who tried to humanise tragedy, *exanthrôpizein tên tragôidian* (Euripides springs to mind), as opposed to others who depicted idealised personages; Sophocles is mentioned lower in the column, evidently as someone who did this, with a reference to 'representing *semnotera*', i.e. representing more earnest characters. Philodemus even rejects the comparison between the ludicrous genres of comedy and iambus and those which are serious, i.e. epic and tragedy. As Hammerstaedt has shown, column III also mentions the adjective *geloios* in line 5; note the contrast between the terms *geloios* and *semnos*, which we already saw paired both in Aristotle's *Rhetoric* (III 3.1406b6-8) and *Poetics* I (4.1449a20-1) and in the *Tractatus* (§18). The following series of columns compares epic with tragedy in exactly the same way as does *Poetics* I 5.1449b9-20. Now at *Poetics* I 2.1448a1-6, comedy and Pauson are alike in that they both represent characters 'worse than us', but tragedy, like the painter Polygnotus, represents those 'better'. The contrast between Pauson and Polygnotus recurs at *Politics* VIII 5.1340a36-8, where Aristotle urges that minors should not see the paintings of Pauson, but rather those of Polygnotus. In column IV of the papyrus, similarly, Archilochus, Aristophanes and Pauson are cited together as representers of objects antithetical to those represented in epic and tragedy. Since this passage occurs in what has now been proved to be a rebuttal of Aristotle, it confirms beyond any doubt that Aristotle regarded Archilochus, whom he never names in the *Poetics* I, and Aristophanes, whom he names alongside Homer and Sophocles

(*Poet.* I 3.1448a25-8), as the best representatives of iambus and comedy respectively.

III

The second area where the *Tractatus* has a major contribution to make is in its analysis of the mechanisms of humour. Plato's theory in the *Philebus* (47b-50e), where he advanced the first superiority-theory of laughter, that we laugh from a sense of superiority at the defects of a base character on stage, lies at the basis of Aristotle's observation (*Poet.* I 5.1449a32-7) that we laugh at some kinds of what is 'inferior' (*phaulos*). However, the cognitive foundation on which Aristotle builds is different: rather than stress our sense of superiority to the object of our laughter, he emphasises our own consciousness of error, not our awareness of the faults of others. Aristotle's central insight is that laughter depends not on inferiority in general ('the ugly'), but on that part of it which is ludicrous – an error or blemish (*hamartêma ê aischos*) which is not painful or destructive (*Poet.* I 5.1449a32-7). This must be supplemented by his remarks on verbal wit at *Rhet.* III 11.1412a19-22: 'most witticisms arise from comparison and the accompanying deception of expectations; for what one learns becomes more clear from its being put in the opposite way, and the mind seems to say, "so it is! But I was wrong (*egô d' hêmarton*)!" ' Note that on this view humour, like *mimêsis* itself, has a cognitive value; and the lesson which it teaches is one's own fallibility, not the inferiority of others. The continuation of this passage develops the same approach, specifically citing comic compounds as an example; the point is that humour depends on our own awareness that we were mistaken, not awareness of the error of other people. But the *Tractatus* enables us to see how Aristotle applied it to actions (§6) as well as to words (§5). I will not recapitulate the different subdivisions here, or the Aristophanic illustrations of them which survive in the Prolegomena to Aristophanes. Even the most sceptical critics of the *Tractatus* have accepted my conclusions about these sections, the authenticity of which was already advocated by Cramer in 1839 and accepted by Bernays in 1853:[37] see, for instance, the review of *Aristotle on Comedy* by G.M. Sifakis.[38] The classification of varieties of humour was applied to Aristophanes most fruitfully and at great length by W.J.M. Starkie in the introduction to his edition of Aristophanes' *Acharnians*,[39] as well as to Eubulus by Campagnolo.[40] One of my students in Los Angeles, who worked as a screen-writer and stand-up comedian in her spare time, was very struck upon reading this analysis between the similarity of its approaches and a recent manual called *Comedy Writing Secrets*, by Martin Helitzer,[41] who made no reference to his illustrious predecessor in the same genre.

IV

The third area where there is much to learn from Aristotle is over the question of comic catharsis. There has been enormous confusion about catharsis. Obviously I cannot here discuss modern versions of the concept. Even to look at the evidence for Aristotle's view will fill the rest of this article, if I am to show how his concept applied to comedy. My previous discussion of this topic[42] was, for reasons of space, so truncated that I have met people who thought I meant the opposite of what I intended. Hence I apologise for traversing some of the same ground again.

Aristotle's starting-point for his approach to catharsis was, I believe, Plato, and especially Plato's theory of education. The *Republic* is the work he had most clearly in view. There, as we saw above, Socrates objected that comedy is not only mimetic, like tragedy and epic, but also habituates us to behaviour of which we would be ashamed in reality, and thus encourages emotional responses which ought to be suppressed (e.g. *Rep.* X 606a-d, especially 606c). These imitative genres are not to be allowed into the state. In *Laws* II 653a-c, we get a more explicit account of this mechanism of habituation, which Plato regarded as fundamental to education:

> A child's first infant consciousness is that of pleasure and pain; this is the domain within which the soul first acquires virtue and vice .... By education, then, I mean goodness in the form in which it is first acquired by a child. In fact, if pleasure and liking, pain and dislike, are formed in the soul on the right lines before the age of understanding is reached, and when that age is attained, these feelings are in concord with understanding, thanks to early discipline in appropriate habits – this concord, regarded as a whole, is virtue. But if you consider the one factor in it, the rightly disciplined state of pleasures and pains whereby a man, from his first beginnings on, will abhor what he should abhor and relish what he should relish – if you isolate this factor and call it education, you will be giving it its true name. (trans. A.E. Taylor)

Exactly the same theory appears in Aristotle's *Politics*, as we shall see; indeed, since the *Laws* was Plato's last work, and Aristotle had been at the Academy, as a student and a teacher, for almost twenty years by that time, I think we must take seriously the possibility that the later Plato was influenced by Aristotle, at least in this dialogue. But from this theory the two philosophers derived very different attitudes to literature. Plato recommends the regulation of melody and the choric art by the state, so that no corrupting influences are allowed in, just as was the case in Egypt; this idea, first introduced in Book II at 657b-c, recurs in Book VII at 799a, and leads the Athenian to propose, to the approval of the discussants, that 'no poet shall compose anything in contravention of the public standards of law and right, honour and good, nor shall he be at liberty to display any composition to any private citizen whatsoever until he has first submitted it to the appointed censors of such matters and the curators of the law, and obtained their approval. These censors we have to all intents appointed by our election of legislators for music and a superintendent of education' (801c-d, trans. A.E. Taylor). When he discusses what poetry should be learned by heart in education, the Athenian recommends their own discourse, the *Laws*. He discusses comedy in the context of dance, and allows it to be performed only by slaves and hired aliens, and only so that the freeborn citizen may learn to recognise what is the opposite of serious, and may never be betrayed by ignorance into saying or doing a ludicrous thing when it is out of place (816d-e). Tragedy, however, is banned completely, unless its ethical approach is totally in harmony with that of Plato's censors, which seems unlikely ever to come about.

Aristotle, on the other hand, regarded literature as worth studying because it represents, according to him, patterns of human action from which we can learn. Whereas Plato did not want serious poetry to show noble characters suffering misfortune, Aristotle accepts this, as long as the nexus of cause and effect is made plain by the representation (e.g. *Poet.* I 7.1451a9-15), and the misfortune originates in a mistake made by the character (*Poet.* I 13.1453a8-17), rather than in either wickedness or an accident.[43] And whereas Plato disapproved of works of literature which affect our emotions, Aristotle thought that tragedy should elicit from us the emotions of pity and fear (*Poet.* I 13.1452b30-2), just as comedy should made us laugh (this is implicit in *Poet.* I 5.1449a31-3). Obvious again, perhaps; so obvious that I shall not argue against those who deny that laughter was, for Aristotle, the emotion at which comedy aimed, on the grounds that it is a physical manifestation, not an emotion (it is of course both, but neither English nor Greek has a separate word for each). Plato (*Philebus* 50a), Longinus (*On the sublime* 38.9) and many others in antiquity treat laughter as a *pathos*.[44] But how could Aristotle approve of comedy, which, as a Platonist would object (*Rep.* X 606c-d), panders to our emotions rather than our reason, encouraging feelings which ought instead to be repressed?

Aristotle's explanation does not directly survive. It is of course his theory of catharsis. Book I of the *Poetics* does not present this theory, but from his *Ethics* and *Politics* we can form a hypothesis as to what he meant. His attitude to the emotions was the opposite of Plato's: for Aristotle regarded emotion as just as important as intellect in determining action.[45] A correct balance in the emotions is essential to attaining the practical wisdom – *phronêsis* – essential to right action. His theory, presented in *Nicomachean Ethics* II-III, runs as follows.

Human beings need to develop a disposition to feel emotion correctly, i.e. in the proper circumstances and to the right degree; our emotions, combined with our understanding, can then become a guide to right action. Take courage, for instance. Aristotle defines courage as feeling fear to the correct degree. We learn to act courageously simply by acting courageously, again and again. Each action we take builds our character; by acting in that way often we acquire a settled disposition to act in that way, a *habit* (*hexis*) of action. This circular pattern is, for him, the origin of character; and it involves both emotion and intellect. We use our intellects to judge the circumstances surrounding an action, and our judgement about these then shapes our emotional response to it; but our emotional response may then influence the action we decide upon, and the aggregate of our past emotional and intellectual decisions creates our character. Poetry can help to habituate us to feel the correct emotional responses, and thereby to approach the mid-point between the extremes; this mid-point is where virtue lies. Put differently, poetry can hold up to us patterns of human action, from which we can learn. Here the process of *mimêsis* is crucial: by watching a representation of the actions and sufferings of *others*, we can benefit ourselves, in that we experience without harm emotions which would be harmful if they were based on reality. This applies, I hold, both to painful feelings like pity, fear and anger in the case of serious genres like tragedy and epic, and to pleasant ones like laughter in non-serious genres like comedy and satire.

We know this from the passage in Aristotle's *Politics* where he is discussing the place of *mousikê* in education, and advances the same theory of education as does Plato in *Laws* II. Like Plato, when Aristotle refers to *mousikê* and to 'songs', he means not 'music' only, but words set to music as well, and hence poetry as well as what we call 'music'; but it has taken a long time for scholars to appreciate this essential fact. This is why the passage had been neglected by previous generations trying to reconstruct Aristotle's literary theory, although since Nancy Sherman[46] and Carnes Lord[47] called attention to it, it has become very fashionable to cite it. I translate:

When listening to representations (*mimêseis*), everyone comes to share in the emotion ... Since *mousikê* happens to belong among pleasant things, and virtue is concerned with feeling delight correctly and loving and hating correctly, clearly one should learn, and become habituated to, nothing so much as judging correctly, that is to feeling delight in decent characters and fine actions. Rhythms and songs contain especially close likenesses of the true natures of anger and mildness, bravery, self-restraint and all their opposites, and of the other character-traits: this is clear from the facts – we are moved in our soul when we listen to such things. Habituation to feeling both pain and delight in things that are like [reality] is close to being in the same state regarding reality.[48]

As I said, this is the same theory as Plato's: Aristotle held that we develop our emotional reactions in the same way, by habituation. It is vital to understand that, throughout Aristotle's discussion in Book VIII, *mousikē* includes poetry as well as the music which goes with it, and that the likenesses referred to are *mimēseis*, of which music in our sense is one kind and poetry is another, according to *Poetics* I 1. The word 'catharsis' does not appear in this passage. However, two papyrus fragments from Herculaneum, which have now been shown to derive from the start of Philodemus' *On Poems* V (*P. Herc.* 1581),[49] have enabled me better to explain what Aristotle meant by it. Philodemus' critique of Aristotle in Book IV apparently continued into Book V, just as his rebuttal of Crates of Mallos continued from Book I into Book II.[50] Criticising an (Aristotelian) theory of catharsis, Philodemus argues that you have to accept three tenets, which are Aristotelian but unacceptable to a good Epicurean like Philodemus. First, 'a poet is a representer (*mimētēs*) of a complete action'; second, 'poetry is useful with regard to virtue, purifying (*kathairousa*), as we said, the <related> part <of the mind>'; and third, 'each of the arts <aims at?> the best of those things (?) which are naturally within it'.[51] The connection between poetry, virtue and 'purifying the related part of the mind', that is catharsis, is clearer here than in *Politics* VIII, but the mechanism is the same. At *Politics* VIII 7.1342a1-15, where Aristotle refers to the *Poetics* for a full account of catharsis, he continues:

> Those [songs] most related to character must be used for education (*paideia*), but those related to action (*praktikai*) and to ecstasy must be used for listening to while others play them. For the emotion that arises violently in some souls exists in all, but differs in its degree, e.g. pity and fear, as well as ecstasy. Some people tend to be taken over by this agitation, but we can see that, as a result of the holy songs they use to rouse the soul to a frenzy, they settle down as if they had attained healing, i.e. catharsis. It follows that this very same thing happens to people who are prone to pity, fear and emotion in general, and to the rest of us to the degree that each participates in such emotions, and a sort of catharsis and relief, accompanied by pleasure, comes about for everyone.

'Songs related to action' include tragedy and epic, which are repeatedly described in the *Poetics* I as representations of action: that Aristotle has tragedy in mind here is shown by the reference to pity and fear. With his statement that everybody can obtain catharsis and relief from tragedy compare the second fragment from Herculaneum, which goes as follows:

Folly is present in the wisest of minds, and lack of self-control in the most moderate. Similarly there are fears in brave minds and jealousies in magnanimous ones.[52]

In Aristotle's moral theory, even those who are generally virtuous can fall into immoderation, and so need catharsis – which is what this fragment implies. Aristotle regarded such poetry as capable of guiding us toward moderation in our emotional reactions. This is shown by allusions to Aristotelian catharsis in the Neoplatonist philosophers Iamblichus and Proclus:

By observing others' emotions in both comedy and tragedy, we can check our own emotions, make them more moderate and purify them. (Iamblichus, *On the Mysteries* I 11)

It has been objected that tragedy and comedy are expelled [from Plato's *Republic*] illogically, if by means of them one can satisfy the emotions *in due measure* and ... keep them in a state suitable for education ... It was this that gave Aristotle and the defenders of these kinds of poetry in his dialogue against Plato most of the grounds for their accusation against him. (Proclus, *Commentary on Plato's* Republic, p. 49 in Kroll's edition)

Terms like 'moderate' and 'in due measure' are references to the Aristotelian mean, that point where virtue lies.

Putting these fragments together, we can see what Aristotle must have said about catharsis. The representation in literature of universalised patterns of human action puts us through a process of reason and emotion which leads us towards the correct reaction, a reaction appropriate to the situation presented to us. A Platonist might object that the play ought not to portray negative situations, in case watching it tempts us to imitate those actions. The Aristotelian reply is that no normal adult would do so. Instead, an adult is put through an emotional experience which would be harmful if one underwent it in person. Instead, Aristotle would claim that we benefit from watching the play: our propensities to diverge from the mean in feeling emotions and judging actions are reduced, and our enhanced perceptions can help to improve our capacity for moral judgement and right action.

The approach to catharsis which I advocate has suddenly become the standard replacement for the purgation-theory of Jacob Bernays,[53] with a number of people advancing much the same interpretation at the same period in the early 1980s, although it goes back to Humphrey House in 1956 or even earlier.[54] The main disagreement amongst us has been whether, in his definition of tragedy (*Poet.* I 6.1449b24-8), when Aristotle wrote 'the catharsis of such emotions' he meant only pity and fear, or a whole group of similar emotions like anger, which he puts alongside pity and fear at *Poetics* I 19.1456b1. I believe that he did mean his entire category of painful emotions: for at *Politics* VIII 7.1342a11-13 he refers to people prone to pity, fear and emotion in general as those who may benefit from catharsis. The same applies to comic catharsis. My own explanation of this has not changed since I wrote *Aristotle on Comedy*,[55] but new arguments to support it can be advanced.

There are two passages in the *Tractatus Coislinianus* relevant to catharsis. The *Tractatus* §4 defines comedy as 'a representation of an action that is laughable and lacking in magnitude, complete, <in embellished speech>, with each of its parts used separately in the various elements of the play; represented by people acting and <not> by narration; accomplishing by means of pleasure and laughter the catharsis of such emotions'. This definition has been emended to make sense (and to make it more Aristotelian) by a number of scholars, myself the last and least; indeed Mesturini's whole article[56] has since been devoted to showing that the unemended text is preferable. Many critics have objected to the statement that comedy brings about the catharsis of *pleasure and* laughter. Surely pleasure is the *effect* of catharsis, not the object upon which it acts, they object (so, e.g., Diego Lanza[57]). Two rival theories have arisen, those of Leon Golden and Dana Sutton, rejecting mine on precisely this point. Golden[58] considers the comic emotion to be purged to be *to nemesan*, 'righteous indignation'. Sutton[59] too is a purgationist, holding that comedy purges pity, fear and other painful emotions by means of laughter, whereas tragedy does the same thing by means of pity and fear; pleasant emotions need no purging, he believes. Moreover, he believes that the later evidence, from Philodemus to Proclus (who refers to Aristotle's defence of poetry against Plato), relates to a later, post-Aristotelian theory of catharsis.

Since 1984 I have come to a better understanding of how Aristotle could have held that pleasant emotions need to be subject to catharsis. First, it is worth recalling that, in the passage of Iamblichus' *De Mysteriis* I 11 where he discusses tragic and comic catharsis, he is investigating the use of obscene language *in ritual*: the same collocation occurs in *Politics* VII 17, where Aristotle says that obscene language ought to be kept from minors, but permitted *in certain rites* and in comedy. The context is not one of fear, pity or righteous indignation, but the kind of behaviour that is appropriate or inappropriate in public, where minors might see or hear it. Second, in summing up his account of the social virtues in *EN* IV 6-7, Aristotle lists the three ways of attaining virtue in social behaviour, and discusses 'those who converse with a view to pleasure or pain' (*hoi pros hêdonên kai lupên homiloun-tes*, *EN* IV 7.1127a18, cf. 6.1126a31). He argues (*EN* IV 6-8, 1126b11-1128b9) that one should seek the mean (i) between obsequiousness and surliness, (ii) between boastfulness (*alazoneia*) and understatement (*eirôneia*), and (iii) between buffoonery (*bômolochia*) and boorishness (the mean here is of course wit). I translate his conclusion:

> The ways we have mentioned of attaining the mean are three. They all concern social intercourse in words or actions of some kind, but differ in that one of them [sc. boastfulness] relates to the truth, but the others relate to what is pleasant [*to hêdu*]. Of those relating to pleasure [*hêdonê*], one [sc. buffoonery] is displayed in our amusements [*paidiai*], the other [sc. obsequiousness] in our social contacts in the rest of life. (*EN* IV 8.1128b4-9)

As I argued in 1992,[60] this shorthand expression points to what is meant in the definition of comedy: not, obviously, that flatterers and buffoons are the only suitable characters for comedy, but that comedy seeks to show us the effects of departures from the mean, i.e. excess and deficiency, in those emotions which relate to laughter and the pleasant side of life. The *Tractatus* §12 duly lists buffoons, ironists and boasters as typical comic characters, just as Aristotle at *Rhet.* III 18.1419b3-9 (*Poet.* fr. II Kassel) indicates they should be.

V

I shall conclude by considering briefly Aristotle's attitude to Aristophanes' *Clouds*. Unlike Plato, Aristotle had a good sense of humour. Even so, one might not expect Aristotle to have approved of the *Clouds*; the parody of his own profession might well have seemed too dangerous, given what subsequently happened to Socrates. When I first perused parodic novels like David Lodge's *Small World* (1973) or Tom Sharpe's *Porterhouse Blue* (1974), each of them seemed a comic masterpiece. Would they seem so hilarious in the light of subsequent historical events – the way in which forces of populist hostility targeted Britain's universities to devastating effect? Their tone is so different from that of Max Beerbohm's *Zuleika Dobson* (1911), so easy for an ignorant, humorless and ambitious politician to take seriously and turn into votes, claiming that students at university 'have every decent value knocked out of them'.[61] Thus I now find myself far closer to G.E.M. de Ste Croix[62] than to A.W. Gomme[63] over Aristophanes' attitude to political questions (and education is always a political question).

Like the *Knights*, the *Clouds* is a comedy of vicious attack. When a play ends with the pupils burning down a school with its teacher inside you need to be part of a very secure and stable society to feel sure that all this is only in fun – unless this dénouement is meant as a graphic illustration of the perils of ignorance (but the action of the play does not encourage this view). As K.J. Dover dispassionately remarked in 1966, Aristophanes' 'portrayal of the effect of Socrates' teaching on the character of Pheidippides is an invitation to violence, or repressive legislation, against such teachers'.[64] Aristophanes may have based the burning down of the Thinkery with Socrates and his followers inside on the torching of Milo's house in Croton in about 454 BC, where the leaders of the Pythagoreans were meeting; from that fire only two or three members of the sect managed to escape alive.[65] However that may be, Aristophanes' attitude did not lack an Athenian context, despite the efforts of Dover and others to argue that Socrates was the Athenians' sole victim.[66] Anaxagoras had had to go into exile in perhaps *c.* 434, Protagoras' books were publicly burned after his condemnation to death, according to the latest investigation, between 420 and 417 BC,[67] and in 415/4 Diagoras of Melos had a price put on his head for what he taught; I think Socrates was lucky to escape prosecution until 399.[68] Those scholars who doubt that teachers of higher learning in Athens had to fear the imputation of impiety may simply have been fortunate in the societies in which they lived, or else unwilling (or happily unable) to imagine the alternative. But those who have seen for themselves the excesses of unbridled arbitrary power, especially when coupled with profound ignorance, know better. Aristotle cannot have been unaware of this danger: when deprived of Macedonian support after the death of Alexander, he left Athens forever when the chief priest at Eleusis brought against him a charge of impiety (Diogenes Laertius V 5).

If the *Tractatus* reflects what Aristotle wrote, he approved of many of the jokes in the *Clouds*, e.g. the one about measuring how far a flea can jump, or the amusing diminutives of Socrates, which the *Tractatus* cites as examples (§5). However, I think he might have classed its plot-structure as going to excess in the laughable, i.e. as 'old' comedy, a play which will go to any length to raise laughter (§18), even to the extent of causing pain to its object, just as does the buffoon in his analysis. The *Frogs*, also cited by the *Tractatus* for tautology and hilarious exchanges of disguise (§5-6), would probably be thought to hit the mean between such excess and becoming too earnest (*semnon*, §18). It was, I would imagine, Aristotle's favourite comedy, which would have appealed to him as much for its intellectualism as for its conservative politics. Oddly enough, the Athenian people agreed with both those verdicts in awarding the prizes.

Notes

1. On the history of this text see my *Aristotle on Comedy* (London, 1984), 63-6. For bibliography see O.J. Schrier, *The* Poetics *of Aristotle and the* Tractatus Coislinianus: *A Bibliography from about 900 till 1996* (Leiden, 1998), 322.
2. *Il nome della rosa* (Rome, 1980; trans. W. Weaver, New York, 1983), at pp. 473-7 of the English translation.
3. See *Aristotle on Comedy*, 89.
4. See R. Kassel, *Aristotelis De Arte Poetica liber* (Oxford, 1965), on *Poet.* I 26.1462b19. As if to typify the timidity surrounding this rectification to the canon, Kassel does not entitle the fragments which follow 'Liber II', although he cites other sources which confirm that the extant *Poetics* is Book I. The *reclamans* is a device which may go back as far as the time when separate rolls of papyrus needed to be kept together in a book-box (*capsa*), before the codex was introduced. Thus Berlin papyrus 16985, a roll dating from the first century BC and containing Books 21-2 of Homer's *Iliad*, cites lines 1-2 of *Iliad* 23 at its end to indicate that Book 23 should be read next.
5. MS Parisinus Coislinianus graecus 120; the text was first published by J.A. Cramer, *Anecdota Graeca e codicibus manuscriptis Bibliothecae Regiae Parisiensis* (Oxford, 1839), I, 403-6. I included a few afterthoughts in my *Aristotle: Poetics I with the Tractatus Coislinianus* (Indianapolis and Cambridge, 1987). Because of the timing I was not able to take into account V. Janković, 'Tractatus Coislinianus', *Živa Antika* 34 (1984), 87-94, C.D. Hill, *A View of Ancient Comedy: Greek and Roman Sources on Comic Theory*, diss. Florida State University 1985, or most of the reviews.
6. *Phronesis* 20 (1985), 103-6.
7. *Mnemosyne* 41 (1988), 166-70; cf. *Gnomon* 65 (1993), 201-4, and for the translation N. van der Ben and J.M. Bremer, *Aristoteles: Poetica* (Amsterdam, 1986).
8. 'Le Comique dans les fragments d'Euboulos selon la critique littéraire antique', *Atti dell'Istituto Veneto di Scienze, Lettere ed Arti* 105 (1991-2), Classe di scienze morali, 411-96.
9. *Humanitas* 35-6 (1983-4), 443-5.
10. *El Tractatus Coislinianus: La obra que salvó el contenido del segundo libro de la Poética de Aristóteles* (Mérida, 2000).
11. 'Aristotelian Comedy', *CQ* 39 (1989), 344-54.
12. *AJPh* 107 (1986), 440-2.
13. 'La Simmetria impossibile', in *Studi offerti a F. della Corte* V (Urbino, 1987), 65-80.
14. *The Catharsis of Comedy* (Lanham, 1994).
15. *CPh* 82 (1987), 156-64.
16. *CR* 35 (1985), 304-6.
17. *Gnomon* 58 (1986), 212-17.
18. *Die attische Mittlere Komödie* (Berlin and New York, 1990), 102-48.
19. 'Puntualizzioni sul Tractatus Coislinianus', *Maia* 42 (1990), 237-47.
20. *An Aristotelian Theory of Comedy, with an Adaptation of the Poetics and a Translation of the Tractatus Coislinianus* (New York and Oxford, 1922).

21. *CQ* 39 (1989), 344-54, at p. 344.

22. 'Ergänzung zu Aristoteles' *Poetik'*, *RhM* 8 (1853), 561-96.

23. E.g. in *Aristotle's Poetics* (London and Chapel Hill, 1986), 273-4.

24. *CQ* 39 (1989), 344-54, at pp. 344-5.

25. Loc. cit. (n. 23).

26. *Aristotle on Comedy*, 244-50.

27. *Die attische Mittlere Komödie*, 145-9.

28. *Die attische Mittlere Komödie*, 124, citing fr. 13 Wehrli. Cf. also I. Rutherford, *'Emphasis* in ancient literary criticism and the *Tractatus Coislinianus* c. 7', *Maia* 40 (1988), 125-9.

29. F 711 Fortenbaugh, from Plut. *Mor.* 631e.

30. Papyrus hypothesis to Cratinus, *Dionysalexandros*, i.47 Kassel-Austin.

31. Jeffrey Henderson, 'The *Demos* and the comic competition', in J.J. Winkler and F. Zeitlin (eds.), *Nothing to do with Dionysos?* (Princeton, 1990), 271-313.

32. 'Die herculanischen Rollen I', *ZOeG* 16 (1865), 717-26, repr. in T. Dorandi [ed.], *Theodor Gomperz: Eine Auswahl herkulanischer kleiner Schriften, 1864-1909* (Leiden, 1993), 3-12; 'Philodem und die aristotelische Poetik', *Wiener Eranos* (Vienna, 1909), 1-7, repr. in Dorandi, op. cit., 256-62.

33. 'Il quarto libro del *Peri poiêmatôn* di Filodemo', *Ricerche sui papiri ercolanesi* I (Naples, 1973) 287-372.

34. 'Philodemus' *On Poems* and Aristotle's *On Poets'*, *Cronache Ercolanesi* 21 (1991), 5-64.

35. 'Aristofane nei papiri ercolanesi', *Papyrologica Florentina* 19 (Florence, 1990), 43-57.

36. 'Pausone, Aristofane ed Archiloco nel quarto libro *Peri poiêmatôn* di Filodemo', *Cronache Ercolanesi* 27 (1997), 105-20. I will publish an updated edition and commentary in *Philodemus: The Aesthetic Works. Volume I/3*, On Poems III-IV (Oxford, in preparation); since many new fragments will be included, the columns will be renumbered.

37. See *Aristotle on Comedy*, 1-3, 164.

38. *JHS* 107 (1987), 202-3.

39. *Aristophanes'* Acharnians (London, 1909), xxxviii-lxxiv; see also 'An Aristotelian analysis of "the comic" ', *Hermathena* 42 (1920), 26-51.

40. See above, n. 8.

41. Writer's Digest, Cincinnati 1987.

42. 'From catharsis to the Aristotelian mean', in A. Rorty (ed.), *Essays on Aristotle's* Poetics (Princeton, 1992), 341-58.

43. For this distinction see *EN* V 8.1135b1-25.

44. See further my *Aristotle Poetics I with the Tractatus Coislinianus*, 169, which develops *Aristotle on Comedy*, 156-7.

45. See W.W. Fortenbaugh, *Aristotle on Emotion* (London, 1975).

46. *Aristotle's Theory of Moral Education*, diss. Harvard University 1982, 162-3.

47. *Education and Culture in the Political Thought of Aristotle* (Ithaca, 1982), 82-9.

48. *Politics* VIII 5.1339b42-1340a27. The translation and those which follow are from my *Aristotle: Poetics I with the Tractatus Coislinianus*, where justifications for them will be found in the notes.

49. For this point see *Philodemus: The Aesthetic Works. Volume I/1*, On

Richard Janko

Poems I (Oxford, 2000), 13 and 114 n. 9. *P. Herc.* 1581 will be re-edited with new fragments (legible with multi-spectral digital imaging) by David Armstrong and Jeff Fish in *Philodemus: The Aesthetic Works. Volume I/4,* On Poems V (Oxford, in preparation).

50. See *Philodemus:* On Poems I, p. 191, where I cite parallels for this procedure from Sextus Empiricus.

51. Frag. I in M.L. Nardelli, 'La catarsi poetica nel *PHerc.* 1581', *Cronache Ercolanesi* 8 (1978), 96-103. In my translation (*Aristotle: Poetics I with the Tractatus Coislinianus*, 61) I may have arranged the fragments in the wrong order.

52. Frag. II in Nardelli, art. cit.

53. *Grundzüge der verlorenen Abhandlung des Aristoteles über Wirkung der Tragödie* (Bratislava, 1857).

54. For a chronological list, which may not be complete, see 'From catharsis to the Aristotelian mean', 356 n. 27.

55. See pp. 139-51; cf. *Aristotle: Poetics I with the Tractatus Coislinianus*, xvi-xx and 181-90, and further 'From catharsis to the Aristotelian mean'.

56. 'Puntualizzioni sul Tractatus Coislinianus', *Maia* 42 (1990), 237-47.

57. 'La Simmetria impossibile', in *Studi Francesco della Corte* V (Urbino, 1987), 65-80.

58. 'Comic pleasure', *Hermes* 115 (1987), 165-74; 'Aristotle on the pleasure of comedy', in A. Rorty, (ed.), *Essays on Aristotle's* Poetics (Princeton, 1992), 379-86; *Aristotle on Tragic and Comic Mimesis* (Atlanta, 1992), 5-39.

59. *The Catharsis of Comedy* (Lanham, 1994).

60. 'From catharsis to the Aristotelian mean', p. 351.

61. Personal experience suggests that most of the predictions which I made in 1988 about the results of Mrs Thatcher's educational 'reforms' ('Dissolution and diaspora: Ptolemy Physcon and the future of classical scholarship', in *Classics: A Discipline and Profession in Crisis?*, ed. P. Culham and L. Edmunds (Washington D.C., 1990), 321-32) have now come to pass.

62. *The Origins of the Peloponnesian War* (London, 1972), 355-71.

63. 'Aristophanes and politics', *CR* 52 (1938), 97-109.

64. *Aristophanes: Clouds* (Oxford, 1968), lvi.

65. See E.C. Kopff, 'Was Socrates murdered?', *GRBS* 18 (1977), 113-22, and for the date B.L. Van Der Waerden, *Die Pythagoreer* (Zurich and Munich, 1979), 217-21, and C.A. Huffman, *Philolaus of Croton* (Cambridge, 1993), 2-3. The parallel is denied by M. Davies, ' "Popular Justice" and the end of Aristophanes' *Clouds*', *Hermes* 118 (1990), 237-42, who considers rather that the school's occupants are to be driven out alive. However, even if Aristophanes did not make the connection with the fate of the Pythagoreans, the story was available for his audience to do so.

66. 'The freedom of the intellectual in Greek society', *Talanta* 7 (1975), 24-54 = *Collected Papers* II (Oxford, 1988), 135-58. Similarly R. Wallace, 'Private lives and public enemies: freedom of thought in Classical Athens', in A.L. Boeghold and Adele Scafuro (eds.), *Athenian Identity and Civic Ideology* (Baltimore, 1994), 127-55. R. Parker, *Athenian Religion: A History* (Oxford, 1996), 199-217, tries to steer a middle course.

67. L. Piccirilli, 'Il primo caso di autodafé letterario: il rogo dei libri di Protagora', *Studi Italiani di Filologia Classica* 15 (1997), 17-23

68. See 'The physicist as hierophant: Aristophanes, Socrates and the authorship of the Derveni Papyrus', *Zeitschrift für Papyrologie und Epigraphik* 118 (1997), 61-94 at 92-4; 'The Derveni Papyrus (Diagoras of Melos, *Apopyrgizontes Logoi?*): a new version', *Classical Philology* 96 (2001), 1-32.

Mimesis in Aristotle's Ethics

Hallvard Fossheim

1. Introduction

The question I want to pursue in this chapter is as follows: How do we, according to Aristotle, become good? Aristotle's reasons for concerning himself with these matters include his determination of the aim of human beings – happiness – as action, as practical activity. 'Both happiness and unhappiness rest on action' (*Poet.* 1450a17), and in order to do good, we necessarily have to *be* good, since for any action, its goodness depends upon the disposition of the agent.

The short version of an answer to our general question, provided in the second book of the *Nicomachean Ethics*, is that we become good by habituation (*ethismos*). What I will attempt is to elaborate a little on that answer, primarily by trying to say something about what, more exactly, habituation might be, or at least what it might include, according to Aristotle. Unfortunately I have not been able to find a way of presenting these ideas except as parts of a much bigger picture, which can in this context only be sketched in very broad outline.

I think it is possible, without too much wild speculation, to find that according to Aristotle's theory of human development and perfection three different principles or aspects of soul-forming are in play. It makes sense to call these principles levels because, among other things, they mark different stages in the history of the individual's development.

According to Aristotle, the three things that make men good are nature, habit and reason.[1] In the *Nicomachean Ethics*, which speaks from the practical point of view internal to an already habituated and reflective agent, the three levels or principles are generally referred to as the pleasant, the noble and the good. In the agent, the three capacities or dispositions roughly corresponding to them are desire, character and reason.

It should be stressed right away that this classification does not imply any real or actual separation of the three principles. For instance, reason is not merely added to pleasure; rather, Aristotle seems to think that practical reason somehow requires and builds on the directives of pleasure and pain, while they again are reshaped and expanded to the extent that reason enters the picture. Still, as principles for human existence, they ought to be treated as different and logically separate sources. Thus, in John M. Cooper's explicating translation of a passage from the second book of the *Nicomachean Ethics* (1104b30-1105a1), 'there are three objects of choice (*ta eis tas haireseis*) and three of avoidance: the *kalon* (the noble, fine, beautiful), the advantageous, and the pleasant, and their opposites, the *aischron* (the base, shameful, ugly), the harmful, and the painful. In relation to all these the good person gets things right, while the bad person gets things wrong, but especially in relation to pleasure.'[2]

I will start by giving a rough sketch of the first and the third principle: on the one hand, pleasure and pain, the pleasant – the basic, sensing existence; on the other hand, the good, reason – where human happiness is realised. Then, I will move on to the middle principle, the noble or fine. I will do this primarily by asking just what Aristotle means by 'habituation' and 'habit', which according to him is the way we develop from being driven only by pleasure and pain to forming a conception of the good. What happens here, and how does it happen? That is, how do we reach the point where human happiness might be actualised? What I hope to show, at least indirectly, is that the all-important main road to human happiness and the good life – habit and habituation – must be something much like what Aristotle describes as mimesis. If this is correct, then one of the most central concepts in the *Poetics* will turn out to play an equally important role in Aristotle's *Ethics*. But let's begin with a brief look at pleasure and pain.

2. Pleasure and pain

Of the three different levels, pleasure and pain is the most commonly shared principle. In the development of the individual, they are present as biological abilities from the very outset, while reason is realised only much later – if ever.

The good is in a sense an aim and measure of practical reason. In the same way, the pleasant is a source of directedness for perception. Pleasure and pain are what determine the striving and avoidance of those who live by perception, whether they be animals or immature human beings. A lack of maturity is, Aristotle reminds us, not necessarily proportionate to a lack in physical age. In both the infant and in the hedonistically inclined adult, the structuring principle remains on the level of perception.

Which is not to say that the life in question must of necessity remain dumbly irrational, at least not according to our understanding of rationality. On the contrary, it is a common experience that the perceptively desiring part of us can be most proficient in arguing its case. Whether it be concerning an illicit love affair or another piece of chocolate cake: the rhetorical ingenuity mustered on the side of what we might call sensible appetites will perhaps never cease in its ability to amaze and impress us. One helpful insight that would appear to be safely exported from psychology to ethics is that the presence of perception implies an ability for experiencing pleasure and pain, that is, for striving or desire.

> if it has sense perception, it has also imagination and desire. For, where there is sense perception, there is also pleasure and pain: and, where these are, wanting also must of necessity be present.[3]

Two inclusive implications are succinctly expressed in this passage: from perception to pleasure and pain, and from pleasure and pain to desire. The first implication tells us that perception should not be thought of as merely a pure disinterested registering, but as something which is somehow deeply bound up with and universally entails concrete effects on the perceiver. The necessity in the latter implication, that if there is pleasure and pain there is also desire of some sort, is possibly even more clarifying. Pleasure and pain are not, indeed cannot be, correctly described as simply mute and acognitive goings-on. Rather, they represent ways of orienting the being in question (animal or human) towards or away from more or less determined parts of the environment.

A life ordered by considerations of that order will nonetheless be only untruthfully characterised as a life of reason, in the Aristotelian sense – irrespective of the subtlety in argumentation and foresight. Not just any instance of calculation or argument can pass as practical reason. No matter the intricacy of the cognitive powers in play, the most important question is whether they are still structured around mere pleasure and pain.

3. Reason

In an important sense, then, the life of the passions remains a life of perception.[4] In cases where the level of more or less perfected practical reason is reached, pleasure and pain have lost their autonomous grip on the individual. In order to suggest what might have occurred between the two levels, it might be instructive if one were to lay out important parts of the difference between a sensual and a rational way of life in terms of presence and distance. The logic of perception implies nearness. The particular object of sensual desire is, *qua* object of sense, close at hand. And to the extent that it is a reaction to unmediated perception that is in operation, the ultimate cause of movement is in the object, not in the organism where the movement takes place. The sensually based life, then, is the life of an entity which is moved by its surroundings. Slightly dramatically phrased, perception as a principle of movement means being driven, through pleasure and pain, by that which is close at hand.

The object of reason, however, is present in another fashion: it is present as reason – as reasons. Thought does not need the physical presence of the thing in question, because its presence as object is assured independently, as thought. Thought somehow makes present, while perception is of that which *is* present. Whereas perception is prevented from strolling away from the objects which move it, reason somehow in its very structure moves away from that which is present. Reason ensures the experience, the possibility, of distance. It does not see a part without placing it in a whole, nor an aim without relating it to one or several means.[5]

Being thus freed from what we might call the spur of the moment, the agent truly becomes just that: an agent. Now, one's general view of things magically overrides the distinction according to which the object should happen to be near or far away. Reason brings together things that to perception remain dispersed and far apart. It deals with the universal, as cases of one in the light of many – both in the sense that the many can be one with each other the way all dogs are dogs, and in the sense of belonging as parts to an organically understood whole the way having a dog can for instance promote one's hunting.[6] Reason's determination of activity is in a new sense up to oneself, even if – in fact, especially as – the decision in question is made when the object, and therefore the act, is still in the distance (or some time away).[7]

The life of perception, in any guise, remains so just because, and to the extent that, it remains within the immanence of mere pleasure and pain as the ruling principles. And the formally oriented sketch of reason I have just presented does not of itself include an alternative guiding principle. Human reason as fully evolved, however, cannot in fact be separated from a substantial conception or experience of the properly good; as a source for the good life, reason enjoys a seeming autonomy that can be attributed truly only to a substantial principle, one which has in view certain goods *as* goods, as worth striving for, as aims, as that which limits and ultimately gives meaning to the other parts. There is no right or correct reason without the right desire, no practical wisdom without a striving that somehow already includes the general directions (e.g., *EN* 1139a20-b7). As a more or less successful transition from the merely pleasant to the humanly good is what takes place in anyone's upbringing, while no substantial source of good appears to be evident so far, the pressing question is: How do we do it?

4. Becoming good

Aristotle devotes some time to presenting a list of possible replies. Do we become good by nature (*phusis*), by teaching (*mathêsis*), by some sort of training (*askêsis*), by divine gift (*dôron*), or is it all up to chance (*tuchê*)? None of the above. To the extent that any one of us comes to the point where he or she might be said to possess the main principle of human goodness, it is – as already disclosed – done through habituation.

But it is at best uncertain that we have replied to the question, as long as no further determination of habituation is available. What is habituation? The basis for an answer lies in the following passage.

> [N]one of the virtues of character arises in us naturally. For if something is by nature [in one condition], habituation cannot bring it into another condition. A stone, e.g., by nature moves downwards, and habituation could not make it move upwards, not even if you threw it up ten thousand times to habituate it; nor could habituation make fire move downwards, or bring anything that is by nature in one condition into another condition. (*EN* 1103a19-24, Terence Irwin's translation)

Nature, of course, does play a part, but not in the direct sense that we become good either 'by nature or against nature. Rather, we are by nature able to acquire them [that is, the virtues], and reach our complete perfection through habit' (*EN* 1103a24-6).

An existence as beings that strive and flee as determined by the perception of pleasure and pain, is in some form inborn with us from nature's part. It is present in us from the very beginning, apparently like the ability to fall back down to earth is present in the stone *before* it is hurled upwards. Both stones and humans are in this loose sense imbued with certain characteristic motions, movements that are present in them as determinate possibilities before they are first tested: in a word, natural abilities or propensities.

We are, however, already verging in on where the attempted analogy breaks down. Whereas the stone will never fail in displaying heaviness, no matter how many times one throws it up into the air, we are all of us examples of a perhaps radically different story. Contrary to fire moving upwards and heavy things moving downwards, our movements can be dramatically altered. In some way or other, it is true that our moving in one direction over and over will actually produce in us the propensity to move differently than before. And not only that, but in the end, this same process is crucial to how we develop from mere pleasure-seekers to good people, to someone who will do the right thing not because it seems pleasant, but because it is the right thing to do.

5. Habituation

As we begin looking into the link between pleasure and habituation as the way to forming a good character, it immediately becomes apparent that virtue and vice are concerned with pleasure and pain. 'Hence we need to have had the appropriate upbringing – right from early youth, as Plato says – to make us find enjoyment or pain in the right things; for this is the correct education'[8] (*EN* 1104b11-13). In fact, even the otherwise perfect action is not really a good action if the agent does not take pleasure in it.[9] Perhaps most important of all, Aristotle takes for granted that pleasure and pain is that by which we steer our children when we educate them (*EN* 1172a22). Besides,

> enjoying and hating the right things seems to be most important for virtue of character. For pleasure and pain extend through the whole of our lives, and are of great importance for virtue and the happy life, since people decide to do what is pleasant, and avoid what is painful. (ib., 23-6)

Habituation, as the human way to goodness, appears to always act in team with pleasure and pain.

So we do have Aristotle's word for the crucial role of pleasure and pain in the ethical shaping of an individual. What we need are pointers that will allow us to form a more concrete image of how they fulfil that role. There is a conspicuous lack of them in the writings that have come down to us, a lack which makes it tempting to turn to interpretations of less direct evidence. The perhaps all-important relation between pleasure and good is rarely brought out more clearly than in the discussion of courage in the *Nicomachean Ethics*. Of course, one inherent danger is that while the habituation we are looking to analyse concerns mostly children and adolescents, most texts of possible relevance to our query deal with adults. Although Aristotle does think most people remain children or worse all their lives, in the sense of living by their passions or never developing virtue to the extent they should, one must take care not to infer too much from one context to another. Remember that the *Nicomachean Ethics* as such is a course for well-adapted adult citizens, people who have already been habituated with a fairly great measure of success; their projects concern furthering personal perfection, even at that level with the help of habituation.

With this in mind, let us turn to the passages just mentioned. In the analysis of courage, six varieties of phenomena that are generally referred to by that name are scrupulously analysed and distinguished from each other. There are many ways of missing the mark and only one perfect hit, and the perfect hit in the case of courage is that which 'chooses and stands firm because it is noble, or because anything else is shameful' (*EN* 1116a12f.). Among the five ways of more or less missing the mark, one stands out as particularly interesting to us: what Aristotle calls citizen's courage. In this class, second only to perfect courage, 'we might also place those compelled by their superiors. However, they are worse to the extent that behaviour is caused by fear, not by shame, by aversion from what is painful, not from what is disgraceful' (*EN* 1116a30-b2). These arguments seem to act strongly in favour of conceiving the development, from being driven to act through pleasure and pain to acting on the basis of a view of the noble or good, as a rather soft and sliding transition, without dramatic breaks or perhaps even clear criteria for the change. The impression is strengthened by how Aristotle conceives the highest realisation of citizen's courage as an imperfect virtue, that is, as a view of what is fine and what is shameful (*EN* 1116a27; but cf. *EN* 1179b11).

At least two remarks seem in order concerning the apparent continuum, the second one hopefully less trivial and repetitive than the first. The pain that functions as a means of correction, here exemplified by physical punishment and injury, is not present as a fact at all, but as the *threat of* physical punishment and injury. The use of pleasure and pain in steering someone is not limited to contact or Pavlovian causality, but relates to the individual in question through his or her view (conceptions, ideas, intentions, interpretations) of the surroundings. That is not to say that experience of causal relations does not lie at the chronological beginning of those views, only that a habituation through pleasure and pain certainly can go beyond it by building on it.

Second, the pain in question proves to include reproaches, that is, shame in the form of oral chastisement. 'For citizens seem to stand firm against dangers with the aim of avoiding reproaches and legal penalties and of winning honours' (*EN* 1116a18-20). While he conceives the range of motivations as a continuum from a practical point of view, Aristotle does allow for two separate (but for the agent perhaps confused) motivations in speaking of some actions as worse 'to the extent that' (*hosôi*, *EN* 1116a31) they are caused by aversion from what is painful rather than by shame. The pleasure and pain in question, then, includes that of punishment and reward in the form of chastisement and approval.

What is implied in the affirmation already quoted, then, that 'pleasure and pain is that by which we steer our children when we educate them'? According to Liddell & Scott, the Greek verb denoting 'steer' (*oiakizô*) is derived from *oiax*, a central meaning of which is the rudder of a ship. The suggestion is perhaps one of a rather direct contact between the one who steers and the directions the one steered is made to take. We get an image of a fairly close and direct control over someone else's general realisation of excellences. The simplest way of construing the general idea has habituation taking place by making the one undergoing it associate pleasure and pain with the right sort of things. Pain will move him or her away from the bad things, and pleasure will move him or her towards the good things, in a fairly simple logic of reward and punishment. If that story is true, some sort of associative ability is at the heart of what goes on. An object or activity, which the child at the outset desires, is made undesirable to it through association with pain of some sort. And correspondingly, an object or activity which is truly good and which ought to be seen as such by the child, is repeatedly associated with something it happens to find pleasurable.

6. The shortcomings of pleasure

Aristotle writes, however, that 'since activities differ in degrees of decency and badness, and some are choiceworthy, some to be avoided, some neither, the same is true of pleasures; for each activity has its own proper pleasure. Hence the pleasure proper to an excellent activity is decent, and the proper one to a base activity is vicious' (*EN* 1175b24-8).

By itself, then, the dimension of association does not allow a bridging of the gap between pleasure and the noble. Mediation, or even argument, cannot open up for the noble. The noble or good is seen by reason as an aim and measure to which the constituents of life must be referred. And no amount of admonition can, by itself, make a cognitive structure of pleasure and pain see anything but a pleasure, as *mere* pleasure, as an aim.

We cannot be brought all the way to the noble or good by a method of steering that takes as its premise a mere external association, whether or not the causal relations are understood by the one being formed. It might bear mention, as part of explaining my meaning, how both we and Aristotle often tend to speak of the good and of pleasure, instead of the good and the pleasurable. It would make sense if it turned out that a reason for the difference is that the good, in a more direct way than the pleasurable, has objective implications. While a mentioning of the good already points to something that is good, pleasure appears to point by itself first and foremost to the subjective experience, without internal reference to an objective standard but only to a cause. My tentative diagnosis is certainly not Aristotle's last word on the subject: after all, some find pleasure in what isn't truly pleasant. But part of his conclusion is, importantly, that pleasures cannot be judged on their own merit, but must always be seen in relation to and judged on the basis of the activities they in some sense complete.[10] The ultimate truth about pleasure and the pleasurable – about what is really pleasant, and what is really not – cannot be decided apart from the goodness of the agent or activity: for the pleasures 'from fine sources are different from those from shameful sources, and we cannot have the just person's pleasure without being just' (*EN* 1173b29-31). Far from being able to spot the good merely through a grid of even correctly tuned pleasures and pains, it's the other way around: we have to 'be in on' the good in order to start passing authoritative judgment on what is and what is not truly pleasant.

It seems unlikely, then, that insight into something as noble or good could arise exclusively from an external, side-by-side relation to a pleasure (or something pleasurable) with which it is associated. Desires, which are themselves cognitive structurings of pleasures and pains, can be reshaped by other pleasures and pains only *as* pleasure and pain. Not that the principle is unimportant, even as seen by itself; pleasure does pervade all of our lives, and has to be correctly tuned in anyone if he or she is to be called good. However, such immanent trimmings are not *by themselves* able to give rise to the orders of the noble or the good.

7. An alternative source for ethical pleasure

What I want to suggest is that there is no way of making sense of the noble (nor, therefore, of the good) without adding at least one separate source, an ability in the child that has to be supposed in addition if we are to get a picture that includes even the possibility of going from pleasure to the good or noble. According to Aristotle, even mature students in his ethics course, known to us as the *Nicomachean Ethics*, should turn to the good man and the good man's actions as the source of insight into the human good: 'virtue, that is, the good person in so far as he is good, is the measure of each thing' (*EN* 1176a17f.). The source of human goodness is good humans. And as we have already seen in the case of pleasure and pain on the perceptual level, the relevant investigating look is not a disinterested one. The question is asked only on the background of some thoroughgoing engagement. This is a premise even when it comes to Aristotle's students, since the purpose of that 'examination is not to know what virtue is, but to become good, since otherwise the inquiry would be of no benefit to us' (*EN* 1103b27-30). We look to the good man not in order to know, but in order to become more of what he already is. The desire or wish to become better, to perfect oneself, is here identified as the desire to in some respect become like somebody else.

What is true of the mature and reflected investigator, is if possible

81

even more so for the earlier stages of life. 'This is why we need to have
been brought up in fine habits if we are to be adequate students of what
is fine and just, and of political questions generally.' As Aristotle says,
'the origin is the that [*hoti*], and if this appears adequately, he will not
at all need in addition the because [*dioti*]. Such a one has origins
[*archas*] or would get them easily' (*EN* 1095b4-9). The 'why', reflective
insight, can only enter the discussion when the 'that', the ideals and
ways of dealing with oneself and the surrounding social world, are
already more or less in place. This is how habituation, the provider of
'thatness', feeds and forms what I have called the substantial conception of practical reason that is in play in Aristotle.

According to the seventh book of the *Politics*, 'we always like best
whatever comes first. And therefore youth should be kept strangers to
all that is bad, and especially to things which suggest vice or hate' (*Pol.*
1336b33f.). The strength of the engagement, the directness with which
it carries back to one's own being, helps explain that the 'steering' in
question is not so much one of activation. Rather, the focus is on
controlling and limiting what is to be available as objects of the child's
engaged attempt to become like what it sees or hears. I think it bears
repeating that 'hearing and seeing' in this context do not exclude what
we, contrary to Aristotle, normally call reason. 'Hearing', for instance,
will include hearing stories. So, in Aristotle's ideal city state, those
responsible for education 'should be careful what tales or stories the
children hear, for all such things are designed to prepare the way for
the business of later life' (*Pol.* 1336a30-2). That hearing implies a
measure of understanding is what makes it so dangerous, because it
makes the distance so short between hearing and saying and doing.
Thus, according to Aristotle, 'there is nothing which the legislator
should be more careful to drive away than indecency of speech; for the
light utterance of shameful words leads soon to shameful actions. The
young especially should never be allowed to repeat or hear anything of
the sort' (*Pol.* 1336b4-7).

In any case, the advice allows us to disjoin a more abstract, or should
I say basic, desire: behind the desire to become this or that is a desire
to simply become (to be like) whatever is presented as an option – that
is, whatever is presented, whatever is present. It is because he sees the
general ability or desire to 'become like' as a condition for the more
specific possibility of becoming good that Aristotle feels the need to
warn against the child being exposed to someone who is seriously
flawed. The exposure in question poses a danger only in so far as it
consists of a cognising engagement on the side of the one exposed, and
this cognising engagement is understood as a desire to 'be like that' (or
'do like that').

Returning to the priority of what Aristotle calls the 'that' in relation to the 'why', it is crucial that the 'that' in question is chosen wholly for its own sake. The pleasure that is taken in activating the ability to 'become like' as such ensures that it could not be conceived as a means, but only as an aim in itself. And at the same time, this pleasure is found in an objective reality that is already present and exemplified as an action or way of appearing.

These two features make it likely that what we are dealing with in some way or other forms the basis that was lacking between pleasure and the good. What was lacking in our previous image of habituation was something that would allow for a combination of objectivity, which was found lacking in pleasure narrowly construed, and perfect choice-worthiness, which was lacking in the previous formal determination of reason. We needed the exteriority of judgment that goes with activity, and a basis for the teleological ordering of life. In habituation, they now combine in an engagement with activity or action, that is also a choice-worthy activity in its own right. And it will stay choiceworthy in that sense for exactly as long as it is still conceived by the agent as a case of 'being like'. The object of the middle level, *to kalon*, is experienced as such both in the sense of beautiful, that is, as surface and outer movement, and as noble, that is, as something honourable and impressive and a measure rod for the rest.[11]

8. Conclusion

The reflexive and in a sense logical problem which opens the *Nicomachean Ethics*, what is the end of all the various things we do and pursue, is at least partly generated by the insight that if it had turned out that we choose everything because of something else, life would go on literally without limit, making desire empty and futile. Now, a merely formal sketch of reason fails precisely in its blindness to the substantiality of reason, to the fact that reason possesses and is arranged around teleological sources of unity.

In fact, practical reason is only fully reasonable when it acknowledges the autonomy of good action. That a good action, in order to be good, must have been chosen for its own sake, is only half the story. The full story is that in order to be good, an action must be chosen for its own sake, *that is, for the sake of the noble*.[12] This is an important relation between the noble and the good: the good is the noble seen not as primarily surface, but as a constitutive part of the greater whole that is life. The noble is that which is acquired by engaged habituation and which is from the very outset perceived as being in itself worth while. It is the teleologically limiting high point of practical reason, it is that which gives meaning to everything else in the practical sphere and without which all would go on without limit. The good, seen by reason, does not set up new aims as much as set up the same aims in a new way. In other words: what I presented as a sketch of practical reason earlier on, was hardly that. It was merely what would have been left if one were to take away the noble as its source. This, I think, is evident from the capacity Aristotle refers to as cleverness (*deinotêta*), which

> is such as to be able to do the actions that tend to promote whatever goal is assumed to achieve it. If, then, the goal is fine, cleverness is praiseworthy, and if the goal is base, cleverness is unscrupulousness; hence both practically wise and unscrupulous people are called clever. Practical wisdom is not the same as this capacity [of cleverness], though it requires it. (*EN* 1144a24-9)

Hence we cannot be practically wise without being ethically good (*EN* 1144b1), that is, good in character, that is, disposed to act in a certain way. In a sense, practical reason is in an ineradicable debt to something that isn't in itself entirely reasonable.

To conclude, it seems to me that according to Aristotle, we take our first steps in an understanding of the human good by the natural propensity, from childhood onwards, to be thoroughly engaged in and formed by the activity of 'being like'.

In the *Poetics*, Aristotle tells us that

> poetry in general can be seen to owe its existence to two causes, and these are rooted in nature. First, there is man's natural propensity, from childhood onwards, to engage in mimetic activity (and this distinguishes man from other creatures, that he is thoroughly mimetic and through mimesis takes his first steps in understanding). Second, there is the pleasure which all men take in mimetic objects. (*Poet.* 1448b4-9, Halliwell's translation)

In the context, it seems to me that the first of the two causes mainly explains the doing of mimesis, while the second one mainly explains the observing and judging of mimesis. In a way, I suppose it would make some sense to say that while the first explains the poet, the second explains the critic. (Provided, of course, that one under 'critic' includes the audience or reader.)

I guess (or at least I hope) it has long been evident that I have tried to establish an affinity between what I have called 'becoming like' and some of what Aristotle says about mimesis. Notice that, according to the model I have suggested for becoming good as a 'becoming like', the 'critic' does not necessarily appear later than the maker (or actor, or agent). Forming one's self requires some judging discrimination from the very start, if one is to pick out the 'that' of appearing like someone or something.

Furthermore, this discrimination always presupposes that its object, explicitly or implicitly, is brought via some universal or at least more general level. Tragic dramatic representation, although it expresses itself through particulars, strives for universals. In some way, the same must also be said of mimesis outside the poet's realm. The mimesis that forms our first steps in practical understanding, too, is only possible as a recognition of something as something else, that is, as a recognition of some common or repeated factor (where oneself, of course, is the repetition). And on the background of what has been said so far, an expression of this recognition could easily include the improvisations involved in child's play.[13]

Let us end by looking at the first cause, man's thoroughly mimetic being. In the same chapter of the *Poetics*, chapter 4, Aristotle gives a rough explanation for the historical development of the various forms of poetic mimesis. In two places, he traces the differentiation of genres to the poets' own characters. First, he states that 'poetry was split into two types according to the poets' own characters' (*Poet.* 1448b24f.). He then tells us that 'when the possibility of tragedy and comedy had been glimpsed, men aspired to either type of poetry according to their personal capacities' (*Poet.* 1449a1-3). If we were to posit a 'practical' mimesis in addition to poetic mimesis, we would have to understand this process in reverse. Habituation does not consist so much in activating a formed character and thereby realising something out there in the world, as in realising something out there in the world and thereby forming a character. (I mean 'realising' in both senses of the word, both as grasping something and as doing it.) All starts with the desire to become like what one sees or hears. Any deeper understanding of the implications, of the totality it fits into, must of necessity come only much later. In this sense, human goodness finds its roots on the surface of the world.[14]

Notes

1. *Phusis*, *ethos* and *logos* (*Pol.* 1332a39, rep. 1334b6).
2. John M. Cooper, 'Reason, moral virtue, and moral value', in id., *Reason and Emotion* (Princeton 1999), 265.
3. *DA* 413b23f; cf. 414b3 (the Hicks/Durrant translation).
4. What are the further relations between perception and pleasure and pain is not the central question for us right now. But it seems to me that the two make for different approaches in philosophical analysis in Aristotle's work. Perception acts as a main divide in the *De Anima*, while pleasure and pain are more in the forefront in the *Nicomachean Ethics*. This difference in approach is probably not an accident: *De Anima* is an investigation into a certain group of

beings, that is, it deals in descriptive psychology; the *Nicomachean Ethics*, on the other hand, is a practical course in ethical betterment. The first, then, is primarily concerned with a biological classification of souls, from plants up, while the latter constantly keeps its focus by asking what can be done to change someone.

5. One interesting consequence of what is, admittedly, a very vague sketch, is that while perception seems to start from the presently realised, that which is already a fact, and moves on to do something about it, reason starts explicitly from that which is not yet realised, not yet a fact, and follows it back to the here and now where the movement starts. In some sense, it must be true of perception, too, that it sees something *as* possibly different (that meat as a possible mouthful); what remains, however, is that the basis of perceptually cognised differences remains with the object as present, while reason not only allows but inherently demands more distance, in time as well as in space.

6. Both uses of *katholou* are represented in the *Poetics*, in chapters 9 (1451b8-9) and 17 (1455a34-b2), respectively, as clearly demonstrated by Malcolm Heath. Cf. Heath, 'Universality in Aristotle's Poetics', in *Classical Quarterly* 41 (ii) (1991), 389-402.

7. Incidentally, and although evidence is lacking, I would like to think that we here see at least part of the reason why Aristotle sometimes, instead of writing 'the good', uses a word that is often translated as 'the advantageous': *to sum-pheron* is that which carries or brings together what is dispersed.

8. The 'education' in question here seems, according to the last two books of the *Politics*, to stretch from infancy to an age of around 17.

9. Likewise, even if they are traceable to a lack of information the agent could not be blamed for, practical mishaps or failures involving a simple error of judgement are still blameworthy if he or she does not truly regret them afterwards (*EN* 1110b18-22). In other words, cases where one might say there is no formal blame are still examples of ethical shortcomings, if it turns out that the individual in question finds pleasure or pain in the wrong aspects of the case.

10. I say 'in some sense', because the two analyses, in Book VII and Book X, divert somewhat from each other when it comes to just that question. According to the formulation in Book VII, pleasure is identical with unimpeded activity (*EN* 1153b12); in Book X, it is some sort of crowning of what is already in a way perfect, the renowned 'bloom on youths' (*EN* 1174b33).

11. Stephen Halliwell and Richard Janko have kindly advised me to move on to an explicit treatment of *Politics* VIII 5 at this point. As a result of the downright frightening complexities brought on by, e.g., the discussion of music in those passages, however, I have been forced to postpone that analysis to some later occasion.

12. Cf. *EN* 1115b12, 16a28, 16b2-3, 17b9, 17b14, 19b16, 20a12, 20a24, 22b6, 23a24, 36b22.

13. For further elaboration on this specific point, see in particular Kendall L. Walton, *Mimesis as Make-Believe* (Cambridge, MA, 1990).

14. I would like to thank Prof. Eyjolfur Emilsson for patiently reading and commenting upon two different versions of this text.

Aristotelian Mimesis and
Human Understanding

Stephen Halliwell

A section from book 30 of the pseudo-Aristotelian *Problemata* poses an arresting question and broaches an intriguing set of alternatives in answer to it:

> Why should one place more trust in a human being than in another animal? Is it, as Plato said when answering Neocles, because humans alone among animals know how to count? Or because humans alone believe in gods? Or because humans are the most mimetic of all animals (for this enables them to learn and understand)?[1]

An ostensibly peculiar choice, then: mathematics, religion – or mimesis? If we take the question to be asking which of these is most fundamentally human, the choice looks a little cramping, at any rate if the alternatives are meant to be exclusive. But this curious, and perhaps not so pseudo-Aristotelian, 'problem' does not say we can have only one of the three possibilities, though it does suggest, perhaps mischievously, that Plato would have been confident of his preferred answer. Even so, the juxtaposition of mimesis with mathematics and religion is likely to strike us as strange, and yet it is the inclusion of mimesis which, from an Aristotelian perspective, ought to surprise us least. For we know from the *Poetics* that it was a genuine conviction of Aristotle's that an instinctive capacity for mimesis is an important component of human nature, and one that distinguishes humans from other animals (though Aristotle certainly recognises the existence of some kinds of mimesis elsewhere in the animal world),[2] whereas we lack good Aristotelian evidence, I think, for the supposition that either mathematics or religion possesses a comparably instinctual status. Furthermore, if we construe the present question as asking what it is that allows humans to understand (and therefore 'trust') *one another*, rather than the world at large, the option of mimesis makes especially cogent Aristotelian sense, since Aristotle regards mimesis as a means by which people

87

explore their own distinctively human world through hypothetical simulation and enactment of some of its possibilities.

We encounter this Aristotelian view of mimesis directly in the first part of *Poetics* 4 (1448b4-19), a passage with which *Problemata* 30.6 has obvious affinities. Aristotle here stresses what he sees as the roots of mimesis in human nature, calling humans the 'most mimetic' of animals and citing the capacity of children to learn/understand (*manthanein*) by mimesis, a concept which even here should not be reductively translated as 'imitation', since it needs to encompass a wide range of play and play-acting. Those who, like Castelvetro, find in this mention of children a reference to elementary copying of fixed models miss the interest of Aristotle's point, which can be much more instructively glossed by some recent work in developmental psychology on the early emergence of children's capacity for, and grasp of, fiction.[3] The scope of mimesis in this context can be confirmed by a glance at a related section of *Politics* 7.17 (1336a28-34). In that passage (which has some Platonic colouring) Aristotle refers to the telling of stories (*logoi* and *muthoi*) immediately before making the general remark that 'most forms of play should be mimetic role-playing of the serious pursuits of adult life'. It is tempting to paraphrase the last part of this clause (*mimêseis tôn husteron spoudazomenôn*) as 'rehearsals for adult life', and it is clear that story-telling and dramatic role-playing are among the forms of mimesis, the forms of imaginative make-believe, Aristotle has in mind there. In the cognate passage from the *Poetics* Aristotle passes directly from children to adults. The proposition that 'everyone takes pleasure in mimetic objects' (1448b8-9), whether or not it marks the second of the two 'causes' (*aitiai*) or explanations of poetry (an old interpretative bone of contention, hardly relevant to my present position), moves the argument beyond children's play-acting or role-playing, not only because 'everyone' (*pantes*) patently includes adults as well as children, but also because the noun *mimêmata* designates the entire class of mimetic works and performances considered as objects of pleasurable contemplation. The thought contained in the sentence as a whole thus embraces both primary participation in and secondary appreciation of mimetic behaviour. What humans are singularly good at producing, according to Aristotle's anthropology, they are also well equipped to respond to when others engage in it; and this means that mimesis has the potential to generate elaborate forms of cultural practice, such as tragic theatre or highly skilful figurative art – practices whose Aristotelian interpretation, even more than with the play-acting of children, is not well served by construing mimesis as 'imitation'.

In *Poetics* 4 Aristotle proceeds to invoke some supporting evidence for the enjoyment taken in mimetic objects/performances. He refers to visual depictions of things whose real appearance would be painful or distasteful, depictions which nonetheless typically provide pleasure. It has sometimes been argued, most recently by David Gallop, that Aristotle is here referring to biological illustrations or diagrams, not to public works of visual art.[4] There are several reasons why this must be wrong. First, in the following sentence, which provides a further explanation for the phenomenon in question, Aristotle refers specifically to the experience of non-philosophers and the pleasure they derive from learning and understanding. The connection between this explanation and the preceding sentence would be weakened if the images (*eikones*) referred to were those used in the context of philosophical teaching or study. That the coherence of Aristotle's argument calls for a wider observation than this is evident, in fact, in the sequence of thought prior to this, at 1448b9-10, where the reference to images is introduced as a sign or index, *sêmeion*, of the pleasure taken in mimesis by 'everyone', non-philosophers as well as philosophers. So the basic logic of Aristotle's case excludes a reading such as Gallop's. But there are further pointers to this same conclusion. Consider briefly two other (and similar) passages, both of which are of broader relevance to the interpretation of *Poetics* 4. The first is from *Parts of Animals* 1.5 (645a7-15), where Aristotle juxtaposes, and to some degree contrasts, the pleasure philosophers can derive from physical inspection of even certain unprepossessing animals with the pleasure 'we' take in contemplating images of such animals. This passage counts against Gallop's reading of *Poetics* 4 because Aristotle's explicit explanation of the second of these pleasures in terms of appreciation for pictorial or sculptural artistry, *tekhnê graphikê/ plastikê*,[5] either excludes the case of philosophical diagrams and models, or, at the very least, makes it perverse to suppose that it is philosophical study-aids rather than regular visual works of art that Aristotle has in mind. Likewise with *Rhetoric* 1.11, 1371a31-b10, which brackets painting, sculpture and poetry together as species of mimesis, indicates that mimesis can create pleasure in objects not found pleasurable in themselves, and, exactly as in *Poetics* 4, links the pleasure derived from mimetic works to a process of learning/understanding (*manthanein*) and reasoning (*sullogismos*). These connecting threads between the *Rhetoric*, *Parts of Animals* and *Poetics* 4 confirm that in the latter Aristotle is not referring directly to philosophical illustrations but to works of visual art for the general public.

The whole impetus of the *Poetics* passage depends on Aristotle's conviction that all humans take pleasure in learning and understanding, an experience which he implies is quasi-philosophical – lower down, certainly, but nonetheless on the same spectrum as philosophical *mathêsis*. He expands this point, whose affinities with the opening of the *Metaphysics* need no iteration, by saying that when people enjoy looking at images they do so because in the process of viewing or contemplating 'they understand/learn and reason what each thing is, for example that "this person is so-and-so"'. There are several questions still worth asking about the force of these words of Aristotle's, questions not for the most part adequately treated by the commentators.[6] First, to deal with what ought to be uncontroversial, though it has been often confused. Aristotle's immediate reference is to depictions of identifiable human figures; there is nothing else that the pronouns in the phrase *houtos ekeinos* can or should mean than 'this man/person is that man/person', 'this is so-and-so'. Several scholars have wrongly rendered the phrase as 'this is that', as though it were equivalent to *touto ekeino*, the neuter expression which *does* occur in the parallel *Rhetoric* passage (1.11, 1371b9) and which some scholars, starting with Gudeman and including David Gallop again, have unnecessarily wanted to introduce by emendation into the text of the *Poetics*.[7] But the masculine pronouns can, in this context, refer only to people, not to objects; moreover – a point to which I will want to return – they can refer only to *individuals*, whether actual or imagined. Nor, by the way, is it at all helpful in this connection to cite the independently attested colloquial usage of *touto ekeino* or *tout'ekeino*, a phrase equivalent to 'just what I said!', 'told you so!', 'there you are!', and the like. This usage, found in Plato as well as Aristophanes, does not fit the experience of identifying figures in a visual artwork, any more than it fits the case of grasping a metaphor's 'identity statement', to which Aristotle applies the phrase at *Rhetoric* 3.10, 1410b19: metaphors do not tell us 'I told you so!', nor do we tell ourselves that when identifying figures in paintings.[8]

Now, *houtos ekeinos*, 'this person is so-and-so', at *Poetics* 4.1448b17, posits, for the sake of convenience and concision, a deliberately rudimentary case of recognising a figure in an artistic image. Aristotle may mean his example to be that of viewing a portrait, though his point must be equally applicable to the identification of mythological individuals, and indeed to much more besides, as I shall shortly explain. The main reason for supposing that he has portraits in mind is the rider which he immediately adds, specifying that if the viewer 'happens not previously to have seen [sc. what is depicted], the image will not give pleasure as a mimetic representation [*mimēma*, picking up its use at 1448b9] but only because of its workmanship [*apergasia*, a known art-critical term],[9] its colour, or for some other such reason' (1448b17-19). Both in Aristotle and in other authors the verb *prohoran* most commonly means 'see ahead' or 'foresee', but here it has to mean 'to have seen previously'. At the same time as it strengthens the inference that Aristotle is thinking immediately, or at least partly, of portraits, this rider raises a *prima facie* problem. For even if we could accept, as we might not want to,[10] that the full appreciation of a portrait *qua* representational work requires prior visual experience of its subject, the principle could hardly be extendable to most visual works of art, as the context requires, and still less (as the fuller context requires) to all works of mimetic art in whatever medium, not least in poetry. The solution (applying a principle of interpretation that itself has Aristotelian credentials) is not to press *prohoran* too literally, and this move is recommendable not only on grounds of hermeneutic flexibility but also by reference to the two passages already cited from the *Rhetoric*. Whatever Aristotle has in mind in the *Poetics*, he has something comparable in mind at *Rhetoric* 1.11, 1371a31-b10; but in the latter, where he uses the neuter expression *touto ekeino* for the identification of the subject of an image, he can hardly be thinking only (if at all) of portraits. Equally, when at *Rhetoric* 3.10, 1410b17-20, Aristotle implies that the semantics of metaphor involve the thought that 'this *is* that', he cannot mean that when we appreciate a (good) metaphor we understand something we have 'seen before'.[11] We might well suppose, however, that in the case of metaphor as in that of artistic representation some familiarity with the 'that' as well as the 'this' does count as a prerequisite. So at *Poetics* 1448b17 we should interpret the force of the verb *prohoran*, as Pierluigi Donini has recently argued too, as an indication that the informed understanding of a mimetic work rests in part on *relevant prior experience*,[12] whether or not that might be taken, in the case of a portrait, to include first-hand familiarity with the actual appearance of the subject.

But we can only make headway with this aspect of the passage by going back, now, to the previous sentence of the text, in particular to the phrase *manthanein kai sullogizesthai ti hekaston* ('to learn/understand and reason what each thing is'). I want to maintain that the vocabulary of that phrase is such as Aristotle would have chosen to use only if he had wanted to ascribe a certain quasi-philosophical respectability and weight to the experience of mimetic art. In one way, this is, or ought to be, uncontentious, since just before this Aristotle has used the verb *manthanein* to make a direct connection between the pleasure taken in works of visual mimesis by ordinary people and the distinctive intellectual pleasure of philosophy itself. Yet there has been no shortage of interpreters who have found the formulation in this passage jejune and inadequate as the basis of a philosophical account of aesthetic experience. To cite a recent example, Malcolm Budd, in his fine book *Values of Art*, deems 'both peculiar and implausible' Aristotle's explanation of 'our capacity to derive pleasure from the accurate depiction of objects, even those we do not like to look at face to face', and he takes this explanation to amount to the claim that 'in recognising what a picture depicts we are acquiring information, namely, the information that this is what the picture depicts'. Budd contends that 'even if the information that a picture depicts such-and-such, acquired by looking at the picture and recognising what it depicts, does on some occasions yield pleasure, the information is too trivial to explain our pleasure in depiction'.[13] His criticism of Aristotle rests, however, on two interpretative mistakes, which he happens to share with a number of specialist scholars who have commented on this passage. The first is to reduce Aristotle's point to one of 'information', and thereby to underestimate the pregnant implications of the terms used in the philosopher's phrasing, *manthanein kai sullogizesthai ti hekaston* ('to learn/understand and reason what each thing is'). The second is the faulty supposition that Aristotle ignores the critical importance of what Budd calls the 'manner of depiction', even though the reference to pictorial art in this context of the *Poetics* actually takes immediate account of the medium and manner of depiction as a factor in aesthetic responses ('we take pleasure', Aristotle says, 'in contemplating *the most precisely rendered images* ...', *tas eikonas tas malista êkribômenas*, 1448b11), while the treatise as a whole (the best test of Aristotle's convictions) repeatedly bears out this point in its treatment of the art-form of tragedy.[14] Budd's rather hasty dismissal of Aristotle's position is cast in a somewhat ironic light by the fact that Budd himself regards a kind of 'understanding' as lying at the centre of the experience of representational art, while seeming not to realise that Aristotle might be making a comparable point by his use of the conjunction of verbs *manthanein kai sullogizesthai*.[15]

Since a reductive or minimalist reading of this part of *Poetics* 4 continues to have many adherents,[16] it will prove worthwhile to scrutinise the terms used here by Aristotle rather carefully. First *manthanein*, a word Aristotle elsewhere treats as having two (overlapping) meanings, to acquire knowledge and to use it – alternatives which I render, provisionally, as to 'learn' and to 'understand'.[17] Aristotle notices this distinction in many contexts, and is alert to ambiguities to which it can sometimes give rise. One context in which he touches on it is *EN* 6.11 (1143a4-18), where he explains the capacity of *sunesis*, 'discernment', a form of understanding related to though importantly different from *phronêsis* (practical wisdom), as being akin to the broader sense of the verb *manthanein*. Since *sunesis* is a form of understanding of a quasi-judicial/spectatorial kind (an ability to judge well *when others speak* about ethical matters),[18] we might reasonably expect it to have some bearing on the kind of learning and/or understanding that *Poetics* 4 ascribes to the experience of mimetic art. In both cases, to put the point succinctly, it looks as though what is involved is an ability to grasp and make sense of human (ethical) behaviour in the judgement of particular situations, but an ability that falls short of, so to speak, ethical expertise (the province of the *phronimos*): 'discernment' is a sort of secondary understanding that enables an audience to follow the deliberations and decisions of others, but does not guarantee an ability to act well in their own lives. Aristotle was conscious of similarities, indeed overlaps, between the audiences of drama and those of deliberative and forensic oratory;[19] it would not be surprising, therefore, if the kinds of understanding he was prepared to attribute to them should turn out to be convergent. So the *Ethics'* concept of *sunesis* might give us a clue to the sort of understanding Aristotle would have been prepared to posit, ideally at least, for audiences of drama. This same passage from the *Ethics* will also turn out to be worth noticing again when I come to the later part of my argument and consider Aristotle's remark about poetic universals in *Poetics* 9.

While Aristotle recognises a distinction in the senses of *manthanein* roughly equivalent to that between 'learn' and 'understand', he certainly does not regard these senses as disjunctive. Indeed, he takes some trouble in the *Posterior Analytics* to explain that all *mathêsis*, in the sense of learning, proceeds from *prior* knowledge and must thus in some degree involve *manthanein qua* understanding: using the verb *epistasthai* as synonymous with *manthanein*, he maintains that it is not absurd to say that the person who is learning something (*manthanein*) in a sense already knows (*epistasthai*) what is being learnt.[20] Moreover, although Aristotle's main concern there is with formal philosophical processes of instruction, his point has larger implications, as he indicates by mentioning that it applies just as much to the learning of a *technê* as to reasoning through arguments, whether deductive or inductive.

Now, it ought to be clear that in *Poetics* 4 Aristotle cannot mean to *limit* the cognitive process involved in experience of mimetic art to the simple registering of something already known, the simple registering of what Budd calls 'information'. If he did, it is highly doubtful, I submit, whether he would call the process *manthanein* at all, let alone compare the experience, however loosely, to philosophical learning/understanding. The point I am pressing is reinforced by the coupling of *manthanein* with *sullogizesthai*. This last term has itself been the object of some dispute in this context, but once we have excluded the extreme though still sometimes advocated view that it here has its strictly syllogistic sense,[21] what matters most is to see that it must mark processes of thought and reflection that even at an apparently rudimentary level open up the possibility of movement from something already known to something newly comprehended. For even in the ostensibly simple case of *houtos ekeinos*, 'this person is so-and-so', the viewer is not simply recognising someone (as it were, in the street), but recognising that this someone is *a subject in the picture*. Nor does Aristotle's argument suggest, though some have certainly taken it this way, that the identification of a depicted figure would properly constitute a complete response to a picture (even in the case of a portrait) rather than the beginning or basis of a response. *Houtos ekeinos* is a shorthand example, though a perfectly serviceable one, since it could hardly be doubted – except by an outright aesthetic formalist – that a necessary part of the understanding of a visual depiction of human figures will often be the recognition of the identity of those figures. And that in turn can be treated, as I claim that Aristotle treats it here, as illustrative of a principle with fundamental and extensive ramifications for the understanding of all artistic representation.

That the phrase *manthanein kai sullogizesthai* in *Poetics* 4 designates, in the Aristotelian lexikon, a potentially rich and intricate cognitive process, and that it can correspondingly accommodate possibilities contained in both senses of *manthanein* (learning and understanding),[22] is an interpretation that receives support from the closely related passage at *Rhetoric* 1.11 (1371a31-b10) already cited. The double link that Aristotle makes there between mimesis and 'wonder' (*thaumazein*), and between wonder and 'the desire to *manthanein*', shows that he takes *manthanein*, where mimetic artefacts are concerned, to be a process, in part, of learning – of coming to see and grasp things which one could not have been previously said to understand. In the *Poetics* itself, a further signal that we need to extrapolate beyond Aristotle's deliberately rudimentary instance of *houtos ekeinos* is supplied by the words *ti hekaston*, 'what each thing is', which form the object of both verbs in *manthanein kai sullogizesthai ti hekaston*. This seemingly humdrum phrase has received virtually no attention from any of the commentators, but I suggest that it makes its own contribution, again as a sort of shorthand, to communicating what Aristotle takes to be the open-ended range of the understanding and learning involved in appreciating mimetic works. I do not think it has been previously noticed that Aristotle elsewhere uses the phrase *ti hekaston* exclusively in connection with philosophical enquiry and method. At *Topics* 1.18, 108b1, he says that discovering differences is useful for knowing 'what each thing is' (*ti hekaston*), and goes on to show that he is referring to the use of differentiae to construct definitions. At *De Anima* 2.4, 415a16, he comments on the need for the student of 'soul' to say what each of its 'forms' – such as thought, perception, nutrition – is (*legein ti hekaston*). *Metaphysics* 13.3, 1077b23-4, cites the possibility of discussing principles of physical motion without referring to particular moving bodies or their properties (*khôris tou ti hekaston esti tôn toioutôn*). At the end of *EN* 7 (7.14, 1154b33) Aristotle concludes the discussion of continence and incontinence, pleasure and pain, by saying that he has analysed 'what each of them is' (*ti hekaston ... autôn*). Finally, early in the *Politics* (1.3, 1253b8) Aristotle undertakes to discuss what each (*ti hekaston*) of three relations comprised by a household (master/slave, husband/wife, father/children) amounts to.

The pertinence of such passages to the interpretation of *Poetics* 1448b16-17 is not straightforward, since all the cases mentioned concern fully philosophical reasoning, and in most if not all of them what is involved is the grasp of concepts, definitions or universals, while in *Poetics* 4 Aristotle is speaking of objects of mimetic representation and his immediate example (*houtos ekeinos*), as I have stressed, designates a case of identifying a particular. There have, however, been attempts to find some reference to universals in this part of *Poetics* 4. Most notably, Gerald Else translated *manthanein kai sullogizesthai ti hekaston* by 'learning, inferring what class each object belongs to: for example that "this individual is a so-and-so" ' (emending the last phrase, grotesquely, to *houtos ekeino*);[23] and he additionally glossed *ti hekaston* as 'to what genus does this individual belong?'. While I commend Else's sense that Aristotle is here designating a potentially serious, quasi-philosophical process of cognition, his textual exegesis is linguistically impossible. Unlike Else, and notwithstanding the usage of the phrase I have cited from elsewhere in Aristotle, I do not think we should take the words *ti hekaston* here to convey a direct reference to the role of universals in the experience of mimetic representation, but rather as a broad indication that the representational content of a mimetic work or performance can be rich and detailed, requiring concentrated attention to a detailed 'field' of significance – as would evidently be so, on Aristotle's own terms, in the case of a complete tragic drama or a Homeric epic. But that field of significance would not, I maintain, actually consist of universals, and to see why that is so is to start to make the transition from my analysis of *Poetics* 4 to the argument I want to present about *Poetics* 9.

It might be thought that to insist, as I do, on the weight of the quasi-philosophical model of aesthetic understanding sketched in *Poetics* 4, while declining to discern an overt reference to universals in that passage, is doubly paradoxical: first, because Aristotelian philosophy paradigmatically deals with universals; and secondly because the *Poetics* itself surely tells us that poetry too engages with ('speaks of') universals. But both these considerations need careful qualification. The first needs qualifying by the observation that it is only the more theoretical, scientific end of the philosophical spectrum that is paradigmatically concerned with universals, and poetry, whose core subject-matter (for Aristotle) is human action and life, does not belong to that end of the spectrum. The second consideration – that the *Poetics* itself tells us that poetry 'speaks of' universals – now calls for fuller examination.

The relationship between chapters 4 and 9 of the *Poetics* is important but complex. That the two passages form a kind of axis within the work seems to me a crucial point about its framework of thought. The vital link between them is the fact that in these two places Aristotle assimilates poetry (in chapter 4, as we have seen, mimesis in general) to philosophy. In chapter 4 the assimilation is expressed in terms of the kind of cognition (the learning/understanding) involved in the experience of mimetic works, and while Aristotle there turns to visual art for a succinct illustration we must bear in mind that his argument expressly purports to uncover the roots, the 'causes', of poetry. In chapter 9 the assimilation is between poetry itself, or poetic works, and the status of philosophy: 'poetry is more philosophical and of greater gravity than history'. Yet, on my reading, there is not only a telling affinity but also an apparent tension between these passages, since chapter 4 exemplifies the understanding of a mimetic art-work by mentioning a case of recognising particulars. What are we to make of this tension? We can best set about the task of lessening or resolving it, I suggest, by acknowledging that chapter 9 has become the subject of considerable misconception, and this has happened both in the scholarly literature and in the wider impact of this celebrated section of the text. I will turn immediately to what I regard as one of the two most damaging of these misconceptions, and will come back to the other at the end of my paper.

It is tempting, but I now think misleading, to suppose that Aristotle claims in *Poetics* 9 that poetry (or, at the least, some poetry – his claim should never have been interpreted as applying to poetry *tout court*) *is*, in the fullest sense, a representation (mimesis) of universals. Here I must admit frankly to a *hamartia* of my own, since I have sometimes drifted towards such a formulation myself in the past.[24] I now wish to make amends. The essential observation called for here is not simply that Aristotle does not use such a formulation himself, but that he betrays a reluctance to make such a strong claim. Now, it can of course be pointed out that while Aristotle does not actually say that poetry is a mimesis of universals, he does say that poetry 'speaks' or 'tells' of universals. But this use of the verb *legein*, perhaps paradoxically, itself marks a subtle nuance in Aristotle's position. Although it was standard usage to refer to poetic texts in terms of what the poet said (*legein*) in them,[25] Aristotle scrupulously avoids such phrasing in the *Poetics*, preferring to use either *mimeisthai* (and cognate expressions) or *poiein* for the poet's relationship to the subject-matter, the representational substance, of his work. Indeed, I submit that Aristotle never in the *Poetics* uses *legein* in this way,[26] and in one much-discussed passage, at 24.1460a7-8, he asserts that 'the poet should say (*legein*) as little as possible in his own person, since it is not in virtue of this that he is a mimetic artist (*mimêtês*)'. We need not trouble ourselves at the moment with exactly what Aristotle means by this last remark; it is enough that he is clearly opposing the idea of the poet's voice, *qua* act of 'speaking' or 'telling' (*legein*), with mimesis. Whatever else, then, may be implied by chapter 9's formulation that poetry 'speaks more of universals', it cannot be synonymous with the proposition that poetry simply *is* a mimesis of universals and it gives us no grounds for the supposition that Aristotle takes universals to form the substance or 'first-order' content of poetic representation.[27] When I have said a little more about how I think universals should be construed in this important passage, I shall return to Aristotle's choice of the verb *legein* in this connection and venture a further suggestion about it.

There are, in any case, further traces in chapter 9 of a characteristically Aristotelian kind of tentativeness surrounding the claim about poetry and universals, traces which implicitly qualify the strength of the claim itself.[28] The first is the adverb *mallon* at 1451b7: poetry 'speaks *more/rather* of universals, history of particulars'. The force of *mallon* here is actually ambiguous; in principle it could mark a difference of kind or of degree, signifying either (i) that while history speaks *only* of particulars, poetry speaks to some extent, and therefore 'more' than history, of universals; or (ii) that poetry speaks of universals *to a greater extent* than history, but with the possibility left open that history itself might in some degree speak of universals, though evidently not, for Aristotle, in exercising its primary function as history.[29] But either way Aristotle's use of the adverb *mallon*, for whose nuances he has something of a penchant, qualifies the force of the proposition that poetry 'speaks' of universals. A further note of qualification is added by the second part of the sentence in which he elucidates what he means by universals (1451b9-10): having said that the term *katholou* covers the probable or necessary connections between the ethical qualities of the agents and their words and deeds, he adds 'and this is what poetry aims at [*stokhazetai*, another note of tentativeness], even though it adds names [sc. to the characters]'. That concessive clause is crucial.[30] It is an implicit reminder that dramatic and narrative poetry is about the actions and experiences of individual characters, characters who, in the depicted world they inhabit, are individuals or particulars in just the same sense as Alcibiades (Aristotle's token historical figure) is – so that we could even legitimately say, in very basic terms (matching the very basic terms in which Aristotle refers to history), that Sophocles' *Oedipus Tyrannus* is about 'what Oedipus did or what he suffered'.[31] It is not, then, the figures of poetry as such who are universals; Aristotle cannot hold a quasi-Johnsonian belief that dramatic characters are (or can be) 'species'.[32] But neither can it be that their actions are universals – for the actions of individuals, whether real or imaginary individuals, are quite certainly particulars. And the same is even true of the agents' qualities of character:[33] whatever Oedipus' characteristics are, they can be no more universals than the characteristics of Alcibiades.

On Aristotle's interpretation, then, universals must enter into poetry, to the extent that they do, at the larger level of plot-structure and of the whole framework of relationships between the agents, their actions and their characters; and that is of course just what Aristotle's explanation of the term *katholou* at 1451b8-9 seems to say. This point is well taken in the most recent discussion of the status of universals in *Poetics* 9, that of John Armstrong, who goes so far as to *identify* universals with plots. Within his larger argument that poetic universals are 'event-types', more specifically 'action-types', Armstrong writes at one point that 'poetic universals *are* plots' (my italics), though later, perhaps under the influence of Aristotle's own tentativeness, he prefers to say that 'the plot is *a kind of* universal' (my italics).[34] Although I find Armstrong's clarification of the issues helpful, I have one rather far-reaching problem with his position. Armstrong seems partly to lose sight of the fact that the agents (including their characters) and the actions of a dramatic poem are – and, unless we are to ascribe a concept of something like allegory to Aristotle, *must be* – represented as particulars, so that if the plot of a poem is a structure of action(s), as Aristotle clearly states (*Poetics* 6.1450a3-5; cf. 1450a15-17, 1450b3-4), it cannot straightforwardly count as a universal. Armstrong may be trying to cope with this point when he says in his conclusion: 'the action-type may ... be conceived at varying degrees of abstractness or concreteness. At its most concrete stage, the action-type is fleshed-out in all the details of a poet's final script. This is what is usually called the plot.' Leaving aside whether it is correct to equate the fully fleshed-out 'script' of the poem with what Aristotle means by 'plot', the more fundamental problem here is that the component elements of a plot – its individual characters, with their individual actions and words – cannot, in Aristotelian terms, simply constitute universals. In other words, even if Armstrong is right to interpret the universals of *Poetics* 9 as event-types or action-types, he cannot be right to suggest that universals in this sense actually make up the fully 'fleshed-out' fabric of a dramatic poem. We need only recall here that when in *Poetics* 17 (1455a22ff.) Aristotle dwells on the need for a composing playwright to flesh out his script as vividly as possible (with maximum *enargeia*), he unmistakably has in mind the dramatic value of a sense of immediacy that creates the impression of real events being acted out. Such vivid immediacy is by definition a property of the particular, not the universal.

My disagreement with Armstrong, then, amounts to a way of restating and reinforcing my earlier observation that Aristotle does not say that poetry is a mimesis, a representation, of universals. Armstrong makes it sound as though that is exactly what Aristotle does think.

98

After all, if the plot is a universal, then whenever Aristotle talks about plots in the *Poetics*, at any rate well-made plots, he would be talking about the representation of universals. But that is patently not so; he is always talking about the mimesis of action and of its agents: that, as we know, is how he *defines* plot (6.1450a3-5).

But if poetry is not, in an unqualified sense, the representation of universals, where does this leave the universals of chapter 9? It must leave them at a level that is at least partly implicit or latent, as a kind of subtext, though a subtext to which the fabric of a well-structured plot is, so to speak, more 'transparent' than Aristotle thinks historical texts usually are. In a larger philosophical perspective, it is only to be expected that poetic universals should exist at the level of subtext, since elsewhere Aristotle regards universals as 'subsisting' or 'underlying' (*huparkhein*) particulars.[35] And there is a further reason for thinking that this makes especially good (Aristotelian) sense for poetry, with its central interest in human 'action(s) and life' (*Poetics* 6.1450a16-17). Here it is germane to remind ourselves, if only very briefly, of the place of universals in Aristotle's own philosophy of human action. Throughout the *Nicomachean Ethics* Aristotle distinguishes between universal and particular considerations on the subject, but he repeatedly insists that the role of universals in ethics (whether in the form of philosophical analysis or in that of practical deliberation) is very different from their status in strict philosophical knowledge or science, which of course involves the grasp of things that are both universal and necessary.[36] Early in book 2 (2.2, 1104a1-7), for example, in a very well-known passage, he states that 'all discussion (*logos*) about conduct should be only an approximate outline, ... since matters of action do not possess fixity', then adding that 'given that this is so with discourse at the level of the universal, still more must it be so with discussion of particulars of action'. A little later in book 2 Aristotle says that in the realm of ethical action universal reasons (*logoi*) are wider in application (or, possibly, 'emptier', *kenôteroi*!), but the particular (those which are *epi merous*) are 'more real' (*alêthinôteroi*, a word here usually but questionably translated as 'truer'), 'for actions concern particulars, and it is at this level that our ideas must be in agreement'.[37] In book 5, in his discussion of the principle of equity, Aristotle observes that all law is couched in universal terms but that this very fact about it creates the possibility of error, and the need for subsequent correction, in those cases where 'it is not possible to speak correctly in universal terms' (5.10, 1137b13-27).[38] In book 6 Aristotle explains that *phronêsis*, because concerned with deliberation about action, 'is not a matter only of universals, but must also grasp (*gnôrizein*) particulars' (6.8, 1141b14-15). Something similar is true of *sunesis*, 'discernment', in a passage of book 6 to which I earlier drew attention for other reasons, where

Aristotle stresses the concern of both *sunesis* and *phronêsis* (as well as related capacities, *gnômê* and *nous*) with the correct judgement of particulars (see 6.12, 1143a28-b5). This gives *sunesis* a twofold pertinence to my own argument: it connects with *Poetics* 4 by contributing to our sense of the kind of broad understanding and judgement of human behaviour which Aristotle suggests that poetry, as a form of mimesis, calls into play; and it connects with chapter 9, on my reading, by exhibiting the Aristotelian conviction that in the domain of action we can only work our way towards universals via a very strong apprehension of particulars.

Material of the kind I have cited from the *Ethics* is very familiar to Aristotelian specialists, but it is rarely if ever brought to bear on the interpretation of *Poetics* 9. If lack of 'fixity' in the sphere of ethical action means that it permits and calls for a grasp of universals only in a partial and qualified sense, whether at the level of practical wisdom (*phronêsis*) or at that of philosophical reflection, why should Aristotle think that poetry – the sort of poetry he regards as the mimesis 'of action(s) and life' – is, or ought to be, overridingly concerned with universals rather than particulars?[39] The answer, I submit, is that he thinks no such thing. What he does think is that poetry 'speaks more of universals' than does history. But as I earlier insisted, the *Poetics* itself affords ample grounds for appreciating that this cannot amount to a claim that in poetry – *any* poetry (of the sorts Aristotle has in mind) – universals are the primary material of the poet's work. The stuff of dramatic and narrative poetry is human actions, characters and thoughts – the three 'objects' of mimesis in Aristotle's classification of the six 'parts' of tragedy. All three of these, as components of a poem, will comprise particulars: that is, each action, each manifested or implied characteristic of an agent, and each expressed thought of a character will be the representation of a particular action, characteristic or thought. It is true that in the case of character and thought we have also to reckon with pronouncements, made by the agents themselves, that have an element of the explicitly universal: Aristotle acknowledges this directly in his definition of 'thought', *dianoia*, at 6.1450b12, and his awareness of this factor might be partly reflected in his remarks on universals. But this cannot have been more than a marginal consideration in his mind; it is poetry, he asserts, that 'speaks' of universals, not its characters as such.[40]

The point I want to emphasise, then, is that the universals of chapter 9 must count for Aristotle as 'weak' universals, falling short of the status of universals in the more theoretical departments of philosophy (for we have seen that the domain of ethical action does not allow for the application of full-blown universals), and also as implicitly or indirectly conveyed universals (for they cannot otherwise be embodied in structures of represented action). In this respect the universals of poetry cannot for the most part have the explicitness that they would have in rhetoric, where Aristotle recognises their expression both in 'examples' (*paradeigmata*) and in 'maxims' (*gnômai*).[41] The rhetorician can spell out his universal propositions, real or purported, but the dramatic poet (as conceived of by Aristotle) can do no such thing: he can only create a tightly convincing structure of events, in which the combination of action and character will possess an intelligibility that conforms to the *Poetics'* ubiquitous canon of probability or necessity, and which will therefore exhibit a higher degree of wholeness and unity than the contingencies of real life (or history) always do. The intelligibility that comes from a causally lucid and powerfully unified plot-structure is at the heart of what motivates Aristotle to mention universals in *Poetics* 9, but we should not underestimate the fact that this still leaves poetic universals at a level much less overt, and less susceptible to propositional formulation, than the examples or moral maxims of the orator, still more those of the systematic philosopher. If the universals underlying, say, a given tragedy *could* be translated into propositional form, it would require a large set of them to encompass the full configuration of its action and character; and Aristotle nowhere suggests, whether inside or outside the *Poetics*, that understanding a tragic plot calls for such explicit cognizance of universals.[42] Understanding poetic universals is a matter of implicit grasp, not – or not necessarily – of explicit articulation, and this points, I believe, to an important dimension of the model of human understanding that prevails in Aristotle's thinking at large.

Now, on the account I have just sketched, it may be helpful to think of the universals of chapter 9 as being a sort of metaphorical presence in poetic works, and I want to suggest that this is why Aristotle himself refers to them at least quasi-metaphorically in his remark that 'poetry speaks (*legei*) more of universals, history of particulars'.[43] We have already seen that Aristotle does not like *poets* to 'speak' in their work, and in the strict sense of the word it is only characters who can speak or tell things, in drama at any rate. So for poetry itself to 'speak', and moreover to speak of universals, looks like a sign that Aristotle is trying to couch the argument of this passage in tentative terms that should not be turned into literal or rigid doctrine. Furthermore, if poetry 'speaks' or 'tells' of universals only implicitly, then it 'speaks' of 'what could/might happen' (*hoia an genoito*, 1451a37-8) equally implicitly and quasi-metaphorically. Indeed, the status of 'what could/might happen' must be precisely equivalent to that of the universals Aristotle goes on to mention. Dramatic or narrative poetry does not, after all, *depict* or represent 'what could/might happen' in the same sense that it depicts or represents the particular actions of particular agents. Neither 'what could/might happen' nor universals are the direct object of poetic mimesis. Yet poetry 'speaks' of them both.

So, on the interpretation I have delineated, the universals of *Poetics* 9 do not vanish, but they do become much less substantial than most scholars and critics have taken them to be: their presence in poetic works is a sub-textual, virtual, even metaphorical presence, though one that still carries the possibility of heightened understanding for the audience. This is, surely, only appropriate. For universals are not, for Aristotle, substances, least of all universals in the province of ethical action; they are a dimension of reality that can only emerge from the mind's processes of experience and understanding. But the degree to which, and the salience with which, universals emerge in understanding varies with the aspects of reality and the kinds of human thinking involved. A corollary of this is that understanding, *manthanein*, is itself not a fixed mental operation – it is a spectrum of ways of making sense, grasping the explanations, of things, extending all the way from the fully theoretical and scientific comprehension of the necessary and unchanging down to the much more partial and local apprehension of the contingent and variable. Where the object of understanding is human life itself, we are at the end of the philosophical spectrum where *manthanein* exhibits continuity with ordinary, common types of reasoning that are not the exclusive preserve of philosophers. We are in the zone of what one might call fully human understanding, an anthropocentric understanding that has to keep close to the local and particular, as opposed to those higher Aristotelian regions of knowledge which, in some sense, aspire to a more-than-human contemplation of reality.[44] This is the zone of understanding to which the human instinct for mimesis (from children's role-playing to artistic representation)[45] belongs, and where philosophy and poetry in some degree converge. *Poetics* 9 indicates that such understanding is linked to poetry's quasi-philosophical capacity to reveal something of the universal in or through the particular. But I have argued that we should not overstate what Aristotle means by talking of universals in this context, both because the *Poetics* as a whole posits particulars (of action, character and thought) as the direct object of poetic mimesis, and also because, as the *Ethics* helps us to see, an Aristotelian understanding of life, *qua* ethical choice and action, cannot be captured to more than a limited extent by a grasp of universals *per se*. It is, then, after all, unproblematic that Aristotle's example of understanding a mimetic image in *Poetics* 4 should be a case of identifying a particular: understanding particulars, in all their contextual complexity (as intimated by that full phrase, 'to understand and reason what each thing is'), *must* play an important part in the appreciation of poetry, as in the appropriately sensitive judgement of ethical issues.

There is one final strand I want to draw out from what I have said about the universals of *Poetics* 9, and this brings me to a second misconception about this section of the treatise. It has often been believed that the universals of chapter 9 presuppose a view of human life that is 'universalist' in the strong sense of predicating what is common to all human experience across time and space, a transhistorically and transculturally 'immutable human condition'. This is, in essence, the neoclassical reading of *Poetics* 9, and it still attracts adherents, though now usually of an unsympathetic cast. A recent instance of this seductive but mistaken reading of the passage occurs in an essay by Edith Hall which confidently identifies this part of the *Poetics* as the *fons et origo* of readings of Greek tragedy that are universalist in the sense just stipulated: 'the supposedly "universal" significance of tragedy posited by Aristotle in his *Poetics*', she writes, '... presupposed an immutable human condition whose teleological imperative [*sic*] was suffering, and which somehow transcended transhistorical [*sic*] changes, and differences in culture and language.'[46] But nothing in *Poetics* 9 invites, still less requires, us to find in it a reference to such a strongly universalist perspective on human life, a perspective which Aristotle's work as a whole does not, I think, actually call for, contrary to the popular image of his philosophy. With immediate regard to the *Poetics*, two succinct objections to this strong reading of chapter 9's declaration about universals should be voiced. First, the concepts of action and character contained in the explanation of that proposition are subject, according to Aristotle's own thinking (especially as we see it in the *Politics*, *Ethics* and *Rhetoric*) to social, political and cultural variables that stand in the way of the strong universalism that is in question here. Secondly, the principle of *eikos* (probability or likelihood) on which that same explanation depends entails circumstantial contextualisation – not an appeal to timeless truths about human nature – if its application is to have persuasive force: as the *Rhetoric* especially serves to underline, Aristotle realises that *eikos* is always relative to the convictions and value-systems of specific audiences. Aristotle may believe in an underlying set of possibilities (one of which is a capacity for mimesis) that constitute human nature, but I maintain that his philosophy does not postulate a global 'human condition' of a kind whose principles and workings poetic dramas and narratives could be expected to disclose. If Aristotle did possess a strong conception of an 'immutable human condition', this condition would be a suitable subject for philosophical knowledge and he would have treated it accordingly. But he nowhere recognises such a branch of knowledge. Instead, he accepts that in the realm of ethical action and experience, we cannot and should not hope for more than an approximate and defeasible search for explanations.[47] In Aristotle's purview, the real importance of

103

poetry, as of other types of mimetic art, resides in its contribution to the
ongoing quest for a fully human form of understanding.[48]

Notes

1. Ps.-Aristotle, *Problemata* 30.6, 956a11-14.
2. See *Hist. Anim.* 8.12, 597b23-6, 9.1, 609b16, 9.49, 631b9.
3. Castelvetro's dismissive view is at *Poetica d'Aristotele Vulgarizzata e
Sposta*, ed. W. Romani (Rome, 1978-9), vol. 1, pp. 94-5. A good specimen of
recent work on the development of children's capacity for fiction can be found
in P.L. Harris, 'Fictional absorption: emotional responses to make-believe', in
S. Bråten (ed.), *Intersubjective Communication and Emotion in Early Ontogeny*
(Cambridge, 1998), 336-53.
4. See D. Gallop, 'Animals in the *Poetics*', *Oxford Studies in Ancient Philosophy* 8 (1990), 145-71, at pp. 161-7; cf. R. Janko, *Aristotle Poetics* (Indianapolis,
1987), 74.
5. This point is ignored by both Gallop and Janko (see previous note).
6. My argument here picks up from my essay 'Pleasure, understanding and
emotion in Aristotle's *Poetics*', in A.O. Rorty (ed.), *Essays on Aristotle's Poetics*
(Princeton, 1992), 241-60, a revised version of which appears as chapter 6 of my
book, *The Aesthetics of Mimesis: Ancient Texts and Modern Problems* (Princeton, forthcoming 2002).
7. *Houtos ekeinos* at *Poet.* 4.1448b17 is wrongly translated as though it were
touto ekeino by e.g. G.M. Sifakis, 'Learning from art and pleasure in learning:
an interpretation of Aristotle *Poetics* 4 1448b8-19', in J. Betts et al. (eds.),
Studies in Honour of T.B.L. Webster (Bristol, 1986), vol. 1, 211-22, at p. 218, J.
Lear, 'Katharsis', *Phronesis* 33 (1988), 297-326, at p. 307 (repr. in *Open Minded:
Working out the Logic of the Soul* (Cambridge, MA, 1998)), E.S. Belfiore, *Tragic
Pleasures: Aristotle on Plot and Emotion* (Princeton, 1992), 46, 48, G. Nagy,
Pindar's Homer (Baltimore, 1990), 44. For the proposed emendation of *houtos
ekeinos* to *touto ekeino* see A. Gudeman, *Aristoteles Peri Poietikes* (Berlin, 1934),
34 (app. crit.), 119, and Gallop (n. 4), 167-8.
8. The colloquial usage of *tout(o) ekeino* is wrongly adduced by e.g. Sifakis (n.
7), 218. This is not, however, to deny that the masculine phrase, *houtos ekeinos*,
may itself have a colloquial ring (cf. *hod' ekeinos*, 'there he is!' or 'this is him!,'
at Aristophanes *Knights* 1331), for this would be in keeping with the deliberately simple formulation of Aristotle's point.
9. Many Platonic passages illustrate the technical sense of this word-group:
e.g. *Prot.* 312d, *Rep.* 6.504d7, 8.548d1, *Soph.* 234b7, 235e2, 236c3, *Laws* 2.656e.
10. See on this point M. Budd, *Values of Art: Pictures, Poetry and Music*
(London, 1995), 63-7.
11. In discussing metaphor at *Rhet.*. 3.10, 1410b10-26, Aristotle favours
those which involve quick but not instantaneous understanding, and he gives
indications of a spectrum of possible forms of *mathêsis*: see 21 for 'quick'
learning, and note esp. 10-15, 21-6, for the clear implication that *manthanein*
cannot be limited to registering things already known.
12. Cf. P.-L. Donini, *Aristotele Opere 10**: Poetica* (Rome, 1997), xxxvii.
13. Budd (n. 10), 48-9.
14. On the art-critical verb *akriboun* at 1448b11 cf. the same verb applied to
literary art at 1450a36; cf. too *EN* 6.7, 1141a9, with reference to visual art. On

art-critical use of related terminology see J.J. Pollitt, *The Ancient View of Greek Art*, student edn. (New Haven, 1974), 117-26; Plato, *Critias* 107c-d is also germane.

15. See e.g. Budd (n. 10), 69, stating that pictures have an 'artistic meaning' which 'the spectator needs to *recognise* if he is to *understand* the picture' (my itals). Moreover, Budd p. 63, 'Perhaps nobody knows what the subject of Piero della Francesca's *Flagellation* is; if so, nobody understands it or can properly evaluate its success as a realisation of that subject', is remarkably, but unconsciously, close to Aristotle's own formulation of his point at *Poet.* 4.1448b17-18.

16. The most recent is G.R.F. Ferrari, 'Aristotle's literary aesthetics', *Phronesis* 44 (1999), 181-98, at p. 185. Cf. my 1992 essay (n. 6), 246-7.

17. One statement of the distinction is at *Soph. El.* 4, 165b30-4.

18. Cf. *Politics* 4.4, 1291a28. For convergence of *phronêsis* and *sunesis* cf. *EN* 6.12, 1143a25-35; 10.10, 1181b10-12 distinguishes *krinein kalôs* (here an exercise of *politikê*) from *eusunetos einai*. Note, interestingly, that at Aristoph. *Frogs* 1483 *sunesis* is ascribed to a tragic playwright (cf. 893) and is said to be a quality of his work from which others can learn (*mathein*).

19. Cf. the explicit analogy between them at *Rhet.* 3.12, 1414a8-12: the immediate point is stylistic, but it conveys a wider awareness of cultural affinity.

20. *Anal. Post.* 1.1, 71a1-b8. Cf. the reiterated point at *EN* 6.3, 1139b25-36.

21. Most recently, Sifakis (n. 7), 219. See D.W. Lucas, *Aristotle Poetics* (Oxford, 1968), 72. For another use of the verb see *Poet.* 25.1461b2.

22. Donini (n. 12), xxxv, rightly speaks of 'un apprendimento e una comprensione'; R. Dupont-Roc and J. Lallot, *Aristote: la Poétique* (Paris, 1980), 165, use only 'apprendre'.

23. G.F. Else, *Aristotle's Poetics: the Argument* (Cambridge MA, 1957), 125; cf. n. 44 below.

24. S. Halliwell, *Aristotle's Poetics* (London, 1986; repr. with new Introduction, 1998), 55, rightly criticised by M. Heath, 'The universality of poetry in Aristotle's *Poetics*', *Classical Quarterly* 41 (1991), 389-402, p. 390 n. 3. I am now rather dissatisfied, let me say, with my own treatment of universals in my 1986 book (above): I particularly regret the use of the term 'propositions' on p. 103 (less so on p. 106), and the statements that universals furnish the 'content' (p. 105) or the 'substance' (p. 162) of poetry. There can, in any case, be no question that Aristotle thought *all* poetry to be a representation of universals, since on any interpretation iambus is said to treat only individuals (9.1451b14-15, cf. 4.1448b23-49a6). Janko (n. 4), p. 12, goes much too far in giving this part of the *Poetics* the heading 'Poetry should represent universals, not particulars'.

25. I discuss Plato's special development of this usage in my article, 'The subjection of mythos to logos: Plato's citations of the poets', *Classical Quarterly* 50 (2000), 94-112, at pp. 103-5.

26. Some merely apparent exceptions are 19.1450b5-7 (definition of *dianoia*), 25.1460b36 (where *legein* is part of a loose formulation that covers more than poetry as such), 25.1461a11 (where *legein* should be translated as 'mean'), and 25.1461b18 (where *legein* belongs in the wider formulation of dialectical method).

27. To avoid misunderstanding, it should be acknowledged that in chapter 9, as most of the time in the *Poetics*, Aristotle is thinking principally of drama and epic; so it would be irrelevant to adduce here other kinds of poetry which might be thought to contain a direct representation of universals – for example, the moralising utterances of didactic or of much Greek elegiac poetry. Whether Aristotle even properly considers such genres to be poetry is a moot point: see Halliwell (n. 24), pp. 276-85. I note that M.E. Hubbard's translation of the *Poetics*, in D.A. Russell and M. Winterbottom (eds.), *Ancient Literary Criticism* (Oxford, 1972), 102 (with n. 1), keeps the full force of *legein* in this context by translating as 'poetry tends *to make general statements*'; but this surely gives a misleading impression. Cf. n. 43 below.

28. We can rapidly discard the suggestion of F. Solmsen 'The origins and methods of Aristotle's *Poetics*', *Classical Quarterly* 29 (1935), 192-201, at p. 198 (repr. in *Kleine Schriften* II [Hildesheim, 1968], 119-28, at p. 125), that the *katholou* of *Poetics* 9 is an offshoot of Platonism, or that it replaces 'reality' as the object of mimesis (p. 143 = 1968, p. 139).

29. This second reading is that of K. von Fritz, 'Die Bedeutung des Aristoteles für die Geschichtsschreibung', in *Histoire et Historiens dans l'Antiquité* (Fondation Hardt, Entretiens IV: Geneva, 1956), 85-128, at pp. 115-22. The significance of *mallon* is remarked on by B. Croce, *Estetica come Scienza dell'Espressione e Linguistica Generale*, 9th edn. (Bari, 1950), 185; but he immediately delivers a lofty dismissal of the whole passage. As regards Aristotle's view of history, it is worth remembering that in the *Rhetoric* he specifically refers to the value of written history in relation to political deliberations: *Rhet.* 1.4, 1360a35-7.

30. The participle *epitithemenê* is rightly taken as concessive by e.g. I. Bywater, *Aristotle on the Art of Poetry* (Oxford, 1909), 190, and Gudeman (n. 7), 207; Lucas (n. 21), 121, hesitates, but his own explanation is indecisive.

31. Belfiore (n. 7), 49-50, flatly states that the objects of poetic mimesis are not individuals, but she seems by 'individuals' to understand 'real/actual individuals'. Later, pp. 62-3, she repeatedly calls dramatic characters and their actions 'instances of universals' – but *instances* of universals are particulars (see p. 67 with n. 52 for apparent acceptance of this), and in this sense historical individuals too are instances of universals.

32. Samuel Johnson, Preface to Shakespeare (1765): 'in the writings of other poets a character is too often an individual; in those of Shakespeare it is commonly a species' (in F. Brady & W. K. Wimsatt (eds.), *Samuel Johnson: Selected Poetry and Prose* [Berkeley, 1977], 301).

33. An individual's character is a particular (e.g. *Rhet.* 2.21, 1394a22-3), even though its qualities instantiate universals.

34. J. Armstrong, 'Aristotle on the philosophical nature of poetry', *Classical Quarterly* 48 (1998), 447-55, at pp. 453, 454 (cf. 455).

35. See e.g. *Met.* 7.13, 1038b12, 22, *Part. Anim.* 1.4, 644a25-6.

36. See *EN* 6.6, 1140b31-2 for this conception of *epistêmê* within the *Ethics* itself; cf. also 10.9, 1180b20-3.

37. *EN* 2.7, 1107a28-32: on the text cf. J.A. Stewart, *Notes on the Nicomachean Ethics of Aristotle* (Oxford, 1892), vol. 1, 211-12; E. Moore, *An Introduction to Aristotle's Ethics* (London, 1897), 98, rightly insists on 'more real' for *alêthinôteroi*, but the point is overlooked by modern translators. For another insistence on the importance of particulars to ethical judgement see 2.9, 1109b20-3.

38. Cf. K. Eden, *Poetic and Legal Fiction in the Aristotelian Tradition* (Princeton, 1986), ch. 2, esp. pp. 48-9.

39. The relationship between ethics 'proper' and poetry is not, of course, entirely straightforward, since the *Ethics'* remarks are addressed to the question of whether and how far universals *qua* normative principles are achievable. But the answer to that question must nonetheless have implications for how far we can discern universals in or through poetic representations of ethical action.

40. In another respect, however, poetic characterisation (*ēthos*) and 'thought' (*dianoia*) are likely to be highly relevant to Aristotle's notion of how poetry can allow universals to be more intelligible in/through the actions it depicts than is usually the case in history: he takes *ēthos* and *dianoia* to be elements in which poetic agents reveal much about themselves, thereby lending to action a clarity, coherence and explanatory fullness which he appears to believe typically lie beyond the scope of the materials available to historians.

41. See esp. *Rhet.* 1.2, 1356b2-6, 2.20, 1393a26-7 (*paradeigmata* as induction), *Rhet.* 2.21, 1394a21-8 (*gnōmai* and universals).

42. The formal setting out of the 'universal' sub-structure of a plot at *Poetics* 17.1455a35ff. is an attempt to describe the poet's compositional procedures and does not carry over directly to an audience's understanding of the plot.

43. *Legein* is applied to the 'statement' of universals at *De Anima* 3.11, 434a17-18.

44. The spectrum of *manthanein* actually continues below the human: for animal learning/understanding see e.g. *Metaph.* 1.1, 980b21-5. Note that Else (n. 23), p. 132, is quite wrong to imply that *manthanein* ('learning') is necessarily or always of universals: this is true of 'knowledge', *epistēmē* (in its strongest Aristotelian sense), but not of everything that Aristotle includes in *manthanein*.

45. One thing that connects children's mimetic play to mimetic art is the experience of *affective* enactment – which means, for Aristotle as for Plato, learning (*manthanein*) to feel pleasure and pain in the right way. For this element in responses to mimetic art see *Pol.* 8.5, 1340a14-18. One might once again paraphrase this aspect of Aristotle's theory of mimesis by saying that art, just as much as children's play, is a sort of emotional 'rehearsal' for life (cf. p. 88 above).

46. E. Hall, 'The sociology of Athenian tragedy', in P.E. Easterling (ed.) *Cambridge Companion to Greek Tragedy* (Cambridge, 1997), 93-126, at p. 94.

47. See A. Savile, *The Test of Time: An Essay in Philosophical Aesthetics* (Oxford, 1982), ch. 5, for a subtle account, starting from Aristotle himself, of aesthetic understanding. M.C. Nussbaum, 'Aristotle on human nature and the foundations of ethics', in J.E.J. Altham and R. Harrison (eds.), *World, Mind, and Ethics: Essays on the Ethical Philosophy of Bernard Williams* (Cambridge, 1995), 86-131, provides an enlightening approach to the question of how Aristotle's view of human nature operates.

48. I am grateful to my fellow participants, and especially to the organisers Øivind Andersen and Jon Haarberg, for discussion of my paper at the Oslo *Poetics* symposium. I would also like to thank a meeting in Leeds of the Northern Association for Ancient Philosophy, in April 2000, for a chance to present a first draft of this paper.

Roman Tragedy and the
Teaching of Aristotle's *Poetics*

Elaine Fantham

When I mentioned to colleagues that I planned to write a paper about the influence of Aristotle's *Poetics* at Rome, more than one of them said, 'That will be a pretty short paper!' And of course I am well aware that we have no Roman *testimonia* for the *Poetics*. Indeed even the earliest Greek mention during the centuries of Classical Latin literature occurs in Diogenes Laertius' list of Aristotle's works – a writer of the third century AD relying on a much earlier Peripatetic source.[1] And I promise that I am not going to fill out yet another paper with the shadowy presence of the *Poetics* in Horace's *Ars Poetica*. So what is there to justify my title?

My theme is the influence, however indirect, of the *Poetics* and its recommended dramaturgy on early Roman tragedy, and my thesis is one I largely owe to a relatively neglected source, a work of the German religious historian, Franz Altheim.[2] But before stating the case, I would like to talk more generally about the problem of how, when and to what extent Aristotle's esoteric works came to be known in Rome.

The best illustration of the different possibilities is the much disputed question of how and when Aristotle's *Rhetoric* reached Rome. When I first started to work on Cicero's *De Oratore* I took as my guide Friedrich Solmsen's wonderful papers on the Aristotelian tradition at Rome[3] and of course Cicero's own statement, through the orator M. Antonius, that he had read both the Aristotelian *Synagoge Technon* and the *Rhetoric*.[4] If we suppose that Cicero here is speaking less for Antonius in 91 BC than for himself, this is a stronger claim of autopsy than his well known report to Lentulus Spinther that he had incorporated into his dialogue 'all the Isocratean and Aristotelian systems'.[5] But this inevitably opens the question 'How could Cicero, writing in 55 BC, have read the esoteric *Rhetorica*?' The tradition reported in Strabo and Plutarch is that the esoteric works, including the *Rhetorica* and presumably the Poetics, had been lost to the world for two centuries, until Sulla's occupation of Athens in 83 BC when he obtained them by appropriation from the bibliophile Apellicon. Assuming these were the first texts of the *Esoterica* to reach Rome, we can see ways in which

Cicero could have access to them; his villa at Tusculum was near that of Sulla's son Faustus, and Cicero writes that he enjoyed the use of Sulla's library:[6] in addition Tyrannio, the scholar who was advising on and cataloguing this library, was also working for Cicero's collection, as Cicero reports in letters from the time when he was composing *De Oratore*.

I at least was content to believe that this was how Cicero had come to see and consult the *Rhetoric*. And no one disputed that by 46 BC, the time of *Brutus* and *Orator*, Cicero was referring to the *Rhetoric* and translated at least one passage verbatim.[7]

There was dispute, of course, from scholars who are not prepared to credit any Roman with intelligent and independent engagement with Greek intellectual argument. William Fortenbaugh in *Cicero's Knowledge of the Peripatos*[8] takes each 'Aristotelian' passage from the dialogue in turn and marks any discrepancies as the product, not of Cicero's choice in the service of his own context and argument, but of carelessness or ignorance. It is not surprising that Jonathan Barnes[9] passes over this treatment and proceeds to a new and more encouraging conclusion. First he considers and regretfully dismisses the idea that Cicero could have gained access to the Library of Apellicon through his exchanges with Tyrannio in 55, when he was composing *De Oratore*, or indeed that Tyrannio himself was familiar with the *Rhetoric* even as late as 46. Instead he infers from Cicero's silence that he had not discussed either Aristotle or Sulla's library with Tyrannio. But then, quite consistently, Barnes takes Cicero's statement through Antonius, and his citation of Aristotle's theories on prose rhythm in *De Oratore*[10] as seriously as his silence. He deduces that if Cicero did not know the three-volume *Rhetoric* from his contact with Tyrannio, he certainly knew its contents, and not through hypothetical compendia and handbooks.

As Moraux acknowledged in his exhaustive discussion of this question, Cicero did consult available esoteric texts of Aristotle:[11] *De Finibus* 3.10 (set in 52 BC) introduces him consulting *commentarii* of Aristotle in Lucullus' library, and the same dialogue discusses the two categories of Aristotle's writings and comments on the contradictions in the *Esoterica*. Hence Barnes' conclusion that 'our three-volume Rhetoric'[12] was available in Cicero's Rome. Distinguishing between the rigorous question 'whether Cicero consulted, himself, a three-volume Rhetoric' which he believes should be answered in the affirmative, and the wider issue of 'whether he knew ... of such a text, whether there was or had been such a text available in or before Cicero's time', Barnes insists that 'a three-volume *Rhetoric* was certainly known and used before Andronicus'.[13] It makes excellent sense that Cicero should have been familiar with the contents of Aristotle's *Rhetoric* before the bringing of Apellicon's library to Rome, since his arguments in *De Oratore* show every sign of having thoroughly absorbed and assimilated its teaching. So why not backtrack and infer that the rhetoric was available in Antonius' generation too? Without pretending that the essentially practical lawyer Antonius had himself read the *Rhetoric* (or the Greek historians whom he has claims to have read earlier in the book), we can say with Barnes, that 'it cannot have seemed absurd to Cicero to imply that a Roman had read Aristotle's rhetorical works in the first decade of the century, and ... such works were available to the interested reader'.[14]

This has been a long digression from the *Poetics*, but I hope that it has illustrated the different levels, direct and indirect, at which knowledge of Aristotle's literary and rhetorical treatises could have circulated among Rome's intellectual elite, even before Cicero's own philosophical work, and the second period of Hellenisation that came with the Greek scholar-critics of the Augustan age. Now let me turn to the earlier period of Hellenisation, the hey-day of Roman tragedy and comedy in the first half of the second century BC. First a counter-example from early drama may show the sort of material we should not use to infer Roman knowledge of Aristotelian teaching. When I argued some years ago that Plautus' *Trinummus* had as the focus of its intrigue an *aporia* discussed by Aristotle in the *Nicomachean Ethics*,[15] I saw no reason to suggest that Plautus himself had read the *Ethics* or Theophrastus' similar studies on the problems of friendship. The comic dilemma between Lesbonicus and Lysiteles in which one friend's financial sacrifice impaired the honour of the other whom he wished to serve, is essential to the plot of Philemon's *Thesaurus*, and was probably adapted by Plautus without the slightest inkling of its origin in Peripatetic ethics.

So when we turn instead to Plautus' younger contemporary, the tragedian Pacuvius, the claim that several of his plays reflect his own knowledge of Aristotle's dramaturgical recommendations in the *Poetics* depends on establishing that Pacuvius did not simply take over these intrigues from his Greek models, but himself invented or remodelled the actions of these tragedies. If the results match Aristotle's recommendations, then they can also be seen as the purpose of his remodelling.

And how, you will ask, could Pacuvius have known the *Poetics*?

There are two unrelated lines of tradition which could have transmitted Aristotelian teaching about dramatic poetry: the philosophical and philological tradition, and the more pragmatic tradition of the working theatre. Let us take the intellectual tradition first.

According to Suetonius *On Grammarians*,[16] the Romans were stimulated to begin the study of literature by the lectures or public readings of the Pergamene critic Crates of Mallos, when he came to Rome on an embassy 'just after the death of Ennius' and had to convalesce after breaking his leg.[17] This can be dated to the end of 168 or beginning of 167 BC, still early in Pacuvius' long career. We know that Crates lectured and wrote about Homer, offering for example allegorical interpretations of the 'shield of Achilles' and identifying the geographical sites of Odysseus' landfalls. He also wrote about tragedy, and the aesthetics of poetry, including euphony, and claimed that the essence of a poem was its form, 'not without the thoughts (*dianoia*) but not the thoughts themselves either'.[18] There is no difficulty in imagining that Pacuvius heard Crates and conversed with him, but, alas, no evidence that Crates' interest in poetry went beyond the text to questions of dramatic presentation.

A second wave of Greek intellectual influence could be expected at Rome when the Athenians sent an embassy in 155 consisting of the heads of the three activist philosophical schools, Diogenes the Stoic, Carneades the Academic and Critolaus the Peripatetic. But memorable as this was, it was the morally ambidextrous arguments of Carneades on justice rather than any known peripatetic teaching by Critolaus, that enthused the Romans and provoked the elder Cato to propose the rapid repatriation of these dangerous talkers.[19]

It is more likely that Pacuvius would learn about Aristotle's dramaturgical preferences from a theatrical source. Like his uncle Ennius, Pacuvius came from the Greek-speaking region of Southern Italy, whose material remains demonstrate their highly developed theatrical culture. What I would hypothesise is that the *Poetics* not only reflected the dramatic tastes of Aristotle's contemporaries but also shaped subsequent theatrical taste, influencing the Greek companies of *hoi peri ton Dionuson tekhnitae*, including directors, and the dramatists who in Pacuvius' time would come to Rome and work in Latin. We still know too little about the theatre in Magna Graecia, but there are inscriptions attesting associations of *tekhnitae* based on Syracuse and Rhegium:[20] O. Taplin argues for theatre companies travelling through Calabria and Apulia, and notes the abundance of Greek vases illustrating tragedy found in Magna Graecia in the fourth and third centuries.[21] Significantly the two instances known to us of Roman commanders hiring the Greek *tekhnitae* for *ludi* come from Pacuvius' time and his aristocratic connections: Livy cites the Asian games of Lucius Scipio, brother of Ennius' patron Africanus, and Polybius the somewhat farcical games of the Praetor L. Anicius twenty years later in 167.

What we find in the surviving evidence for Pacuvius' tragedies is a substantial interface between Pacuvius' practice in what was to Aristotle the most important aspect of tragedy – plot-structure – and Aristotle's own recommendations. It is probably unnecessary to linger here over the discrepancies between Aristotle's praise of recognitions that lead to an unhappy reversal in chapter 13 of the *Poetics* and his enthusiasm for the recognition plays of 'averted disaster' in the very next chapter: the two chapters also offer competing accounts of the 'best' or 'strongest', 'most impressive' forms of recognition and reversal. However, consulting both the definitive chapter in Stephen Halliwell's 1986 monograph and his commentary,[22] and following through Elizabeth Belfiore's discussion in *Tragic Pleasure*, I seem to find unanimity in treating the options reviewed by Aristotle, and in taking as his considered view the report in chapter 14 that the plot which makes the most powerful impression of terror or pity involves 'cases where the sufferings occur within relationships' and 'where the person is on the point of unwittingly committing something irremediable, but recognises it before doing so'.[23] Aristotle's examples here are a lost play of Euripides, the *Cresphontes* 'where Merope is about to kill her son, but recognises him in time', and the *Iphigenia in Tauris*, where Iphigenia as Priestess is obliged to sacrifice the man whom she then discovers to be her brother. Despite its complete difference in tone from Sophocles' *Oedipus Tyrannus*, this play is one of Aristotle's favourites, cited six times in the *Poetics* between chapters 11 and 17 for various features of its plot structure.[24] In chapter 13 Aristotle declares that the dramatist cannot change inherited myths, but must invent and make good use of the traditional material (1453b22). And this, I will argue, is what Pacuvius has done. He has twice deliberately reshaped a Greek myth – not a particular Greek tragedy – to conform to the general type of 'catastrophe averted' described above, and in one case to produce what we might fairly call a spin-off of Aristotle's favourite *Iphigenia among the Taurians*.

The first case-study must be the one so brilliantly analysed by Franz Altheim over sixty years ago, Pacuvius' play *Atalanta*. Altheim himself was building on a foundation of Otto Ribbeck's great *Römische Tragödie* and *Tragicorum Romanorum Fragmenta*, and Friedrich Leo's *Geschichte der Römischen Literatur*:[25] since Altheim's study none of the serious work on the fragments of the *Atalanta* has found reason to challenge his conclusions. I shall use as basis for my presentation an ordering of the known fragments more or less agreed among the Loeb edition of Pacuvius by E.H. Warmington, the only English-language edition, H.J. Mette's analytical *Lustrum* survey of 1964, and Giovanni D'Anna's full edition and commentary on Pacuvius' plays of 1967. I also consulted the useful introductory monographs by M. Valsa and Italo Mariotti from the late 60s.[26]

As Mette notes, we know nothing about any Greek plays about Atalanta or her son Parthenopaeus: nothing survives of the *Atalante* of Aeschylus, or that of Aristias. Again plays called after Atalanta's son

Parthenopaeus were composed by the younger Astydamas and by Spintharos, but they are quite lost; there is no evidence that either play introduced the young Parthenopaeus in search of his mother, as does the Pacuvian tragedy. We can approach the mythical basis of this drama from two directions; from the account of the two known Atalantas, and the family of the Arcadian Atalanta in Apollodorus' *Bibliotheke* and from the genealogical synopsis offered by the version of Hyginus which survives from the third century of our era.[27]

For this play we can forget the Boeotian Atalanta, daughter of Schoeneus and cousin of Meleager who won the prize in the Calydonian boarhunt which led to his quarrel with his uncles and tragic death at his mother's hands.[28] Pacuvius' play is concerned with Arcadian Tegea and involves the Arcadian Atalanta, and two young kinsmen from her family, the house of Arcas.

According to Apollodorus, Arcas' grandson Aleus was father of three children, including Lycurgus, Atalanta's grandfather, and Auge. Lycurgus' son Iasus exposed his baby daughter Atalanta to die, but she survived, suckled by a bear, to become an athlete and huntress and protect her virginity as best she could. Atalanta's ruse was to challenge all suitors to a footrace: if the suitor was overtaken he was penalised by death on the spot, but if he beat her he was rewarded by marriage. Only her cousin Milanion was able to outrun her, by using the golden apples provided by Aphrodite as decoys to distract her. (Apollodorus has difficulty disentangling the contamination of her legend with the Boeotian Atalanta, daughter of Schoeneus.)

What matters for our play is that Atalanta conceived a son Parthenopaeus, whether by Milanion or Meleager, and in her turn exposed him. Now her kinswoman Auge had also conceived a son by Hercules when she was a priestess of Athena on Mount Parthenios, and this son was Telephus, whom she also exposed on the mountain. With Apollodorus' version of the family tree Auge would actually be Atalanta's great-aunt, and Pacuvius' play, which brings the two young men together, would leap across two generations in presupposing that the two exposed heroes grew up as friends and set out together to find their mothers. However nothing is more likely than that the women in a complex family tree should have been attached to the wrong generation.

This plot, which we will examine more closely, is reflected in Hyginus' synopsis XCIX, entitled AUGE, as follows:

> Auge daughter of Aleus, when seduced by Hercules gave birth to her son on Mt Parthenius and exposed him there. At the same time Atalante daughter of Iasus exposed her son begotten by Meleager.[29] Now Hercules had his son suckled by a doe. The shepherds found the babies and brought them up, calling them ...

Telephus and Parthenopaeus. Now Auge feared her father and fled to Moesia to king Teuthras, who had no children and adopted her as his daughter.[30]

But neither Hyginus nor Apollodorus narrate the drama which is presented by the twenty-five identified and five conjectural fragments of Pacuvius' play.[31] Several fragments show that the play opened with the young men on their journey together 'in order to find their unknown parents' and already regretting that they had begun the quest. Someone – perhaps Atalanta herself – warns them to be off and control their dangerous confidence, and the next fragment explains this: someone – surely Atalanta – has overtaken even Parthenopaeus himself on the last bend of the racetrack (fr. VI D'Anna *extremum intra campterem ipsum praegradat / Parthenopaeum*). So it seems Parthenopaeus, probably also his companion Telephus, if we give weight to *ipsum*, has challenged Atalanta to the race. Here indeed is a *pathos* waiting to happen: if she wins he is doomed to be executed, if he wins, he is fated like Oedipus to marry his mother. And some editors have even amended the text to make sure he does win, reading 'Parthenopaeus overtakes even her' *ipsam praegradat / Parthenopaeus*, while Altheim himself surmised[32] that Atalanta only overtook him temporarily and he was able to recoup and finish as winner. You can see how this dramatic situation prompts pity, if not also horror, even in the audience response of textual critics! To continue with the action; other fragments make it clear that the boys begin to narrate the mystery of their births and she offers to help them determine which of them is her own child, mentioning a recognition token (*signum*) (frr. IX and X D'Anna) which she left with her baby. It must be the ring, which one of them now shows he is wearing on a chain around his left arm (fr. XI), but there is an intervening stage of suspense when it is not clear which of them is her child. Shortly after a fragment 'O my son, shame leads me to fear speaking out' (XIII) and another reference to the approach of her labour pains (XIV) show that Atalanta now tells the tale of her pregnancy and exposure of the baby.[33] But we have only resolved the perplexities of one hero, Atalanta's own son. It is far more difficult to see how the needs of young Telephus are to be met. Editors usually explain two further excerpts: 'what troubles you? What sadness mars your features?' and: 'for I will now explain what I was attempting to say when the disturbance arose ...' as a transition to Atalanta's narrative of the birth of Telephus. Certainly a very Pacuvian invocation of 'women who suffer enslavement, violence, poverty, slander, fear and shame' (XVII) seems to suggest that she turns to the victimisation of Auge by her male kinsmen, who 'threaten her with death, drive her from the kingdom and renounce her as their sister' (XXII). Other fragments relate to the family history of Auge and the current ruler of Tegea.

What is most problematic is that there can be no resolution of Telephus' search for his mother without either a whole new intrigue centred around the narrowly averted union of Telephus with his own mother, or at the very least, a major change of location to Moesia. My own suggestion, which is no more than speculation, is that Telephus could hear of his birth and parentage from Atalanta but receive only a partial knowledge of his mother's fate, since his own drama to come depended on continued ignorance of her identity. He would need to be sent to Moesia in quest of her, and this direction could be given by a *deus ex machina* at the play's end.

Now, as Altheim has argued step by step,[34] the details of this action, guaranteed in some sense by Hyginus' introduction to the *Auge*, can hardly have occurred in any version of the myth, or any Greek play. To translate Altheim's conclusion, the playwright 'could only generate an anagnorisis in the Atalanta story by fusing both versions of her myth, even though it robbed the race of its meaning. He did so because he considered the structure of the tragic action as a pure literary form, as more important than meeting the requirements[35] of the myth. Tragedy as *genos* had won its liberation from myth.'[36]

But a number of near absurdities result. If we eliminate the generation gap beween the youthful companions there is still the race episode. For why would a women old enough to have a grown son and long past virginity, have set up the fatal race to protect her from suitors? And why would the young man have wanted to marry her at the risk of his own death, and why would he not be able to outrun her? The story can only have been created by deliberately transferring to Parthenopaeus a variation of the recognition and reversal undergone by Telephus in the traditional Greek account, perhaps found in Sophocles' lost *Mysoi*. Pacuvius must have consciously manipulated his action to include the recognition between close kin that averts the catastrophe, with all the poignancy of Atalanta's own birth-narrative and probable narrative of the expulsion of Auge. In this confection we have then the suspense of an Oedipal union narrowly averted, a Merope-like mother at risk of killing her son after the model of *Cresphontes*, a Creusa-like tale of a lone girl in labour as in Euripides' *Ion* to provoke pity, and some advance sampling of the story of Telephus, one of the families which Aristotle cites in *Poetics* 13 as suitable context for tragedy.[37]

Let me take the next step, beyond Altheim's argument. The play we have just discussed is most unlikely to have been adapted from a comparable but unknown Greek play. But it is not the only 'new' plot offered by Pacuvius on the model of Aristotle's preferred type in *Poetics* 14. As far as we know no Roman tragedian before Pacuvius had adapted

Aristotle's favourite, the *Iphigenia in Tauris*. So Pacuvius could have made his own adaptation: but he chose not to. Instead he continued the Taurian adventure in a play called *Chryses*, whose plot is constructed around Orestes and Iphigenia, but introduces a third sibling ignorant of his kinship with the two of them.[38] This Chryses was the son of Chryseis, daughter of the Priest of Apollo, who had been taken as booty by Agamemnon before the narrative of *Iliad* 1 began. When she was reclaimed by her priest father she was returned, supposedly unharmed, by Agamemnon. Again we seem to have the plot of Pacuvius' tragedy under the heading *Chryses* in 'Hyginus'. This is how Hyginus ends CXX *Iphigenia Taurica*:

> The king obeyed the words of the priestess; Iphigenia seized the opportunity and having removed the statue embarked on shipboard with her brother Orestes and Pylades and came with a favourable wind to the island of Sminthe to Chryses, priest of Apollo.[39]

His next section, CXXI *Chryses*, starts from Agamemnon's surrender of Chryseis to her father at Troy. She was then pregnant, and although he declared he had not touched her, she duly gave birth to the younger Chryses and said she had conceived by Apollo.

> (3) Afterwards when Chryses wanted to surrender them (i.e. Orestes, Pylades and Iphigenia, from the previous story) to Thoas, the elder Chryses heard that Iphigenia and Orestes were the children of Agamemnon ... and <Chryseis> revealed the truth to her son, that they were brothers and Chryses was Agamemnon's son. Then after recognising the facts Chryses with his brother Orestes killed Thoas and they all reached Mycenae unharmed with the statue of Diana.[40]

This action could hardly be a more obvious sequel to the Taurian adventure; here too the Greek hero and his friend are saved by a recognition (note the Latin of Hyginus *re cognita*) but this time the threatening Thoas is not temporarily escaped but permanently killed. The fragments of Pacuvius' play include a narrative of the landing (or shipwreck?) by Orestes, a pursuit scene in which our heroes call on the servants to bring weapons to drive off Thoas, and may include some interesting groups of lines attributed to Pacuvius but not specifically to this action. There is an exchange between a speaker who is considering a portent, and his citizens or fellow citizens: this could be Chryses: there is what look like a choral meditation on the instability of fortune and the new helplessness of Orestes, reduced from royalty to beggary (these

117

lines do not seem to fit very well). The most significant element is a scene in which Orestes and Pylades compete to die for each other by claiming to be the real Orestes. This scene, much praised by Cicero in both his *Laelius: On Friendship* and *De Finibus*, is closely modelled on the scene of mutual self-sacrifice in Euripides' *Iphigenia among the Taurians*. But in that play Orestes was the one whom Iphigenia was prepared to save: this time, it is Orestes who is in danger, as son of Agamemnon the supposed enemy of Chryses' family. Both ask to be killed, until the third party announces that he has divined which of them is Orestes: *inveni, opino, Orestes uter esset tamen* (D'Anna XIII, XIV).

The chief uncertainty over this scene is the possibility that it is taken not from *Chryses* but from another of the three Orestes plays by Pacuvius, the mysterious *Doulorestes*, a play slightly resembling Sophocles' *Electra*, but a product of no known Greek model.[41] But Cicero's statement that the young men are disputing before an anxious and confused king[42] surely eliminates the possibility that they are disputing before the hostile Aegisthus: the king is Chryses, and he is disturbed precisely because of the ambivalence he feels before these young strangers, one of whom will be revealed in the peripeteia to be his very own half-brother.

Here then we have reconstructed from fragments and Hyginus' narrative a piece of Pacuvian dramaturgy echoing the merits of the *Iphigenia in Tauris*, with a timely recognition between kin (*philoi*) reversing the imminent threat that Chryses would surrender the three Greeks to their enemy Thoas. Instead they unite in vengeance on Thoas with the bonus that by the sheer discovery of his fatherhood Chryses has now gained both friendship and his Greek heritage. Yet we should not underestimate the emotional charge of his reaction when he is told by his mother that he is not a child of Apollo: we have a precedent for this kind of shock and loss of emotional identification with the god in the reactions of Euripides' Ion.

Identity will be the major theme of several other Pacuvian tragedies which conform in various degrees to the *Poetics'* preferred model of catastrophe averted, plays which probably faithfully reflected a Greek original. Pacuvius would be showing his principles, then, not in composing but in choosing pre-existing tragedies. Thus his *Antiope*, adapted from Euripides, is a rescue drama in which her twin sons avert catastrophe from the victimised Antiope, but there is no reason to assume they were ever about to harm her: indeed they probably were searching for their mother before the action of the play. In contrast, the plot of *Ilione* presupposes the unwitting (*imprudens*) killing of a kinsman – his own son Deipylus – by the villainous Polymestor, who believes he is killing Polydorus son of Priam to oblige the Greeks. Meanwhile the real

Polydorus, like Oedipus, has consulted the oracle of Apollo, and applies its oracular response to the wrong parents, Ilione, his actual sister and Polymestor. When Ilione tells him that he was switched with her own child Deipylus for fear that Polymestor would murder him, the discovery of his true identity, far from preventing the murder of a kinsman, resolves both Polydorus and Ilione to avenge the murder on the greedy Polymestor. The outcome is indeed the triumph of good kinsmen and aversion of misfortune through an anagnorisis, but there has been no risk of harm between them.

Only Pacuvius' *Medus* echoes the model of *Cresphontes* praised by Aristotle, and this play is worth a few minutes of special attention. The other Pacuvian tragedies we surveyed depend for their happy outcome on pure recognitions rather than a combination of recognition and intrigue – what Solmsen calls *mechanema*.[43] But the *Medus* is constructed on the basis of a double deception: both Medea and Medus, her longlost son by Aegeus, converge separately on the kingdom of Colchis. Colchis is in the hands of a tyrant, Perses, who has imprisoned the rightful king, Medea's father. Now Perses has been warned by an oracle to beware of death at the hands of Aeetes' children, and they presumably expect his hostility. Hence Medea claims to be a priestess of Artemis, while Medus pretends to be the son of Medea's old Corinthian enemy Creon. Hearing that her enemy's son is at court, Medea, unaware (*imprudens*) that this is her own son, tries to have him killed, and the family crime is only averted through her timely recognition of Medus as her child. Once reunited they act together to kill the usurper and release the king. The surviving fragments can be matched against the story as told by Hyginus under the title *Medus*.[44] Like the secondary murder plot of the *Ion*, the strong element of intrigue in this play probably rather diluted the possibility for genuine sympathy and the suspense of pity or horror, but it again matches the formula put forward in *Poetics* 14 and the peripeteia of the *Cresphontes* cited by Aristotle.

There is however one added detail worth a moment's thought. Aristotle does not discuss titles, but from chapter 6 on he sees tragedies as constructed around the *praxis* of persons who make a moral decision, a *prohairesis*. The titles of three of these Pacuvian tragedies, *Atalanta*, *Chryses* and *Ilione*, name not the adventurous figure who strays into a new world, but the character with the authority to make the crucial decision for good or ill. Only *Medus* seems to go against this pattern and its moral implications, if, as we may assume, the mother guided her son in their joint actions. But Pacuvius could hardly have called his play *Medea*! The titles suggest that these plays were constructed in an ethical spirit, to embody a decisive moral *praxis* by their protagonist.

So how plausible is it, that Pacuvius knew or knew of Aristotle's recommendations in the *Poetics* and designed his plays to satisfy them?

At the colloquium Daniel Javitch courteously suggested a highly plausible alternative: that Aristotle is, alas, marginal to the whole narrative; that he was himself influenced by a successful theatrical plot type, and so, two hundred years later, was Pacuvius. I have only one counter-argument. If the plot type was such a continuing success, why did Pacuvius' uncle Ennius not use it in any of his twenty-two tragedies as far as we can tell?

And why did Pacuvius innovate in this way? It would be over-speculative to argue he had actual access to the text of *Poetics*, and there are no pointers to suggest that dramaturgy was an interest in later Peripatetic theory. We may have to admit coincidence rather than influence.

Why, in contrast, is Horace's treatment of tragedy in *Ars Poetica* so disappointing? Clearly he is not interested in *plot*. He approaches tragedy only indirectly via diction and metre, marking the iambus as common to tragedy and comedy, though he does praise it as 'made for action' *natum rebus agendis* (80). He devotes most of the poem to *lexis* and to *ethos*, urging consistency with traditional characterisation – and internally. Only thirty lines deal with dramaturgy, focussing in fact on what Aristotle passes over; what should be kept offstage (the horrible and incredible), the number and separation of acts, the number of speakers and restriction of divine intervention to resolving crises beyond human control. The nearest he comes to considering types of dramatic reversal is when the chorus is commended for praying to the gods 'for a change of fortune for both the humble and the arrogant'. Neither pity nor fear, as emotional implications of conflict between kinsmen, nor ignorance and revelation, fallibility and recognition, get a line.

You may have wondered, when I launched on this discussion of Roman tragedy in the light of the *Poetics*, whether I was intending to say something about Seneca's tragedies, and if so, what I could possibly find to link Senecan practice with Aristotle's ideal tragic action.

It is now generally accepted that Seneca did not adapt, closely or loosely, existing Greek tragedies, but was his own dramaturge, choosing what to include in his plot and how to order it. It is well known that his *Medea* and *Thyestes*, if staged, would violate Horace's few principles of dramaturgy, with scenes of on-stage killing. But it is equally clear that Senecan tragedy almost deliberately inverted the Aristotelian criteria or ethical code for dramatic composition that we have been considering. Only three of his plays have a recognition scene, and in two cases that recognition is not of personal identity. In the *Hercules Furens* the maddened hero comes round to recognise that he has killed his wife and children, or if you prefer, he recognises who it is that he killed when he thought that he was killing the Tyrant Lycus and his family. And if we consider whether the outcome of the play is a single *peripeteia* from

120

prosperity to downfall, we have to offset the obvious disasters by the dubious moral victory of his final decision to go on living and bear his own sorrows.

Several other plays offset the downfall of the innocent as in *Trojan Women* or *Agamemnon* or *Phaedra* by affirmations of this kind of dubious moral victory, or a future reversal of fortune beyond the action. In *Trojan Women* we are closer to the spirit of Euripides' related tragedies than in any other Senecan play, but because the victims are not autonomous males, nor free agents capable of moral action, nothing seems to redeem their bad fortune. Seneca can offer only the vindication that the sacrificed children die nobly, their spirit unbroken, and Hecuba herself threatens to bring doom on her enemies even as their captive. Cassandra too triumphs by forecasting the doom of Clytemnestra and Aegisthus at the end of *Agamemnon*, and Phaedra after causing Hippolytus' death achieves a moral victory in confessing her guilt and punishing herself by suicide.

But let us keep to the plays with an element of recognition. Thyestes' recognition of having eaten his own sons brings no turn for the better and no hope at any level, even metaphysical. The outcome is as bleak and contrary to divine justice as the end of the *Medea*. The most interesting tragedy to consider is of course *Oedipus*, which covers the same complex of actions as the Sophoclean masterpiece. But whereas Sophocles' hero is driven by his love of the city and passion for knowledge to extort the record of his infancy that exposes his own unwitting crimes, Seneca's Oedipus acts almost from the beginning under a conviction that he is somehow to blame – the protracted recognition rises to explode in his unredeeming self-imposed blindness and isolation from humanity. It might not be unfair to call these plays anti-tragedies; whatever traces we may find of Aristotle's poetic principles in Roman drama, there are none here. What I have tried to argue is that Rome, regrettably, was closest to Aristotle's poetics, whether with a large or small p, at the beginning of her literature.

Notes

1. Diogenes cites the Life of Aristotle by the Peripatetic Hermippus (together with a number of other sources for particular details). In his list of Aristotle's works (5.22-4) the literary works (ch. 24) include *Synagoge tekhnon* (2 books), *Rhetoric* (2 books: NB not 3), then a work called *Tekhne* (?), a second *Synagoge* (2 books), then the *Poetics* (*Pragmateia Tekhnes Poietikes*) (2 books); after that an abridgment of Theodectes' *Rhetoric*, and two books *On Style* (*Peri Lexeos*) which probably constitute what we call the third book of the *Rhetoric*.

2. *Epochen der Römischen Geschichte* II (Frankfurt, 1935), 283-98.

3. 'Aristotle and Cicero on the orator's playing upon the feelings', *CP* 33 (1938), 390-404 and 'Aristotelian tradition in ancient rhetoric', *AJP* 62 (1941),

35-50; 169-90 reprinted in *Kleine Schriften* II, 178-216; 216-30: the latter can also be found in *Rhetorika*, ed. Stark/Steinmetz (Hildesheim, 1968), 312-50, and *Aristotle: The Classical Heritage of Rhetoric*, ed. Erickson (1974), 278-310.

4. *De Oratore* 2.160 praises Aristotle *cuius et illum legi librum, in quo exposuit dicendi artes omnium superiorum* (the *Synagoge Tekhnon*), *et illos, in quibus ipse sua quaedam de eadem arte dixit* (the *Rhetoric*). See n. 1 above for Diogenes' record of both works.

5. *Fam.* 1.9.23.

6. See Jonathan Barnes, 'Roman Aristotle' in *Philosophia Togata II: Plato and Aristotle at Rome*, ed. Jonathan Barnes and Miriam Griffin (Oxford, 1997), 1-70 here p. 16f., noting Cicero's report *Ad Att.* 4.10.1 of browsing on Faustus' library.

7. At Cic. *Orator* 114. The *Rhetoric* was also known and quoted a decade or so later by the Greek critic Dionysius of Halicarnassus in his *Letter to Ammaeus*.

8. Ed. W.W. Fortenbaugh and P. Steinmetz: Rutgers University Studies in Classical Humanities, 4 (New Brunswick, NJ, 1989).

9. In fact Barnes rightly pays far more attention (see p. 18 n. 84) to Paul Moraux's detailed and painstaking reconstruction in *Der Aristotelismus bei den Griechen* I (Berlin/NY, 1973), 16-50 which allows for the existence of other versions of the *Esoterica* before the arrival of Sulla's library and the undatable edition of Andronicus. But unlike Barnes, Moraux believes (pp. 43-4) that Cicero did not use this opportunity to read the texts himself but relied on compendia, doxographies and handbooks.

10. Barnes loc. cit., 52 adducing *De Orat.* 3.182 where Crassus cites as Aristotle's views on prose rhythm material which is discussed in Ar. *Rhet.* 3.

11. Op. cit., 40; the further discussion of Aristotle's *Esoterica* is at *Fin.* 5.12.

12. Scholars infer from Diogenes Laertius 5.24 (above n. 1) that the three books of the Rhetoric represent Diogenes' two books on Rhetoric plus the two books 'On Style'.

13. Barnes, 53-4.

14. I do not see it as an obstacle that Cicero's student manual from the 80s, the *De Inventione*, reflects a much more pedestrian form of teaching organised by the successive parts of the speech.

15. 'Philemon's Thesaurus as a dramatization of Peripatetic ethics', *Philologus* 105 (1977).

16. This is the simplest but not the most accurate way of translating *De Grammaticis*. *Grammatici* were as often serious literary editors and interpreters (Greek *kritikoi*) as teachers of language.

17. According to Suetonius *Gramm.* 2 (on which see Kaster's full commentary, pp. 58-61), Crates gave a great many *akroaseis* (lectures or recitals). Crates' visit can be dated by the death of Ennius in 169. On Crates' theories see R. Janko, 'Crates of Mallos, Dionysius Thrax amd the tradition of Stoic grammatical theory', 213-33 in *The Passionate Intellect*, ed. Lewis Ayres (New Brunswick, NJ, 1995), also J.I. Porter in *Homer's Ancient Readers*, ed. J.J. Keaney and R.D. Lamberton (Princeton, 1992), 89-114. See also Janko's article 'Reception of Aristotle in antiquity', 104-7 in *Encyclopaedia of Aesthetics* I (NY/Oxford, 1998). I am most grateful to Richard Janko for the suggestion and bibliographical references.

18. On this see Porter, loc. cit., 111. 'Crates' inheritance was pluralistic and

culled from every imaginable discipline ... his critical activities extended to Hesiod, the tragedians, Aristophanes and Aratus.'

19. What is known of Critolaus suggests that he was hostile to rhetoric, and was more interested in Aristotle's scientific heritage.

20. See Poland s.v. *Tekhnitae* (*RE* 5A 2473-558). He lists (2475) *IG* XIV 12 and 13 for Syracuse, and 615 for Rhegium, but it is impossible to believe there was not also an association in the wealthy theatre-loving Tarentum. Poland's article is my source for the occasions in Livy 39.22 from 186 BC, and Polybius 30.14.2 (found in Athenaeus XIV 615b) from 167 BC, when Roman commanders overseas hired the *Tekhnitae* to put on *Ludi*.

21. Taplin, *Comic Angels* (Oxford, 1993): see esp. 20-8, and vases illustrating the legends of Oedipus, Iphigenia Taurica and Telephus cited below.

22. S. Halliwell, *Aristotle's Poetics* (London and Chapel Hill, 1986), and *The Poetics of Aristotle* (London and Chapel Hill, 1987); E. Belfiore, *Tragic Pleasure: Aristotle on Plot and Emotions* (Princeton, 1992).

23. This is the Loeb Classical Text translation of Halliwell 1995, which differs slightly from that accompanying his commentary of 1986.

24. See Stephen White, 'Aristotle's favorite tragedies', 221-40, and Elizabeth Belfiore, 'Aristotle and Iphigenia' 358-78 in *Essays in Aristotle's Poetics*, ed. A.O. Rorty (Princeton, 1992). Taplin, *Comic Angels*, 23-4 notes the great quantity of vase paintings found in Magna Graecia that show the crucial letter scene from this play.

25. F. Altheim, *Epochen der Römischen Geschichte* II (Frankfurt, 1935), 283-98. The first detailed systematic treatment of Roman tragedy is O. Ribbeck, *Die Römische Tragödie* (Stuttgart, 1875): Ribbeck also edited the fragments *Poetarum Romanorum Fragmenta*, vols I and II (Leipzig, 1871) with further editions. The best literary historical study from the twentieth century is still F. Leo, *Geschichte der Römischen Literatur* (Berlin 1912).

26. *Remains of Old Latin*, vol. 3, ed. E.H. Warmington (Cambridge, MA, 1936), H.J. Mette, *Lustrum* 9 (1964), Pacuvius pp. 78-107; *M. Pacuvii Fragmenta*, ed. Giovanni d'Anna (Rome, 1967). The monographs are M. Valsa, *M. Pacuvius: Poète Tragique* (Paris, 1957 and I. Mariotti, *Introduzione a Pacuvio* (Urbino, 1960).

27. On the nature of this peculiar text see *Hygini Fabulae* ed. H.J. Rose (Leiden, 1935), iii-xv. Behind the clumsy Latin of the redactor is a genuine learned text which in at least one case – *Ilione* – is agreed by Welcker and Ribbeck to reproduce the synopsis of a Pacuvian tragedy.

28. Hyginus tells the story of Atalanta daughter of Schoeneus and her race against Hippomenes in CLXXXV.

29. Cf. Hyginus LXX, describing Parthenopaeus in the list of the seven leaders against Thebes as an Arcadian son of Meleager by Atalanta, daughter of Iasius (*sic*) from Mt. Parthenius. CLXXIII and CLXXIV, on the Boeotian huntress and the tale of the Calydonian boar, do not mention any children by Meleager.

30. Auge Alei filia ab Hercule compressa cum partus adesset, in monte Parthenio peperit et ibi eum exposuit. eodem tempore Atalante Iasii filia filium exposuit ex Meleagro natum. Herculis autem filium cerva nutriebat. hos pastores inventos sustulerunt atque nutrierunt, quibus nomina imposuerunt Herculis filio Telephum, quoniam cerva nutrierat, Atlantes autem Parthenopaeum, quoniam ... in monte Parthenio eum exposuerat. Ipsa autem Auge patrem suum timens profugit in Moesiam ad regem Teuthrantem, qui cum esse orbus liberis hanc pro filia habuit.

31. Our sources for Pacuvian excerpts ascribe about three-quarters of their quotations by name to a specific play; the rest are asscribed simply to Pacuvius.

32. Op. cit., 291.

33. Altheim oddly argues that Atalanta's birth narrative preceded the recognition by tokens (p. 294), and only the distinction between the two young men is resolved by the *signum* of the ring. This would make, he notes, the recognition a case of Aristotle's fifth, preferred type *ex auton ton pragmaton ... di' eikoton*. If so although the composer of this tragic action imitated the model of the Telephus saga, he will have changed the anagnorisis.

34. *Epochen der Römischen Geschichte* II 283-98.

35. Altheim's word is Erfüllung.

36. Altheim, op. cit., 296.

37. 1453a18-22: 'nowadays the finest tragedies are composed about only a few families – such as Alcmaeon, Oedipus, Orestes, Meleager, Thyestes, Telephus and as many others as have suffered or perpetrated terrible things.' Taplin, *Comic Angels*, notes (37 and n. 21) the frequency of vase paintings from Magna Graecia depicting the altar scene from the Euripidean *Telephus* (as also of its Aristophanic parody). It may be a coincidence that, as Taplin notes, p. 29, the most unambiguous vase painting from tragedy, by the *Capodarso* painter, illustrates the moment of Jocasta's realisation at *Oedipus* 1042f. singled out by Aristotle *Poetics* 1452a24.

38. Scholars since Wilamowitz have believed that Sophocles' tragedy *Chryses* concerned a quite different adventure of the same hero. Wilamowitz argued (*Hermes* 18, p. 257) that the plot of Pacuvius' *Chryses* must depend on that of Euripides' *Iphigenia among the Taurians* which was written after Sophocles' *Chryses* (dated by Wilamowitz to 414 BC). Cf. A. Lesky, *Greek Tragic Poetry*, tr. M. Dillon (New Haven, 1983), 300.

39. Rex sacerdoti dicto audiens fuit; occasionem Iphigenia nacta, signo sublato cum fratre Oreste et Pylade in navem ascendit ventoque secundo ad insulam Zminthen ad Chrysem sacerdotem Apollinis delati sunt.

40. postea Chryses Thoanti eos cum reddere vellet, Chryses audiit senior Agamemnonis Iphigeniam et Orestem filios esse; qui Chrysi filio suo quid veri esset patefecit, eos fratres esse et Chrysen Agamemnonis filium esse. tum Chryses re cognita cum Oreste fratre Thoantem interfecit et inde Mycenas cum signo Dianae incolumes pervenerunt.

The text must be damaged; although either the elder Chryses or Chryseis could have told Chryses of his birth, *filio suo* means the informer must be Chryseis. Rose surmises that old Chryses heard the news and spoke to his daughter; she then revealed his true and mortal parentage to her son.

41. In Warmington's edition the lines discussed above are frr 163-6 tentatively assigned to *Doulorestes*.

42. Cic. *Fin.* 5.63: cum autem etiam exitus ab utroque datur conturbato errantique regi.

43. Compare F. Solmsen, 'Zur Gestaltung des Intrigenmotivs in den Tragödien des Sophokles und Euripides', *Philol.* 87 (1932) and 'Euripides *Ion* im Vergleich mit anderen Tragödien', *Hermes* 69 (1934), repr. in *Kleine Schriften*, vol. 1, 142-57 and 158-87.

44. 'Perses, son of the Sun, had been warned by an oracle to fear death at the

hands of Aeetes' offspring: then Medus in quest of his mother was carried there by a storm: royal attendants seized him and brought him to the king. When Medus, son of Aegeus and Medea, saw that he was in enemy hands, he lied that he was Hippotes, son of Creon. The king investigated more thoroughly and had him thrown into prison. When Medea arrived in her chariot yoked with serpents, she lied to the king that she was a priestess of Diana and could expiate the drought. Then when she heard from the king that he had Hippotes, son of Creon, in prison, she thought he had come to avenge his father.

'Then she unwittingly betrayed her son; for she persuaded the king that this was not Hippotes, but Medus "son of Medea" sent by his mother to kill the king, and she begged him to hand the man over to her to be killed, convinced that he was in fact Hippotes. So when Medus was brought out to pay for his lie with death, and she saw it was not as she thought, she said she wanted to talk with him, and gave him a sword, telling him to avenge his wrongs. Once he understood, Medus killed Perses and took his grandfather's kingdom, and they called it Media after his name.'

On the Rise of Genre-specific
Poetics in the Sixteenth Century

Daniel Javitch

Late fifteenth-century Italian humanists no longer had to depend on
medieval refractions of Aristotle's *Poetics* (e.g. Hermann the German's
thirteenth-century translation of Averroes' 'Middle Commentary') once
they acquired some Greek and could consult manuscript versions of the
original text. Yet despite the availability of the Greek text from the
1470s, and, eventually, of Giorgio Valla's (less than reliable and incomplete) Latin translation of it in 1498, the evidence suggests that, at the
start of the sixteenth century, Aristotle's theory had little relevance and
value for its readers. It is telling that Giorgio Valla's own treatise on
poetry, his *De Poetica* (largely devoted to metrics) was much more
indebted to Diomedes' *Ars Grammatica* than to Aristotle, cited by Valla
only occasionally and mostly for his views on the origins of drama.[1]
Even after Aldus published the Greek text in 1508 (as part of an
anthology entitled *Rhetores Graeci!*), it had little impact. To be sure the
Poetics was not dismissed or totally disregarded in Italy, as it was in
other parts of Europe, but interest in the treatise only begins to grow
once the Italians become more familiar with ancient Greek tragedy. It
is hardly accidental that Alessandro Pazzi de' Medici, the first writer to
provide a relatively reliable Latin translation of the *Poetics* (composed
in 1524 but not published until 1536) was also responsible for the first
Latin and then vernacular translations of Sophocles and Euripides.

Pazzi's translation served to make Aristotle's text more accessible
but only somewhat more intelligible. In the dedication to his first
tragedy *Orbecche* (1541) G.B. Giraldi Cinzio indicates how obscure and
perplexing the text remained to contemporary readers. It was at this
very moment, at the beginning of the 1540s, that the first sustained
exegeses of the *Poetics* began. Bartolomeo Lombardi's lectures on the
Poetics at Padua in 1541, continued by Vicenzio Maggi (who also
lectured on the text at Ferrara in 1543), inaugurate a series of explica-
tions and retranslations by professors connected to the school of
Aristotelian philosophy at Padua. With the appearance of Francesco
Robortello's *Explicationes* (1548), the first of the commentaries to be
published, a real upsurge of interest in the *Poetics* begins to manifest

itself. Robortello's commentary was followed by Segni's first Italian translation of the treatise in 1549, and then a series of rival commentaries which mark as well as contribute to the full assimilation of Aristotle's theory in the latter half of the Cinquecento. The entry of the *Poetics* into the mainstream of poetic criticism can be noted, too, by the way Aristotle's art of poetry is correlated, from the mid 1540s on, with Horace's in commentary on the *Ars Poetica*, and by unprecedented references to Aristotle's authority in mid-century literary disputes, some of which I will be describing shortly. But even though Aristotle's treatise quickly acquires an authority equal to Horace's *after* the mid-century, one has to keep in mind that it was not until the 1540s that the treatise began to be more widely read, understood and invoked by the Italian intelligentsia.

In the course of the 1540s one also notices the emergence of a body of discourse about poetry that is much more genre-specific than discussions about the art of poetry or about poetic composition had been beforehand. On this occasion, I cannot dwell on these prior considerations but simply point out that they didn't concern themselves with genres or individuate them. If one looks at early sixteenth century Italian poetics in the Horatian vein, Vida's *De Arte Poetica* (1527), for example, one is struck by how general its precepts of composition are. For a young man being initiated to poetic art, Vida proposes to follow Virgil as a model regardless of the kind of poetry he undertakes. And, indeed,when he cites exemplary aspects of Virgil's practice he doesn't do so to prescribe norms for epic poetry specifically, but for all kinds. One is seldom if ever made aware in Vida's treatise that the poetic genres observe different structural or thematic principles shaped by their particular identities.

I am not proposing that before the 1540s educated readers were unaware of the differences between traditional genres such as epic, tragedy, comedy or different lyrical forms. Obviously they were able to recognise the basic differences between them, but apart from Aristotle's *Poetics* – which, as I have just pointed out, did not enter the mainstream of criticism and theory before the 1540s – one cannot find extended discussions of the respective genres and of their differences in the poetics that were dominant in the first decades of the Cinquecento. Consider, for a moment, Horace's *Ars Poetica*, which continued to dominate thinking about poetry even beyond the middle of the sixteenth century. True, a section of the *Ars* is devoted to drama, most of it about satyr drama, but besides a number of genre-specific interdictions, it does not offer any definition of comedy or tragedy or any guidelines on how to compose them. When it is not discussing the origins of poetry or the qualifications of a good poet, it consists of formal or organisational precepts applicable to all poems. The *Ars Poetica* had such lasting value for would-be poets precisely because its brief, memorable *dicta* about unity, order, consistency, and decorum transcended particular kinds of poems and poetic practice. One can find in the *Ars Poetica* an implicit awareness that certain guidelines may have to be differentiated for respective genres, and that what applies for one kind of poetry may not be appropriate for another. But this awareness remains largely implicit; it is not articulated to any extent. What happens in Italy in the 1540s is that such awareness does become increasingly articulated. There begins to appear in this decade critical discourse that seeks to formulate extensive definitions of individual genres, but that seeks also to differentiate quite explicitly the genre being defined from one or more other genres with which it may share features. Much of this initial discourse is concerned, for reasons I will take up shortly, with defining tragedy. And some of the first sustained efforts to differentiate genres are devoted to distinctions between tragedy and comedy.

In fact, one of the pioneering efforts to codify genres is G.B. Giraldi's *Discorso over lettera ... intorno al comporre delle comedie e delle tragedie* which, though first published in 1554, seems to have been composed in large part as early as 1543. Giraldi's *Discorso* provides the best example of the new effort to formulate ampler definitions of their genres and of their differences. With more space I would examine in some detail the sort of differentiation between comedy and tragedy that Giraldi provided. Let me simply say that he really expands upon the differences between the two genres indicated in Horace and simply itemised by the ancient grammarians: the different subject matters, plot outcomes, the different social status of the protagonists, and the ensuing differences in speech and style.[2] Giraldi's account of these distinctive features not only significantly expands and elaborates what had been summed up beforehand. In some cases he modifies traditional claims quite drastically. For example, Giraldi challenges the Donatian commonplaces that tragedy must end woefully, or that tragic plots have to be based on historical matter. As original as are these departures from prevailing *topoi* about the two genres, more innovative is Giraldi's elaboration of distinctions that his contemporaries may have been aware of, but had not seen so fully articulated. For example he takes the traditional assertion that tragedy concerns the highest born individuals while comedy deals with ordinary citizens and he elaborates on what these differences will and won't allow in terms of language, verbal intercourse, characterisation, and general comportment. He devotes quite extensive and, to my knowledge, unprecedented discussion to the different behavourial decorum that obtains in each genre. For example, toward the end of his treatise, Giraldi goes on for several paragraphs as to why unwed maidens cannot have speaking parts in comedy, but why, on the other hand, it is permissible for high-born virgins to speak in tragedy. Then he points out that it is improper for serious ladies ['donne gravi'] in comedy to engage in love affairs, but that the same does not hold for tragedy in which serious married women are shown to succumb to the power of love, and as a result create some of the woes and disasters that characterise the genre.[9] Such preoccupation with generic decorum is related to Horatian theoretical strains, although, as I suggested earlier, one would be hard put to derive anything like Giraldi's extensive directives about what is appropriate in comic and tragic characterisation from Horace's few and very brief interdictions in the *Ars Poetica*.

I deliberately start off by pointing to innovative aspects of Giraldi's *Discorso* that are *not* of Aristotelian origin, but it is usually the Aristotelian characteristics of his treatise that are identified by modern commentators, myself included.[4] Giraldi defines comedy as well as tragedy in his *Discorso*, which is more than we find in the *Poetics* (at least in the text as we have it), but when he starts off by showing that comedy and tragedy have in common means and modes of mimesis, even though their objects of imitation differ, it is clear that he is inspired by chapters 2 and 3 of Aristotle's treatise where kinds of mimesis are distinguished on the basis of means, objects and modes. The methodology he uses to define both tragedy and comedy, namely considering first their qualitative and then their quantitative parts, obviously imitates Aristotle's procedure and terminology. By privileging plot and devoting most of the discussion to it, he again imitates Aristotle, and some of the guidelines – for instance, his recommendation to resolve plots without having recourse to divine interventions – are derived directly from the *Poetics*. More often he will begin by reiterating one of Aristotle's directives (see my brief discussion, later in this paper, of his call for tragic protagonists neither totally good nor totally wicked), but then he makes a significant modification consistent with some of his broad departures from Aristotle. Still, his debt to the *Poetics* is undeniable, and he depends throughout his treatise on Aristotle's authority, however singular his interpretations of the Greek master may sometimes be.

Giraldi is not the only writer to produce the genre-specific discussion of poetry that emerges in the 1540s. Discussions of what constitutes proper tragedy can be found in the anonymous and polemical *Giudizio* against Speroni's *Canace*, a treatise composed in 1542 that I will soon return to, and at the end of the decade Giovan Giorgio Trissino provides extensive definitions of tragedy, epic, and comedy in 'La Quinta e Sesta Divisione' of his *Poetica*. As one examines these treatises one is further struck by the debt these authors have to Aristotle's *Poetics*. In the case of Trissino's 'Quinta Divisione', which is devoted to tragedy, the text often consists of a translation of chapters 6 to 20 of Aristotle's *Poetics*.[5]

It is in these very treatises, beginning with Giraldi's *Discorso*, that one actually discerns the first appropriations of Aristotle's theory in sixteenth-century poetics.[6]

What does this mean? That the new genre-specific discourse emerging in the 1540s is all due to the dissemination and impact of Aristotle's *Poetics*? So Bernard Weinberg wanted us to believe in his *History of Literary Criticism in the Italian Renaissance* (1961), and his claims have been widely accepted. Actually, Weinberg did not really acknowledge the newness of the genre-specific poetics emerging just before the mid-century. Intent as he was on revealing how indebted they were to Aristotle's *Poetics*, he gave his readers the impression that these poetics were simply the continuation of a tradition established by Aristotle rather than the innovative development they represent. Even though Weinberg's view has been the most influential, he was not the first to promulgate the argument that genre theory in the sixteenth century stemmed directly from the impact of Aristotle's *Poetics* in the 1540s. Already Joel Spingarn's pioneering *Literary Criticism in the Renaissance* (1899) had proposed that it was due to the translation and unprecedented exegesis of the *Poetics* that poetic genre theory was revived in early modern Europe. One cannot deny – and I have already given evidence of it – that early genre theorists such as Giraldi were quick to appropriate the newly recovered *Poetics*. Nor can one doubt that the Greek treatise had a discernible, and, in some cases, even a decisive impact on Italian thinking on genre in the mid-century. What can and must be called into question is that the Greek treatise was the direct cause of the new theorising. Elsewhere I have maintained that it was because of certain literary and cultural needs that genre-specific approaches to poetic art developed in Italy in the 1540s, and these needs can serve to explain the new importance granted Aristotle's theory, and, consequently or conjointly, its impact.[7] However, I did not demonstrate sufficiently what specific needs or what factors external to the *Poetics*, as such, brought about this new discourse on the genres. What follows is an attempt to make to make up for this omission.

It seems evident to me that a desire to define tragedy, and to understand its rules of composition, plays a foundational role in the development of genre-specific poetics. It is very significant that tragedy is the first genre to be given extensive theoretical attention and that Italian efforts to codify tragedy in the 1540s precede the codification of other genres. Someone might immediately counter that it had to be Aristotle's primary concern with tragedy, and his privileging of the genre, that prompted Italians to understand tragedy better and to reconstitute the genre in the vernacular. This, again, remains a widely held view, but the trouble with it is that it puts the cart before the horse. Italians did feel a need to reconstitute tragedy in their own language, but that Aristotle directly provoked this need is dubious. It is quite likely that the Greek philosopher's particular esteem for and extensive treatment of Greek tragedy was one of several reasons why the genre acquired a higher status in the eyes of Renaissance humanists. The admiration for and citation of Greek tragedies by other Greek and Latin authors also made learned Renaissance readers aware of the importance of the genre in ancient culture. Furthermore Italians could admire the imposing remains of the magnificent theatres and amphitheatres that had been erected in most ancient cities, architectural evidence of the important role that the performance of tragedy and comedy had in both Greek and Roman culture.[8] Still, it was primarily the rediscovery of the texts of ancient Greek tragedy from the late Quattrocento onwards, and the gradual and ensuing appreciation of the significance of Sophocles' and Euripides' achievement, and to some extent of Aeschylus', that gave tragedy a prestige it had not enjoyed for nearly a thousand years.

Why sixteenth-century Italian writers deemed it necessary to produce modern tragedies is connected, too, to the esteem which the genre had enjoyed in ancient Greek and Roman poetic and rhetorical theory (e.g. Quintilian's *Institutio Oratoria* X.i.67-9, and 97-9). Many sixteenth-century literati may have still considered epic the supreme genre, but they were gradually acknowledging that no type of poetry approached tragedy in *gravity*, and that it was necessary to restore this most serious of genres, disregarded for so long, if vernacular literature was to achieve the dignity of ancient poetry.[9] The writing of vernacular tragedy was seen, too, as a means to achieve in Italian the stylistic power of Greek and Latin.

Yet, despite the desire to recreate it in Italian, tragedy, especially in its ancient Greek form, remained an arcane, rather mysterious kind of poetry. One has to take seriously Giraldi's claim, in the dedication to his first tragedy *Orbecche* (1541), that the writing of tragedy had been neglected for so many centuries that the art of composing it had been forgotten. Part of the difficulty of reconstituting it 'all'antica' was that there was no master text nor a master author that could serve as an indisputable model. Authors of comedy had Terence's practice to turn to as a paradigm, but tragedy had no equivalent. Seneca's tragedies, though known in the Middle Ages (Seneca inspired Albertino Mussato's *Ecerinis* of 1314, the earliest post-classical attempt to write tragedy), available in various editions after the advent of printing, and some even published in translation by the end of the fifteenth century, did not spur imitations by the start of the sixteenth century. Despite a few efforts to stage one or two of them in the late fifteenth century, the tragedies never came to enjoy a place in the repertory of court performances the way Plautus' and Terence's comedies had by the turn of the century.

Nor, when Italians started to compose tragedies 'all'antica' in the first decades of the Cinquecento, did Seneca's practice become exemplary. These writers turned, rather, to the Greek corpus for inspiration, and to Sophocles and Euripides in particular. But despite the appeal and influence of some the Greek plays (e.g. Sophocles' *Antigone*, Euripides' *Hecuba*), no single work of either Greek playwright became the pre-eminent model. Sophocles' *Oedipus Tyrannus* gradually gained such paradigmatic status in the 1560s, but until then, despite an awareness of Aristotle's admiration for it, Sophocles' play was not the unchallenged master text.[10]

Given this situation, Aristotle's *Poetics*, difficult a text as it was, became the guide for anyone who wanted to understand more about the nature of ancient tragedy and sought to comprehend its principles of composition. Yet useful and inspiring a text as Aristotle's treatise may have been for poets and *literati* who wanted to define tragedy for their time, the impulse to formulate such definitions was almost always generated by dramatic practice, not by some sheer desire to produce some modern equivalent or translation of Aristotle's *Poetics*. I maintain that it is the production of modern instances of tragedy, and, in particular the criticism these new texts encounter that stimulates debate and theorising on the genre, and that theorising is then carried over to other genres.

To be more precise, disputes are provoked by the dramatic experimentation of the early 1540s, specifically by the tragedies composed by G.B. Giraldi and Sperone Speroni. I am thinking of the criticism and defence provoked by Giraldi's *Didone*, his second tragedy, and especially by Speroni's *Canace*. These were not, to be sure, the first efforts to write formal tragedies in Italian. Trissino had pioneered the genre as early as 1514-15 with his *Sofonisba*, and some more tragedies in the Grecian mode (i.e. modelled primarily on Sophocles' and Euripides' practice) were composed by Florentine writers in the next two decades: Rucellai's *Rosmunda* (1515); Pazzi's *Didone in Cartagine* (1524), Alamanni's *Antigone* (1533); and Martelli's *Tullia* (1533). One has the sense that these Florentine tragedies 'alla greca', especially Pazzi's, were more of a philological than a dramatic experiment. There is no evidence that any of them were staged, although some were presumably recited. On the other hand, Giraldi and Speroni clearly wanted to produce tragedies that could be performed. In fact, Giraldi's first tragedy, *Orbecche* (1541), was the first Italian tragedy to be staged, and with success. To make their plays work as dramatic productions they moved away from the Greek form. They resorted to five-act structure; they reduced, though they did not eliminate the role of the chorus. As far as plot material, they sought more affective, even sensational subject matter to secure the attention of their auditors. It was, to some extent, because both playwrights consciously departed from the prior attempts to imitate Greek models that their plays provoked hostile reactions. Consider the dispute provoked by Giraldi's *Didone*, a drama he composed soon after the success of his first tragedy, *Orbecche*, in 1541. The criticism of the *Didone* never appeared in print. The objections raised by an unnamed individual who attended the recitation of the play at the Ferrarese court were reported to Giraldi. He sums up the objections in a lengthy letter he wrote to his patron Ercole II in 1543, before he proceeds to refute them.[11] Giraldi reports in this letter that he stands accused of violating norms established by Horace, but also, and more interestingly, by Greek tragedians 'from whom', his critic maintains, 'should be taken the laws and true rules for composing such plots well, as Aristotle did'.[12]

For instance, the critic objects that tragic plots should not be divided, as the *Didone* was, into acts and scenes. Giraldi acknowledges that the Greeks had no such divisions and always had the chorus on stage when other actors left it. But Giraldi wanted to reduce the role of the chorus, and preferred following the Roman practice of emptying the stage between acts as opposed to having the chorus standing there. One reason for resorting to act division with discrete scenes, he explains in his rebuttal, was to be able to depict his royal protagonists addressing important affairs of state in more private, confidential situations than the ones regularly represented in Greek tragedy where the protagonists are always shown speaking and conducting their affairs in public, in the eyes of the community (often represented by the chorus). 'It is not at all verisimilar,' writes Giraldi, 'that great persons who rule want to conduct their very important affairs, such as those that arise in tragedies, in the presence of a multitude of people, however familiar. When engaged in such affairs … they only have secretaries, or counsellors attending them, or wise persons whom they trust.'[13] Giraldi implies that a realistic depiction of the action of tragedy's high-born protagonists, moving as they do from public to more private spaces, requires a shift of scenes not made available by Greek dramatic practice. He repeatedly justifies features of his play criticised by his anonymous critic on the grounds that they make possible a more verisimilar representation of the 'royals' or high-born characters appropriate to tragedy.[14] His whole effort is dedicated to convey a 'signorile imagine di discorso e di pensamento' which is appropriate to tragedy, and which distinguishes it from the popular and demotic discourse (and manners) of comedy. He believes that what one might call this 'aristocratisation of discourse' can make modern tragedy believable and more stageworthy. In his view, one of the major shortcomings of ancient Greek tragedy is its failure to depict the 'majesty' of royal comportment, a fault already detected and corrected to some extent by Roman poets: 'If the Greeks were not aware of this decorum, the Romans were, and knew how to provide for the majesty of royal actions, persons that conducted them in a manner appropriate to such majesty' ('E se i Greci non conoberro questo decoro, lo conobbero i Romani e seppero dare alla maestà delle azioni reali, le persone, che in quel modo le maneggiassero, che si conveniva a tanta maestà', I.477). His conservative critic, determined to set ancient Greek tragedy as the norm, fails to realise that the imitation of such models will result in an unbelievable depiction of the intercourse and behaviour of the ruling class that make up tragedy's *dramatis personae*. Giraldi, on the other hand, seeks to devise a tragic language and a comportment on the part of his protagonists which, to be credible, more closely reflects the language and comportment of those presently at the centre of power and sovereignty, namely rulers of modern courts, like his very own patron Duke Ercole.[15]

In addition to ancient Greek practice, some of Aristotle's prescriptions, or what are taken to be his prescriptions, are invoked by the anonymous critic of *Didone* to condemn Giraldi's deviant practice. For example, the critic maintains that the gods should not be introduced in the plots of tragedies (Mercury appears on stage in Act III of *Didone*). Giraldi counters that his critic mistakes Aristotle's advice to avoid using divinities to resolve the outcome of a play as a general injunction against having the gods partake in the action. A more significant violation is that the play does not conform to the model represented by the *Oedipus Tyrannus* which the unnamed critic takes to be the paradigm 'from which Aristotle has taken his precepts, as from the true idea of the perfection of tragedy' (I.472). Giraldi refutes this charge by denying, first of all, that Aristotle's norms were derived from a single master text. 'However greatly Aristotle esteemed the *Oedipus*,' Giraldi writes,

> nonetheless he did not have so little esteem for the other tragedies as not to avail himself of them too in giving directives and laws for the praiseworthy composition of tragic matter. I will confess then … that the *Dido* in its matter is different from the *Oedipus Tyrannus*. But I do not wish to concede that in the parts proper to tragedy and in its workmanship it is not of the same sort as the *Oedipus*.[16]

Giraldi admits that his *Didone* differed from *Oedipus*, but he points out that the ancient dramatists – Euripides and the Romans – modified Sophoclean and then Greek tragic practice, and serve therefore as justifying examples for his own modern departures from prior conventions.

The dispute that Giraldi engages in illustrates, in my opinion, how theorising about a genre like tragedy began. Clearly, at the time that *Didone* was composed and recited there were no fully articulated rules established for Italian tragedy. Some *literati*, like Giraldi's conservative critic, may already have held notions of what a proper tragedy should be, notions derived from their readings of Greek tragedies, or of Trissino's *Sofonisba*, and from their interpretations of Aristotle and other ancient authorities, but there was yet no fixed generic code in place. These individuals may have declared that one ancient model was to be the measure against which modern writings in the genre had to be written and judged, but someone like Giraldi, who was a modernist exponent of a changing paradigm over time was ready to challenge such claims. The absence of an indisputable paradigm allowed for contestation, and, as Giraldi's own *Discorso* on composing tragedies illustrates, the contestation itself developed into theoretical discourse about what should (and what should not) constitute the modern revival of the genre. I believe that both the dispute over the incorrectness of his *Didone*, as well as the unrecorded reactions to his first tragedy *Orbecche*, actually prompted him to set down the more elaborate rules for composing a modern Italian tragedy, which we find in his *Discorso*, itself initially written in 1543, not long after he composed his letter in defence of *Didone*.

Let me turn to another dispute that erupted at about the same time that Giraldi's *Didone* was criticised; the quarrel over Sperone Speroni's *Canace*, which some modern scholars believe may have been instigated by none other than Giraldi. In the *Canace*, first published in 1546, but composed in 1542 for the Accademia degli Infiammati in Padua, Speroni set out to wring the hearts of his audience by representing the disastrous consequences of the incestuous love between Canace and Macareo, children of Eolus. Speroni's main source was Canace's epistle to her brother in Ovid's *Heroides* 11, but the drama actually includes the delivery of the baby that results from the incestuous union of the brother and sister, and also their respective suicides. When Eolus becomes aware of Canace's offspring he orders that the baby be thrown to the dogs, and forces Canace and her nurse to kill themselves. Macareo takes his own life upon learning what happened to his sister and their child. Eolus regrets his vindictive fury but too late to prevent the death of his son. The play had quite a success and influenced subsequent Italian drama (especially Tasso's *Torrismondo*). But it also provoked a polemic which lasted half a century. The main attack against it was composed in 1542-43 and, when first published in 1550 (along with a pirated version of the play), this anonymous work was entitled *Giuditio sopra la Tragedia di Canace & Macareo con molte utili considerationi circa l'arte Tragica et di altri poemi*. I don't want to broach the debate about its authorship. It has been attributed to Giraldi himself, an attribution I find unconvincing, and not simply because the published edition was dedicated to Giraldi. It is likely that the attack on Speroni was Ferrarese in origin, and Giraldi may have been involved in the polemic, but if we are to believe his younger rival, G.B. Pigna, Giraldi was not its author.[17]

The *Giudizio* takes the form of a dialogue, or rather of two discussions, the first set in Bologna, and the second in a gondola returning from a visit to Trissino's house in Murano. The main speakers in each, who remain anonymous, generally object to *Canace*'s subject matter, its characters, its style of writing and its prosody (incidentally, the author of the play also remains anonymous in the course of the discussion). The first and basic contention is that *Canace* cannot be called a tragedy because it does not satisfy the basic requisites for pity and fear. If these emotions – essential to the genre – are to be produced, the hero must be the kind of person who can elicit them. He or she cannot be a 'persona scellerata'. 'For what pity,' asks the first major speaker (referred to as 'il dotto uomo'), 'can be aroused in the minds of the spectators by a wicked person who falls into unhappiness and misery through his own malice?' (Perché qual misericordia può nascere nell'animo delli spettatori da una persona scellerata, la quale per sua malvagità incorra nelle infelicitadi e nelle miserie?')[18] Both Canace and Macareo commit their crime of incest with full knowledge of it, and then the sister gives birth to a baby conceived by her brother. Who will not deem, asks the first main speaker, that both of them deserve every kind of punishment and torment?

However un-Aristotelian the moral indignation of the criticism levelled at Speroni's protagonists by the first major speaker, he quickly reveals the Aristotelian basis of his objections. His critique is supported by the injunction in chapter 13 of the *Poetics* against showing a 'thoroughly villainous person falling from good fortune into misfortune', since 'such a structure can contain moral satisfaction but not pity or terror' (1452b35-1453a3, in R. Janko's translation). Aristotle, it will be recalled, then recommends a 'middling' protagonist, possessed of good reputation and good fortune until some error brings about his misfortune. Aristotle's prescription notwithstanding, one of the participants in the dialogue staged in the *Giudizio* then asks the main speaker to justify Greek tragedies which depict protagonists who have not only committed 'scelleratezze', but also incest, Oedipus and Jocasta being the most famous case. The main speaker vindicates these two notorious protagonists because their crimes were not committed knowingly, and they are not therefore deserving, as are Speroni's brother and sister, of the punishments they suffer. Moreover, Oedipus, as this speaker points out, is singled out by Aristotle as a paragon among tragic heroes worthy of compassion, and he goes on to explain why Electra and especially

Orestes, though matricides, also qualify as 'persone mezzane', that is, somewhere between good and evil, and therefore apt to be pitied.

To my knowledge, it is in the *Giudizio* that we find for the first time, at least in print, the requisite for a middlingly good tragic hero mandated for Italian tragedy. Giraldi, as I will shortly point out, also argues for a protagonist 'di mezzana condizione' in his *Discorso* on comedies and tragedies, published four years later. Even Speroni agreed that tragic protagonists had to be less than totally wicked. In the defence of his play, eventually presented as five *Lezioni* to the Accademia degli Elevati in Padua in 1558, Speroni began by vindicating his lovers. He did so not by arguing that tragic protagonists can be wicked, but by making a case for the brother and sister in his play on the grounds of their youth, and the fact that they were made to fall in love by a vindictive Venus: the overwhelming, irresistible force of love could explain and excuse their trespass. Moreover their sinning because of love has been a trespass that has always provoked great compassion, as numerous prior poems, ancient and Italian, can attest (cf. the first *Lezione* in Roaf, pp. 210ff.). Much of the thrust of the defence of Canace and Macareo was to show that they were not as unforgivably wicked as his opponents maintained, but had some redeeming virtues. The very fact that he needed to show that the young lovers were 'mezzane' and 'acconce alla compassione' confirms how necessary it became to conform to this requisite of middling goodness. Indeed, the demand for a middlingly virtuous protagonist, originally recommended by Aristotle, became a virtually undislodgable requisite for tragedy in the second half of the Cinquecento.

The point I wish to make is that a criterion such as the middlingly good protagonist doesn't become a standard for tragedy merely because Aristotle posits it, and his authority makes it become a law of the genre. The criterion begins to take hold after Italian practice *that has defied it* is met with criticism, and that criticism in turn is countered but not refuted. Undoubtedly Aristotle's authority is then appropriated to justify, and, even in the long run, to institutionalise the criterion of the middlingly good protagonist. But it doesn't happen without modern dramatic practice, and often deviant practice, to provoke debate and reflection about it. And if a criterion of Aristotelian origin such as this one does become established, it is usually established for reasons that are quite unlike the ones Aristotle had in mind. Let me briefly illustrate.

Aside from the *Giudizio* against *Canace*, the first time we find this requisite for a middlingly good individual is in Giraldi's *Discorso* on comedies and tragedies, composed, as I mentioned earlier, in 1543, that is, at about the same time as the attack against Speroni's play. When Giraldi considers the kind of protagonists that should be represented in tragedy (*Scritti critici*, 181-2) he seems to reiterate Aristotle's call for protagonists who are neither totally good nor totally wicked. But when he explains why one cannot show totally good men falling into misfortune his reasoning already betrays a Christian and didactic conception of catharsis that is not to be found in the Greek text. A plot representing a good character suffering a wretched fate 'will not introduce any good morals', he states, 'because no sin is committed in such action' ('ne potrà ciò introdurre buon costume alcuno, non essendo in tale azione peccato'). Tragedy purges the souls of men, Giraldi explains, because of the horror and pity produced by the sufferings of its protagonists, but these afflictions are brought about by the errors they have committed. He then goes on to rationalise why characters of middling virtue need to be represented. He appreciates that such protagonists will generate greater pity because of the disproportion between the error they commit and the suffering they undergo, especially when the tragic error is committed in ignorance. But then the disproportion between the suffering and the error committed is taken to have a moralistic effect on the spectator of a sort never suggested (nor imagined) by Aristotle. 'And this wonderfully purges the minds from such errors,' writes Giraldi, 'because the spectator, drawing a silent conclusion, says to himself: if this character has suffered as much as I now see because of an involuntary error, what would happen to me if I should voluntarily commit such a sin? and this thought makes him abstain from errors.'[19] The cautionary and didactic effect that Giraldi imagines tragedy will exert on the viewer is quite consistent with his moralistic view of tragedy's purpose but is quite remote from Aristotle's catharsis, elusive as that term remains. Giraldi's directive about the 'middling protagonist' may well be indebted to Aristotle's but one can see how it becomes significantly modified by being made to serve a different, post-Aristotelian and post-classical conception of tragedy. This kind of modification, I contend, characterises a number of other criteria prescribed for tragedy whose origins are clearly Aristotelian.

To return to the *Giudizio*, some of the basic criteria for the genre that emerge as the critique of *Canace* progresses have to do with the observance of *decorum*, which is of primary importance in Horatian poetics, and not a central concern in Aristotle's. Besides being incorrect about his choice of characters, the author of the *Canace* is repeatedly attacked for depicting his high-born protagonists comporting themselves in ways not appropriate to their stations. Certain events so transgress good taste that they produce effects quite improper to the genre. For example, Canace shown suffering the pangs of childbirth is a 'brutezza' which provokes laughter instead of maintaining the 'gravità' that should characterise tragedy (Roaf, pp. 120-1).

More extensive than the objections to the improprieties of character portrayal is the critique of the play's versification and style as generically inappropriate. By resorting to rhyme, and also by experimenting with other kinds of verse than unrhymed hendecasyllables, the *Canace* does not observe the kind of verse forms and prosody proper to tragedy. The intent of the tragic author, it is reasserted, is to generate pity and terror, and the language in which this is done has to seem natural and believable. Various speeches in the *Canace* are criticised for being too embellished, or too affected, or for using registers that are not fitting for the lamentable predicaments they depict. In such a rapid account of the *Giudizio* I cannot consider the analysis of the play's diction and prosody in the detailed manner in which specific passages in the play are criticised. Suffice it to say that 'Il Fiorentino', the second major speaker, cites numerous instances in which the author of *Canace* fails to relate verbal style and tone to respective characters' emotional states, or to their situations. These lapses, as indeed all the violations of *decorum*, are seen to be part of the play's disregard for naturalism and verisimilitude, essential features to maintain if the audience's belief is to be secured.

As I suggested earlier, the recurring concern with the observance of decorum of character, of comportment and of style, can be identified as an Horatian rather than an Aristotelian strain in the *Giudizio* against the *Canace*. Also more Horatian than Aristotelian is its overarching concern with having the tragic poet create a moral world that represents human agents who are true-seeming enough that his public will believe them. I wish to reiterate, however, that one cannot find in Horace's *Ars Poetica*, or in any of the neo-Horatian Italian criticism produced earlier in the century, any critique of violated generic decorum as specific or as detailed as one finds in this treatise. Horace does bring up in *Ars Poetica* (see lines 99-111) the need to match style and diction to the emotional state of characters if the poet wishes to convince and move his audience:

> Si vis me flere, dolendum est,
> primum ipsi tibi; tunc tua me infortunia laedent,
> Telephe vel Peleu;

But the correct procedure often has to be inferred from advice about what *not* to do:

> male si mandata loqueris,
> aut dormitabo aut ridebo, ... (*AP* 102-5)

And the interdiction remains most general: 'if the words you utter are ill suited,/ I shall laugh or fall asleep.' In the case of the *Giudizio* against

Canace, correct stylistic procedures also have to be inferred from the negative instances criticised in the play, but the critique is much more specific and more extensive.[20]

My account of the judgments against *Canace*, hasty though it is, should suffice to reveal how one can derive from its sustained critique a set of criteria which provide a definition of tragedy unprecedented in its amplitude and precision. The conception of tragedy that underlies the critique will be challenged, primarily by Speroni himself, or it will be modified when, soon after the *Giudizio* is written, Giraldi will, for the first time, formulate generalised rules for composing tragedy in Italian. But, despite subsequent modifications and counter-claims, the critique of the *Canace* establishes terms, issues and criteria which will remain central to the definition of tragedy for the next century (for example, many of the same issues and criteria of judgment are still brought up in Dryden's 1668 *Essay on Dramatic Poesy*).

Finally, it is also important to note that many of the terms of the debate will be transposed to the codification of other genres. For example, in the subsequent debate on the nature and definition of heroic poetry, the criteria that are repeatedly brought up are: the character of the heroes; whether decorum of character is observed or violated; verisimilitude and the quest for naturalistic mimesis; the style of writing, including versification, and whether it is appropriate to the genre. True, that structural criteria such as unity of action will become more prominent in the codification of heroic poetry, but it is nonetheless striking how many of the same criteria originally brought in the disputes about tragedy will be invoked again and argued about.

I wish to point out, in closing, that even though the first debates about what constitutes a proper heroic poem occur very soon after the disputes over tragedy, they come after these disputes, not before them. One of the first reports of neo-Aristotelian criticism of modern Italian narrative poetry is the letter G.B. Pigna wrote to Giraldi in 1548 listing the objections that devotees of ancient epic practice were levelling at the *Orlando Furioso*. Ariosto's poem is not a proper heroic poem, so these critics maintained, because it has many actions instead of one; it lacks continuity as well as unity; it lacks verisimilitude; it regularly violates decorum of character and of style; and its author has not chosen a proper protagonist by focusing on a wise man who goes mad. Overall the critics object because 'si è del tutto scostato dalla Poetica d'Aristotele'.[21]

I mention this letter of G.B. Pigna's because the critics cited by its author have the same inclination that the critics of new tragedies had in the 1540s of erecting norms for the genre by negation. One starts understanding what requisites have to be met in an epic poem by being told how Ariosto's poem failed to meet them. This tendency to define epic poetry by using the deficiencies of the *Furioso* and other chivalric 'romanzi' as counter-examples recurs in most of the theorising about epic produced in the second half of the sixteenth century. I cannot dwell on this tendency, but I insist on our being mindful of how this manner of defining a genre by contrasting it to some recent transgressive practice, is a pattern that was set by the debates about tragedy I have sketched here. I am quite convinced that these debates over tragedy were what served as an example, and also provided many of the criteria for the eventual codification of other genres, beginning with epic. It may take more than these rapid closing remarks to persuade the scholarly community that these early disputes were so influential, but it should now, in any case, be more evident how the experimentation with tragedy in the early 1540s and the debates it provoked generated the first genre-specific theorising in the early modern period. There were various ways in which Aristotle's *Poetics* could enable some of this thinking, or could be appropriated to legitimise certain principles or rules. But Aristotle's theorising did not engender this new thinking about tragedy. To finish with a mixed metaphor, Aristotle may have been a midwife, but he didn't lay the egg.

Notes

1. Giorgio Valla's *De Poetica* appeared as the thirty-eighth book in his encyclopaedic *De expetendis ac fugiendis rebus opus*, published posthumously in 1501. On this treatise as well as for perceptive observations on the late Quattrocento reception of the *Poetics*, see E.N. Tiegerstedt, 'Observations on the reception of Aristotle's *Poetics* in the Latin West', *Studies in the Renaissance* 15 (1968), 7-24.

2. For a useful account of these minimalist definitions of tragedy and comedy see Timothy Reiss, 'Renaissance theatre and the theory of tragedy', *Cambridge History of Literary Criticism*, vol. III. *The Renaissance*, ed. Glyn Norton (Cambridge, 1999), esp. 233-5.

3. See G.B. Giraldi Cinzio, *Scritti critici*, ed. C.G. Crocetti (Milan, 1973), 215-19.

4. For a more detailed account of Giraldi's indebtedness to Aristotle in the *Discorso … intorno al comporre delle comedie e delle tragedie*, see my article, 'The emergence of poetic genre theory in the sixteenth century', *Modern Language Quarterly* 59 (1998), esp. 148-56.

5. The last two divisions of Trissino's *Poetica* are reprinted in *Trattati di poetica e retorica del cinquecento*, ed. Bernard Weinberg (Bari, 1970), II.5-90. So much of the 'Quinta Divisione' reiterates Aristotle that Weinberg considered it the second Italian translation of the *Poetics* (*Trattati*, II.654).

6. One of the reasons that the *pioneering* aspects of these treatises tend to be overlooked is because of their delayed publication: Giraldi's *Discorso* on comedies and tragedies is first composed in 1543 but only published in 1554; the *Giuditio sopra la Tragedia di Canace & Macareo … was composed soon after Speroni wrote his *Canace* in 1542, but only published in 1550; the 'Quinta

e Sesta Divisioni' of Trissino's *Poetica*, composed *c.* 1549, were only printed in 1562.

7. See 'The assimilation of Aristotle's *Poetics* in sixteenth-century Italy', *Cambridge History of Literary Criticism*, vol. III. *The Renaissance*, ed. Glyn Norton (Cambridge, 1999), esp. 59-64.

8. These various testimonies of the high worth that the ancients accorded tragedy are brought up by Alessandro Pazzi de' Medici (best known for his Latin translation of Aristotle's *Poetics*) in a dedicatory letter (dated 1524) to Pope Clement VII, preceding his composition of *Didone in Cartagine*, one of the earliest tragedies in Italian. To what extent tragedy was esteemed by Aristotle, he writes, 'si può conoscere che d'esso [i.e. tragedy] principalmente scrive, et di tutte le parti pienissamente tracta. Puossi oltre di questo comprendere in che conto sia sunto et quanto conveniemente sempre approvato dalli antiqui secoli non solo da quel che molti doctissimi et approbatissimi authori greci e latini ne scrivono, dalli quali frequentemente allegati si truovano i versi tragici, ma etiandio dalle reliquie delli superbi theatri e amfitheatri, che ancora alli occhi nostri non senza maraviglia appariscono.' *Le tragedie metriche di Alessandro Pazzi de' Medici*, ed. Angelo Solerti (Bologna, 1887), 44.

9. In the opening sentence of his *Discorso* on comedies and tragedies, Giraldi states that 'tra quante composizioni si fanno da noi, e si son fatte prima dagli antichi, e greci, e latini, non ve n' è alcuna che in gravità vada appresso la tragedia'. The notion is derived ultimately from an Ovidian tag, 'Omne genus scripti gravitate tragoedia vincit', cited regularly in summary definitions of tragedy, e.g. the prefaces of early sixteenth-century editions of Seneca's tragedies.

10. See Daniel Javitch, 'La canonizzazione dell' *Edipo re* nell'Italia del sedicesimo secolo', in *Teatro e palcoscenico. Dall'Italia all'Inghilterra. 1540-1640* (Rome, 2001), pp. 17-42.

11. The entire 'Lettera sulla tragedia', as Bernard Weinberg calls it, is reprinted in *Trattati di poetica e retorica*, ed. B. Weinberg, I.470-86. It was first published with *Didone* and the other tragedies in 1583.

12. '... da' quali si deono trarre le leggi, e la vera regola di comporre lodevolmente favole tali, come gliele trasse Aristotile.' See *Trattati di poetica e retorica*, I.472.

13. '... non è punto verisimile che le grandi e signorili persone vogliano trattare le azioni di molto importanza, come sono quelli che vengano nelle tragedie, nella moltitudine delle genti, quantunque famigliari. Ma in simili negozi ... hanno solamente con loro i segretari, i consiglieri e le altre persone prudenti e sagge delle quali si fidano.' *Trattati di poetica*, I.477.

14. For example, his critic objected that the extended soliloquies voiced by his protagonists violate decorum, since he presumed that rulers would not utter such personal thoughts in the public urban space that the stage of ancient Greek tragedy represents. Giraldi responds that his critic foolishly ignores that when they do not share their thoughts with their intimate advisers, rulers are wont to reflect *alone* on their true sentiments or their future but secret course of action, in the privacy of their chambers, and he seeks to represent their soliloquies 'non altrimenti che se essi si facessero nelle più segrete e più riposte stanze de' signori', *Trattati di poetica*, I.483.

15. For a more detailed, and also more abstruse, discussion of Giraldi's defence of the representation of his royal characters, see Marco Ariani, 'La trasgressione e l'ordine. L'"Orbecche" di G.B. Giraldi Cinthio e la fondazione del linguaggio tragico cinquecentesco', *Rassegna della letteratura italiana*, LXXXIII (1979), 117-80.

16. 'Quantunque Aristotele istimasse molto l'*Edipo*, non fe' nondimeno sì poco conto delle altre [tragedie] che non si servisse anche di loro nel dare gli ordini e le leggi di comporre le materie tragiche lodevolmente. Confesserò io adunque ... che la *Didone* in quanto alla materia è diversa dall'*Edipo tiranno*. Ma non voglio già concedere che nelle parti che alla tragedia convengono e nell'artificio ella non sia tale quale è l'*Edipo* ....' *Trattati di poetica*, I.484

17. Bartolomeo Cavalcanti, who has been the other main contender for the authorship, though Florentine, was in Ferrara, in the service of Ercole II d'Este, from 1537. When G.B. Pigna was asked by Speroni whether Giraldi was the anonymous author of the *Giudizio*, he assured him thet Giraldi did *not* write it, and Pigna was in a position to know, embroiled as he was in Ferrara with Giraldi, after accusing his former mentor of plagiarising his ideas in his *Discorso intorno al comporre dei romanzi*: 'La faccio sicura,' writes Pigna in a letter to Speroni of 5.xi.1553, 'che il giudicio scrittole contra non fu mai del Giraldi: perciochè lo stile e la materia il dimostrano ...'; cf. S. Speroni, *Opere* (Venice, 1740). For the argument that Giraldi was the author of the *Giudizio*, see Christina Roaf, 'A sixteenth-century anonimo, the author of the Giuditio sopra la tragedia di Canace e Macareo', *Italian Studies* XIV (1959), 49-74; and her edition of Sperone Speroni, *Canace*; G.B. Giraldi Cinzio, *Scritti contro la Canace* (Bologna: Commissione per i testi di lingua, 1982), esp. xxv-xxix.

18. Sperone Speroni, *Canace*; G.B. Giraldi Cinzio, *Scritti contro la Canace*, ed. Christina Roaf (Bologna: Commissione per i testi di lingua, 1982), 98. Hereafter cited in text as Roaf.

19. *Scritti critici*, op. cit., 182. '... E questo purga maravigliosamente gli animi da tali errori. Perché lo spettatore con tacita conseguenza seco dice: se questi per errore commesso non volontariamente tanto male ha sofferto quanto vedo io ora, che sarebbe di me se forse volontariamente commettessi questo peccato? e questo pensiero il fa astenere dagli errori.'

20. See, for example, the critique of Macareo's grief, at the news of his sister's death in Act V, for being expressed in the sort of Petrarchan diction one enjoys in a canzone, but inappropriate when a person is 'empito di dolore' (Roaf, 152). Later in the discussion 'Il Fiorentino' accuses Speroni of violating stylistic decorum by imitating affective and highly charged scenarios in prior poetry but failing to place them in similarly appropriate situations. For example, in the scene preceding Canace's suicide, the author imitates some of Dido's speech prior to her self-inflicted death in *Aeneid* IV, but because Canace lacks Dido's tragic grandeur and her predicament therefore is really not similar to Dido's, the transposition does not work (Roaf, 156).

21. For Pigna's letter to Giraldi, see G.B. Giraldi Cinzio, *Scritti critici*, ed. C.G. Crocetti (Milan, 1978), 246-7.

Poetic Marvels: Aristotelian Wonder in Renaissance Poetics and Poetry

Kirsti Minsaas

O wonder!
How many goodly creatures are there here!
How beauteous mankind is! O brave new world,
That has such people in't!
Shakespeare, The Tempest

An important feature of Aristotle's *Poetics* is its grounding in an affective orientation towards the art of poetry. Ignorant of what twentieth-century critics have dubbed 'the affective fallacy', Aristotle formulates in his little treatise a poetic theory that permits a literary work to work its imaginative spell on the minds of the readers in the widest possible sense, engaging them both cognitively and emotionally. At the centre of this affective poetics is Aristotle's belief that the end of tragedy is to bring about the catharsis of pity and fear. But of no less interest is his emphasis on the effect of wonder, or what he alternately referred to as the marvellous (*to thaumaston*) or the astounding (*to ekplêktikon*). It is, however, noteworthy that while the idea of catharsis still invites critical attention, wonder has almost disappeared from contemporary critical debate. The number of works dealing with this term today is highly limited, and if one searches literary dictionaries or glossaries for some entry that will explain its meaning, one is likely to be disappointed.

This evaporation of wonder from today's critical scene stands in marked contrast with what we find in the Renaissance. Beginning with the explosion of critical activity in sixteenth-century Italy, the notion of wonder came to take a central place in the Renaissance literary imagination, evolving into what may be called a poetics of *la maraviglia*. For some Italian theorists, *la maraviglia* even constituted a defining feature of poetry, shared by all the individual genres. Thus Giason Denores defined poetry as the imitation not just of an action but of an action that is marvellous;[1] and Francesco Patrizi, adopting an anti-mimetic (and anti-Aristotelian) approach, viewed the arousal of wonder as the primary task of all poets, writing that the poet 'must tend to ... his proper end of exciting admiration (*eccitare maraviglia*), and to this he must direct the whole texture of marvellous things (*di mirabili*) in his poem, which invest it with its proper form'.[2] Although few went as far as Denores and Patrizi, most sixteenth-century critics made the marvellous a primary concern in their poetic theories, seeing it as a vital means of producing the desired effect of wonder.

On the theoretical level, this cult of *la maraviglia* can be linked to the revival of interest in Aristotle's *Poetics* that occurred in Italy during the latter half of the sixteenth century. Although Aristotle, through his insistence that a well constructed plot should develop according to the principles of probability and necessity, traditionally is seen as a spokesman for poetic realism, his brief concessions throughout the *Poetics* that the most effective plot is one that includes the unusual and the unexpected also made him a major source for the Renaissance concern with the marvellous. However, while in Aristotle the marvellous played a subordinate role, serving mainly as a means of enhancing the cathartic effect of a tragic work through its power to excite wonder, it came during the Renaissance to play a much wider role, taking on meanings and functions that went far beyond the Aristotelian conception.

A major reason for this was the common tendency, pointed out by Bernard Weinberg and others, to conflate Aristotle's *Poetics* and Horace's *Ars Poetica*, so that Aristotelian precepts, including the notion of wonder, acquired a utilitarian dimension drawn from the Horatian emphasis on the need to combine profit and delight (*utile et dulce*). But another reason for the expanded role attributed to wonder was the extensive use of marvellous material in poetic forms and practices that had evolved since Aristotle's day. Not only was the marvellous a staple ingredient in post-Aristotelian popular genres such as the romance and tragicomedy, but it also dominated individual masterpieces like Virgil's *Aeneid*, Ovid's *Metamorphoses*, Dante's *Divine Comedy*, and Ariosto's *Orlando Furioso*. Faced with a sudden plethora of poetic marvels, the Italian critics tried to account for their functional role in terms that while drawing on Aristotle also transcended him. Far from engaging in mere translation and exegesis of Aristotle's text, they conducted their theorising in close alliance with poetic practice, sometimes bringing in important innovations. As Daniel Javitch has argued, the reason for the unprecedented interest in Aristotle among the Italian commentators was precisely the fact that his treatise served as a useful model for the analysis of the many generic changes and developments that had occurred since antiquity.[3] It would thus be an exaggeration to say that Aristotle inspired the Renaissance interest in the marvellous; rather, he provided a method and a vocabulary that came in handy for the critic desirous to analyse and codify the poetic use of the marvellous.

146

In this chapter I wish to consider some aspects of the Renaissance preoccupation with the marvellous, as it manifests itself both in theory and in practice. In so doing, I shall be especially concerned with the ways in which much of the critical debate on the topic, although taking Aristotle as its starting point, also went beyond him, moving into new and interesting directions. But first I need to say a few words about wonder in Aristotle.

Aristotle on wonder

The first thing to be noted about Aristotle's conception of poetic wonder is that it involves a special link between emotion and cognition.[4] Not only is wonder a feeling that has a cognitive foundation, being like the other emotions an evaluative response founded in thought, but it is also a feeling that stimulates cognition. Cognition, that is, constitutes both the departure and the end point of the act of wondering. In fact, Aristotelian wonder is best seen as a form of intellectual desire. Confronted with objects and events that appear strange or unusual or out of the ordinary, we are brought into a state of perplexity or amazement that stirs our desire for understanding, challenging us to a process of thought that may still this desire. It may even challenge us to philosophical thought – a point Aristotle makes in his *Metaphysics* when he writes that 'it is owing to their wonder that men both now begin and at first began to philosophise' (982b12), and also in the *Rhetoric* when he states that 'philosophy consists in the knowledge of many things that excite wonder' (1371b27-8).[5] For this reason, wonder also brings pleasure, both through the fact that it may lead to learning, thus satisfying the desire, and in that anticipates learning. As Aristotle explains further in the *Rhetoric*: 'learning and admiring (*thaumazein*) are as a rule pleasant; for admiring implies the desire to learn, so that what causes admiration (*to thaumaston*) is to be desired, and learning implies a return to the normal' (1371a31-4).

In the *Poetics*, Aristotle makes this intellectually charged wonder the peculiar response to three different components of a plot: (1) an unexpected reversal (*peripeteia*) in the flow of events, (2) a character's recognition (*anagnôrisis*), and (3) events that occur contrary to reason (*alogon*).

Of these, the unexpected reversal is perhaps the most important. Its link to wonder is mentioned for the first time in Chapter 9, where Aristotle indicates how such a reversal, through the arousal of wonder, makes the emotional impact of the tragic mimesis more effective:

Since tragic mimesis portrays not just a whole action, but events

147

which are fearful and pitiful, this can best be achieved when things occur contrary to expectation yet still on account of one another. A sense of wonder (*to thaumaston*) will be more likely to be aroused in this way than as a result of the arbitrary or fortuitous, since even chance events make the greatest impact of wonder (*thaumasiótata*) when they *appear* to have a purpose (as in the case where Mitys' statue at Argos fell on Mitys' murderer and killed him, while he was looking at it: such things do not *seem* to happen without reason. (1452a1-10)[6]

An important implication of this passage is that the effect of wonder seems to rest conjointly on an element of surprise and an element of coherence. That is, an unexpected and apparently inexplicable turn in the events will not arouse proper, or thought-provoking, wonder unless it is also perceived as causally plausible. Even if an event happens quite accidentally, it will. Aristotle indicates, have a wondrous effect only if it has the *appearance* of happening with a purpose, as in the Mitys example. On the other hand, a fully coherent chain of events will also fail to produce a cognitively satisfying wonder if it only unfolds according to expectation, with no surprise element. Thus, Aristotle seems to regard poetic wonder as a site of experience situated in a mean position between shocking surprise and causal plausibility. Mere surprise without plausibility will be experienced as something weird and incomprehensible and so cognitively frustrating; mere plausibility without surprise will be experienced as predictable and so cognitively unchallenging. In neither case will there be the pleasure of understanding that Aristotle in the *Rhetoric* associates with the learning as well as the anticipation of learning produced by wonder, naming 'sudden changes (*peripeteiai*) and narrow escapes from danger' as one type of things that may stimulate such pleasure-producing wonder (cf. 1371b10-12).

In Chapter 18, Aristotle adds a comment which indicates that the wondrous effect of the *peripeteia* is best achieved when it concerns the downfall of a man with superior skills but flawed morality:

In the case both of reversals (*peripeteiai*) and of simple dramatic actions, poets use wonder (*to thaumaston*) to achieve their aim; for the effect gained arouses the tragic emotions as well as humane sympathy (*philanthrôpon*). Examples are the outwitting of a clever man who is flawed by evil (like Sisyphus), or the worsting of one who is manly but unjust. Such things conform to probability, on Agathon's principle that probability allows for the occurrence of many *im*probabilities. (1456a19-25)

148

Whereas in *Poetics* 13 Aristotle rejects the fall of a deeply flawed hero on the grounds that it fails to excite the tragic feelings of pity and fear, appealing only to one's moral sense (*philanthrôpon*) (1453a1-6), he now seems to accept the fall of such a man as tragic as well. The likely explanation for this apparent inconsistency is that in this particular case we have the improbable and yet (according to Agathon) probable spectacle of a superior man being defeated by someone else and so will be inclined to experience his fall as wondrous in a way productive of pity and fear.

Closely connected to Aristotle's emphasis on the unexpected reversal is his emphasis on recognition (*anagnôrisis*) as an important stimulus to wonder – especially when it is of the kind that occurs in *Oedipus Rex* when a character does harm to a close friend or kin (*philia*) in ignorance of who the person is and then discovers the victim's identity later, after the act has been done. For such a discovery, Aristotle suggests in Chapter 14, is emotionally striking:

There is a better way [of handling the tragic plot situation], one in which the agent acts in ignorance [of who the intended victim is] and then recognises what he has done, for there is nothing repugnant here and the recognition is striking (*ekplêktikon*). (1454a2-4)[7]

And better still is the case of Iphigenia and Orestes in *Iphigenia in Tauris* where the discovery prevents the harmful act as 'the sister recognises the brother and does not kill him' (1454a6-7).

As in the case of the surprise reversal, Aristotle sees the wonder aroused by *anagnôrisis* as a means of enhancing the tragic effect. The type of wonder he refers to, however, is that of *ekplêktikon*, a word that with its connotations of something astounding or shocking, even terrifying, is much stronger than the word *thaumaston*, which Aristotle used about the plausible surprise in Chapter 9.[8] In Chapter 16, he adds the point that such 'ekplectic' wonder is not merely contingent upon the *anagnôrisis* occurring in connection with a terrible crime but also upon its springing logically from the events rather than from artificial signs or logical inference:

The best of all recognitions is that which arises from the events themselves, when the striking effect (*ekplêxeôs*) comes through probabilities, such as that we find in the *Oedipus [Rex]* of Sophocles; another appears in *Iphigenia [in Tauris]*, for it is probable that Iphigenia should wish to be sending letters home. Such recognitions are the only ones that occur without the use of contrived signs or amulets. The next best are the recognitions which arise from inference. (1455a16-21)

It seems clear that Aristotle in both the above passages has in mind the impact an *anagnôrisis* makes on the spectator rather than on the character. The *anagnôrisis*, that is, is a structural element in the tragic plot that in conjunction with certain other conditions strikes the spectator with a wonder that serves to reinforce the cathartic effect generated by pity and fear. We may, however, note an interesting parallel between the emotional response of the spectator witnessing the *anagnôrisis* and the emotional response of the character actually experiencing it. As D.W. Lucas comments, Aristotle's formulation in Chapter 16 indicates that '*ekplêxis* is the emotion that an *anagnôrisis* naturally evokes'.[9] Thus Orestes responds to his sudden recognition of Iphigenia in Euripides' play by being 'wonder-struck (*ekpeplêgmenos*) (795) at the 'marvellous' (*thaumast'*) news (797). That this *anagnôrisis* is equally striking for those witnessing it is suggested by the comment made by the Chorus that the meeting between brother and sister is a 'marvel of marvels' (*thaumastoisi*) beyond 'fabled lore' (900), a comment that guides the spectators watching the scene in the theatre to a similar response by inviting them to partake in Orestes' *anagnôrisis*-provoked wonder.[10]

The third and final source of wonder in Aristotle that needs to be mentioned is the irrational, or that which is *alogon*. The locus for this kind of wonder is Chapter 24, where Aristotle turns his attention from tragedy to the epic:

> While the marvellous (*to thaumaston*) is called for in tragedy, it is epic which gives greater scope for the irrational (*to alogon*) (which is the chief cause of the marvellous), because we do not actually see the agents. The circumstances of the pursuit of Hector would be patently absurd if put on stage, with the men standing and refraining from pursuit, and Achilles forbidding them; but in epic the effect is not noticed. The marvellous gives pleasure: this can be seen from the way in which everyone exaggerates in order to gratify when recounting events. (1460a11-18)

Aristotle's main point here is that there is greater scope for the inclusion of marvellous incidents in epic than in tragedy. Yet again his emphasis is on a wondrous effect held in check by the probable, since the greater tolerance for that which is *alogon* in the epic is precisely that in this particular context it is perceived as plausible, the incongruity of the situation being less noticeable in a narrated work than in a theatrical performance. As with the statue of Mitys in Chapter 9, the important point is not whether the represented action really *is* logically plausible but that it *seems* to be – a point Aristotle accentuates in his contention at 1460a26 and later at 1461b11 that what is probable

150

though impossible is preferable to the possible but implausible. Ideally, he believed, a poetic work should contain no impossibility unless camouflaged by apparent plausibility. Then, however, it was acceptable, that is, if it could serve its goal of increasing 'the emotional impact (*ekplêktikoteron*) either of the particular part or of some other part of the work' (1460b25).

An interesting point regarding Aristotle's inclusion of the irrational as a source of wonder is that it marks a shift from his earlier concern with structural plausibility to a concern with subject matter. Whereas wonder aroused by the unexpected *peripeteia* and the *anagnôrisis* relies on an intra-textual standard of probability, derived from the logic of the events, the wonder aroused by that which is *alogon* relies on an extra-textual standard of normality, derived from generally accepted considerations of what is reasonable. That the distinction is not too clear in Aristotle's own mind is suggested by his use of the Mitys example in connection with the unexpected reversal in Chapter 9, since it in fact exemplifies an incident that is *alogon* (or contrary to extra-textual normality) rather than a surprise *peripeteia* (or contrary to intra-textual logic). When he does use it, it is probably because it serves to underscore his major point, namely, that the marvellous occupies a mean site between shocking surprise and causal plausibility, involving a tensional balance between the improbable and the probable.

During the Renaissance, this point was elevated into a principal literary doctrine, informing theory as well as practice. As Baxter Hathaway has argued, the tension that can be found in Aristotle between what appears to be contradictory demands for the wondrous and the verisimilar became a central issue in Renaissance poetic theory, especially in Italy, rising to the forefront of critical debate.[11] In spite of disagreeing about how the proper balance between the marvellous and the credible was best achieved, the Italian theorists largely concurred that the poet's skill had to be measured above all by his ability to astound his audience while staying within the bounds of the plausible.

In part, this preoccupation with balance can be explained by the power Aristotle's authority exerted on the individual critics. But it can also be explained by their need to come to grips with the abundance of marvellous objects and incidents in practical poetry, not only in the romance but also in other, more established, genres like tragedy, comedy and epic. Added to this comes the fact that the proper use of the marvellous came to play a vital role in the common Renaissance concern with the moral effects of poetry. As a result of their injection of the utilitarian doctrines of both Plato and Horace into Aristotelian theory, Renaissance theorists forged a link between the marvellous and the moral never hinted at in Aristotle. One clear manifestation of this can

151

be observed in contemporary notions of tragedy, the genre at the centre of Aristotle's attention.

Renaissance theories on wonder in tragedy

To some extent, wonder evoked by tragedy retained for the Renaissance commentators its basic Aristotelian function as a feeling that reinforces or intensifies the cathartic effect generated by pity and fear. Thus Torquato Tasso believed that the marvellous helped facilitate the arousal of the tragic emotions, writing that 'marvellous events make horror and pity easier to induce'.[12] Similarly, Lodovico Castelvetro notes that the marvellous 'engenders and intensifies pity and fear'.[13] The extent to which this line of thinking also penetrated practical tragedy is indicated by the frequency with which the adjectival forms 'wondrous' and 'marvellous' were used as epithets to describe the shocking or amazing quality of painful emotions. Thus Othello describes the moving impact his wooing tales make on Desdemona with the following words: "twas strange, 'twas passing strange / 'Twas pitiful, 'twas wondrous pitiful' (*Othello* I.3.159-60). Given the fact that the response here described concerns a story, it is not unlikely that Shakespeare is drawing on contemporary theories about the effect of tragedy. But he may equally well be drawing on a commonplace Renaissance belief that strong emotion, even when painful, was strengthened and made more intense when infused with a sense of wonder. In Philip Sidney's *Arcadia*, for example, Amphialus, after a tragic mishap where he mortally wounds a beautiful lady disguised as a knight, is described as being 'astonished with grief, compassion and shame' for what he has done.[14]

In addition to emphasising this reinforcing function, however, Renaissance tragic theorists also came to see wonder in tragedy as an independent tragic feeling, giving it an autonomous status that it does not have in Aristotle. For Francesco Robortello, for example, the wonder aroused by a tragedy with a complex plot (or one having both a *peripeteia* and an *anagnôrisis* in it) became a third tragic emotion, working its effect alongside both pity and fear (when the reversal was toward a tragic outcome, as in *Oedipus Rex*) or just pity (when the reversal was toward a happy outcome, as in *Iphigenia in Tauris*).[15] This elevation of wonder into an autonomous tragic feeling is even more radical in Philip Sidney, who defines tragedy as a genre that 'with stirring the affects of admiration and commiseration, teacheth the uncertainty of this world'.[16] Although Sidney's use of the words 'admiration' and 'commiseration' reveals a likely indebtedness to Robortello's Latin translation of Aristotle, he goes beyond the Italian in making admiration a substitute for and not just an addition to fear – something Robortello reserves for tragedies with a fortunate reversal. Interest-

152

ingly, this replacement of fear with wonder can also be observed in Shakespeare's *Hamlet*, where Horatio describes the tragic catastrophe as 'aught of woe or wonder' (V.2.368).[17] Evidently, both Sidney and Shakespeare attached profound significance to wonder as a tragic feeling.[18]

But the most notable way Renaissance tragic theorists expanded the role of wonder in tragedy can be observed in their emphasis on its power to make tragedy an enjoyable experience. Thus Castelvetro, although acknowledging the role of wonder in intensifying pity and fear, also emphasised its power to intensify pleasure. Since, as he wrote, 'the end of poetry ... is to produce pleasure; and since the marvellous is especially capable of giving pleasure, it follows that the tragic poet must do his utmost to achieve the marvellous'.[19] And one way of doing this, he tells us, is to have tragedies where the marvellous induces the pleasure of watching the deserved fall of 'a depraved person'. For such a fall 'brings consolation to the audience and thereby intensifies their pleasure'. To substantiate this view in Aristotelian terms, Castelvetro seeks support in Aristotle's statement in *Poetics* 18 that the wonder excited by such things as 'the outwitting of a clever man who is flawed by evil (like Sisyphus)' and 'the worsting of one who is manly but unjust' (1456a19-23) will contribute to the tragic emotions. Castelvetro, however, significantly ignores Aristotle's emphasis on the tragic potential of these situations as a result of their wondrous quality of being at once probable and improbable, claiming instead that this quality makes them pleasurable.[20]

In addition to pleasure, though often in combination with it, Renaissance critics exalted wonder for its usefulness in helping effect the moral ends of tragedy, commending it as an important means of achieving the Horatian ideal of pleasant utility (*utile dulci*) or of a 'delightful teaching' as Sidney phrased it.[21] But the precise understanding of how the marvellous could contribute to such delightful instruction in tragedy varied with the individual critics.

One common view – ultimately derived from Lucretius in *De Rerum Natura* – was that the marvellous in tragedy consists in a kind of sugar-coating through which the lesson of the horrible material could be made more pleasant and so more palatable to audience tastes. In part, this sugar-coating was to be achieved by means of unusual subject matter, ranging from fantastic and extraordinary events to striking spectacle and interludes with song and dance. But it could also be achieved by artistic means, such as skilful handling of the plot and elevated verse and diction. Yet whatever the means, the pleasant marvels were made subservient to the utilitarian goal of making the moral lesson taught by the tragic work easier to swallow.

Of greater interest than this sugar-coating theory was the view –

relying on a Horatian interpretation of Aristotelian catharsis – that the arousal of a pleasurable wonder in tragedy could contribute to its educative impact by enhancing its end of effecting a moral purgation. One critic who adhered to this view was Giason Denores, who argued that the task of tragedy was 'to purge the spectators, by means of pleasure, of terror and pity, and to make them abhor the life of the tyrants and the most powerful men'.[22] Similarly, Antonio Minturno held that tragedy's end was to purge undesirable 'passions from the minds of the spectators' by demonstrating the tragic consequences of these passions, thereby imprinting the lesson that 'in prosperity we must not place our trust in worldly matters'.[23] Although differing somewhat in their descriptions of what was the message absorbed through the tragic purgation, as well as what emotions were purged, the two critics agreed that the purgation achieved its instructive effect by being accompanied by a pleasurable sense of wonder.

It must here be noted that even if theorists like Denores and Minturno both saw the marvellous in tragedy as instrumental in the cognitive enlightenment of the spectator, what they had in mind was a type of mental processing very different from what we find in Aristotle's conception of tragedy. Although recent scholarship indicates that Aristotelian catharsis may have involved a form of cognitive learning experience effected through the emotions of pity and fear and assisted by wonder,[24] the Italians adhered to a more clearly didactic view of the educative role of tragedy. Instead of seeing catharsis as a form of heightened insight into man's tragic condition, situated in the tragic emotions, they saw it as a form of moral purgation through which the spectator was cleansed of vice, learning to abhor all forms of sin by watching their fatal consequences of the erring hero. A good insight into the nature of the reasoning process believed to take place in the spectator's mind during such purgation is offered by Giovambattista Giraldi Cinthio. Commenting upon the feelings aroused by those situations (discussed by Aristotle in *Poetics* 13) in which a morally middling hero, having acted in ignorance rather than out of wickedness, suffers a penalty in excess of his crime, Giraldi writes:

> From this can be seen that ignorance of the sin committed, when the evil doer incurs punishment for the evil he has done, causes the greatest horror and the greatest compassion. And this wonderfully purges the mind from such errors, because the spectator drawing a silent conclusion says to himself: If the tragic character has suffered as severely as he does because of an involuntary error, what would happen to me if I should voluntarily commit such a sin.[25]

154

This is an ingenious, if contrived, way of accommodating Aristotle's notion of catharsis to the utilitarian view of tragedy as a form of warning against sin. By experiencing pity and fear for the erring hero's misfortune, Giraldi holds, the spectator learns the 'wonderfully' purging lesson that he must abstain from doing deliberately what the hero does accidentally lest the same misfortune befall him. The sense of wonder, it appears, becomes the product of learning and not its stimulator, as in Aristotle.

A more sophisticated interpretation of the role played by wonder in the tragic learning experience is found in Sidney, although he too relies on the customary Renaissance conflation of Aristotelian catharsis with Horatian utilitarianism. But unlike the Italians, Sidney does not locate the utilitarian value of wonder, or admiration as he terms it, in its power to produce pleasure but in its emotional shock effect on the spectator's mind, a shock effect productive of rational reflection. As Geoffrey Shepherd comments,

> For Sidney, *admiration* is a kind of emotional shock, the amazement felt in face of an exceptionally heroic order of behaviour …. The tragic effect as Sidney understands it is primarily in this emotional shock followed by a feeling of pity that men should have to do and suffer horrible things. The tragic effect produces moral effect. The shock, followed by reflection, brings a man to a consideration of the true nature of life. Sidney plays down the sensationalism in some of the Italian critics and accentuates the rational usefulness of tragedy.[26]

As Shepherd's gloss indicates, Sidney seems, more than his Italian contemporaries, to have grasped the cognitive value of wonder, its power to affect the mind in a way productive of tragic understanding. What is more, since in his definition of tragedy admiration works its effect in conjunction with pity and not fear, which it replaces, Sidney put a stronger emphasis on wonder as a reinforcer of pity, holding up compassion with human suffering as a morally ennobling feeling in its own right. Whereas the Italians were primarily concerned with the negative effect of tragedy, its power to make the spectator shun vice, Sidney anticipates the neo-classical view that tragedy could serve the positive aim of inducing fellow-feeling – as illustrated by his example (taken from Plutarch) of the 'abominable tyrant Alexander Pheraeus' who, although being a cold-blooded murderer 'without all pity' was moved to 'abundance of tears' when watching a tragedy, unable to resist its 'sweet violence' (though not sufficiently to change his wicked ways).[27]

It should by now be clear that the idea of wonder fulfilled a wide variety of functions in Renaissance tragic theory, ranging from its reinforcing role in the arousal of pity and fear to its utilitarian role in effecting moral instruction. A similar variety can be observed in discussions of what constituted the best means of eliciting wonder in tragedy. To a large extent, however, sixteenth-century tragic theorists followed Aristotle in emphasising striking and unexpected turns in the plot as a major source of wonder in tragedy, commending plots with surprising reversals that take the protagonists either from happiness to misery or from misery to happiness. But as a result of their changed views on the function of wonder, they liked to amplify Aristotle's viewpoints, offering their own versions of his prescriptions.

One interesting example here is Castelvetro's contention that depictions of 'men doing some horrible deed accidentally against their will' constitute one class of plot situations that, because they have, as he says, 'the element of the marvellous in them', help reinforce the feelings of pity and fear. Clearly drawing on Aristotle, Castelvetro attributes the marvellous quality of this type of situation to its unexpectedness, ranking as most marvellous and hence most tragic those cases where a character tries to avoid the horrible deed. For 'we marvel greatly', he argues, 'when [the horrible deed] results from one that should normally have a different issue, and most of all when it results from one that was designed to lead to its opposite'.[28] Yet Castelvetro goes beyond Aristotle in that he seems to locate the wondrous effect of this situation in its moral incongruity, or in the discrepancy it involves between will and act – as exemplified by the case of Oedipus who having given 'the surest proof of his intention to avoid a deed of horror merits greater pity and inspires greater fear because of his strivings to remain guiltless'.[29] Thus, while Aristotle in *Poetics* 13 finds the spectacle of a morally perfect man falling into misfortune through no fault of his own shocking (*miaron*) rather than tragic, preferring the causally more plausible fall of someone of lesser stature who comes to grief because of an error (*hamartia*) (1452b35-8, 1453a7-11), Castelvetro believes that the greatest tragic effect is to be found in the fall of moral innocence. As he asks, 'who shall be pitied if not the saintly man who falls into misfortune?'[30]

This link between the marvellous and moral incongruity in the tragic response is less apparent in other Renaissance critics who, concerned with the task of accommodating Aristotle to the ideal of moral utility, express their preference for unexpected reversals that by conforming to the demand for causal plausibility are productive of a morally enhancing wonder. Thus Minturno writes that 'the business of the tragic poet is to put his reader into a condition of astonishment, and we consider those accidents astonishing that move us to compassion or horror, and yet the more when they come about with probability against our hopes and opinions'. Minturno here clearly follows Aristotle's insistence in *Poetics* 9 that those plots are most wondrous where the reversal comes as a causally probable surprise. Interestingly, however, he departs from Aristotle when he goes on to suggest that this causal probability resides in our impression that the accidents come about 'through the divine will or as the result of a plan'.[31] While Aristotle in his example of the Mitys statue may have had in mind divine intervention as the probable cause without making it explicit,[32] Minturno here explicitly makes a case for supernatural interference as the causally ordering factor. And his reason for doing so is his desire to make the tragic reversal not only astonishing but also morally acceptable in providential terms.

Another manifestation of the Renaissance concern with the morally enhancing reversal can be observed in the preference for reversals that are accompanied by an *anagnôrisis* – especially of the kind that Aristotle commends in his favourite play, *Iphigenia in Tauris*, where the recognition averts a tragic outcome by triggering an unexpected turn in the plot from misery to happiness. It is here notable that Renaissance commentators tend to differ from Aristotle in that they postulate for tragedies containing such reversals an effect markedly different from that of tragedies with an unhappy outcome. While Aristotle saw the *anagnôrisis*-induced aversion of the tragic outcome as a means of heightening the tragic emotions by means of wonder, on a par with regular tragedy, Renaissance commentators tended to view it as a means of making tragedy more pleasurable, because more morally satisfying, and hence also more profitable. This was especially true when the happy reversal came about quite unexpectedly, after the audience had been held in suspense about the final outcome, since it would then be experienced as more stunning. As Giraldi Cinthio, the most vocal spokesman for happy end tragedies, prescribes, 'the happenings in these less terrible tragedies should come about in such a way that the spectators are suspended between horror and compassion until the end, which should leave everyone consoled'. To justify this view, he refers to Aristotle, noting that 'In this kind of tragedy the recognition or, as we prefer to call it, the identification of persons is especially in place; through this identification those for whom we feel horror and compassion are taken from perils and from death.'[33]

Although Giraldi here leans on the authority of Aristotle, his main purpose was not to exalt Aristotle but to defend his own practice of writing happy end tragedies.[34] In this, he was not alone, as the Renaissance abounds in plays with tragedy-averting reversals, many of them achieved through stunning recognitions. In many cases, however, these plays are better classified as tragicomedies than as tragedies. Notable here are some of Shakespeare's latest plays, traditionally classified as either tragicomedies or as romances, especially *The Winter's Tale*, which has a whole series of wondrous recognitions that produce unexpected twists and turns in the plot, first from happiness to misery and then from misery to happiness – climaxing with the final scene where the statue of Leontes' supposedly dead wife, Hermione, comes alive and permits Leontes to enjoy his remaining days with her after many years of sorrow and penance for believing that he has caused her death through his delusions of jealousy. Not only is the shock effect of this scene truly stunning when experienced in the theatre, but it also illustrates Shakespeare's play on the greater power of drama over narrative in achieving wonder since the scene is dramatised, relying on the vividness of that which is shown and not merely told. It thus comes as a striking contrast to the moments of recognition in the preceding scene, which are narrated in language heavily loaded with exclamations of wonder but still falling short of the amazement effected by that which is seen and not just overheard.

To some extent, *The Winter's Tale* serves to illustrate not only how wonder is generated through striking changes in the plot but also how it can be aroused through inner changes of character – as highlighted in Leontes' dual metamorphosis of first falling into jealousy and then gradually being restored to a more rational self by undergoing a process of regeneration. The full effect of this kind of inner metamorphosis, however, is something Shakespeare explores more profoundly in his regular tragedies. While Aristotle in his notion of tragedy assumed relative stability of character, locating the tragic situation in the hero's external change of fortune from happiness to misery, or his *metabasis*, Shakespeare presents tragic situations in which the hero's tragedy is marked by an inner disintegration as a result of his suffering losses so severe that they totally upset his moral and mental being. The hero's *metabasis* is thus accompanied by his spiritual metamorphosis, often of a kind that turns him into his own opposite by causing him to move from a state of apparent perfection to a state of madness or bestiality. The result is a type of tragedy deeply disturbing in its effect, arousing a sense of wonder at the changeability and corruptibility of human character.

Interestingly, there seems to be an absence of critical commentary on tragedies of this kind. Here, evidently, we are faced with a type of poetic practice that owes more to tradition and creative innovation than to theory, the practice transcending the limits set by theoretical prescription. Unrestrained by such prescription, Shakespeare's use of tragic metamorphosis may owe more to the pattern set by Euripidean tragedy, and developed by Senecan tragedy, where characters under the pressure of external misfortune break down morally and psychologically.[35] But another source for the metamorphic pattern of Shakespeare's tragedies could be Ovid's *Metamorphoses*. As Jonathan Bate has argued, what happens literally in Ovid's tales of men turning into animals becomes in Shakespeare's tragedies 'metaphors for the internal changes effected by emotional and behavioural extremity'. Drawing on the Ovidian idea expressed in *Titus Andronicus* that 'extremity of griefs would make men mad' (IV.1.19), Bate argues that Shakespeare shows us heroes who under severe pressures of passion and desire are turned into moral if not physical beasts.[36] What makes this explanation appealing is that it makes it possible to see the wondrous quality of Shakespearean metamorphosis as deriving from the marvels associated with Ovidian metamorphosis. Exploiting the Ovidian art of metamorphic marvels, Shakespeare turns it into a subtle instrument for the presentation of human instability of character.

In this he has moved into a landscape of tragic wonder never envisioned by Aristotle. Yet, though Shakespeare may be transcending Aristotelian theory in the pattern of his tragedies, he may still owe something to Aristotle in his handling of this pattern. For in its effects, Shakespearean metamorphosis invites a wonder that coheres with Aristotle's conception of a wonder that not only intensifies the tragic emotions but that also stirs the desire to grasp causal connections in the apparently irrational. Watching the inner transformations that take place in his heroes, we are shocked into a feeling of wonder where perplexed amazement mingles with a desire to comprehend the deeper reasons for these transformations, to detect in them some pattern of causal coherence and meaning. It is part of Shakespeare's mastery of the effect of wonder that it is a desire that while it illuminates also frustrates, stirring us into further wondering.

Othello, one of Shakespeare's most wonder-arousing tragedies, may serve as example. When in Act IV Othello, poisoned by jealousy and losing command over himself, strikes Desdemona in public, Lodovico, a Venetian nobleman, responds with amazed disbelief, asking

> Is this the noble Moor, whom our full senate
> Call all in all sufficient? Is this the nature
> Whom passion could not shake? Whose solid virtue
> The shot of accident nor dart of chance
> Could neither graze nor pierce?
>
> (IV.1.255-9)

What causes Lodovico's stunned response is first of all the magnitude of Othello's change, the awareness of the difference between what he was, a man renowned for his noble self-command, and what he has become, a man totally in the grip of uncontrolled passion. It is a response we, as spectators, are invited to share, although as witnesses to the whole play, we are privileged with a deeper understanding of the causal pattern of Othello's disintegration and hence better able to experience an intellectually illuminating wonder.

Kirsti Minsaas

A similar play on wonder occurs in Shakespeare's *Timon of Athens*,
where the metamorphosis of Timon from near-divine philanthrope to
misanthrope stirs his servant Flavius into an exclamation of wonder –
aptly taking the rhetorical form of the *thaumasmus* (or *admiratio*) –
when he discovers his former master living the life of a wild animal:

> O you gods!
> Is yond despis'd and ruinous man my lord?
> Full of decay and failing? O monument
> And wonder of good deeds evilly bestow'd!

> (IV.3.461-4)

The wonder Flavius expresses here is not just that of questioning
disbelief at witnessing the transformation effected in Timon; it also
involves a feeling of amazement stemming from the paradox that what
has led to his ruin, both financially and spiritually, is his own goodness.
Again, we as spectators are invited to share this response, although
treated to the whole play we are also in a position to resolve the
paradoxical nature of Timon's metamorphosis – to see it as at once
strange and causally coherent.

As indicated by these two plays, Shakespeare's tragedies forge a close
link between tragic metamorphosis and Aristotelian wonder – a wonder
that as exploited by Shakespeare takes us into an ever-deepening
inquiry into the causal nature and meaning of the metamorphic
changes that we witness. When Shakespeare's tragedies rank as perhaps the highest achievement in the genre, this is in no mean degree
the product of his mastery of the poetics of wonder. In his hands,
wonder becomes a sophisticated instrument for the exploration of
tragic experience, transcending the Renaissance tendency to see in
wonder either a cognitively empty sensationalism or a cognitively sim-
plified didacticism.

The Renaissance concern with wonder was, however, not restricted
to tragedy. Although wonder was regarded as essential to the affective
appeal of tragedy, it also came to be seen as a feeling that could work
its effect severed from the tragic context, serving a distinctive function
in other types of poetry. Again, however, the general tendency was to
link wonder to moral instruction, to see it as a means to the production
of both profit and delight. According to Torquato Tasso, for example,
comedy could be made more effective by producing a wonder that helped
reinforce the laughter it evoked, 'baseness alone without wonder being
insufficient to make us laugh at things that seem ugly'.[37] Although some
theorists, most notably Jacopo Mazzoni and Giangiorgio Trissino, saw
the marvellous and the laughable as antithetical, the first involving the
ridiculous and undignified, the second the noble and admirable, others

160

believed that the two could be combined in a profitable manner.[38] Thus Antonio Riccoboni, the first critic to attempt a systematic codification of comedy, viewed the marvellous as essential to the purgative effect of a comic work, arguing that, as Weinberg phrases it, 'through our marvelling at some ridiculous deception, we are purged of that same kind of deception' while 'our marvelling at wickedness teaches us not to fall into similar forms of wickedness'.[39] The most important generic vehicle for a morally instructive wonder, however, was the heroic epic.

Renaissance theories on wonder in epic

In his brief discussion of epic in the *Poetics*, Aristotle does not reserve any distinctive function for epic but treats it as essentially similar to tragedy, viewing both genres as imitations of 'elevated matters' (1449b9-10). Where epic differs from tragedy, Aristotle holds, is mainly in its 'length of plot-structure and its metre' (1459b17) and in being 'in the narrative mode' (1449b11). This generic identification of epic and tragedy started to fall apart in the Renaissance, as theorists under the pressure of changing modes in epic as well as romance composition began to formulate new theories of the meaning and function of epic poetry. Although these formulations usually took their point of departure in Aristotle, leaning on Aristotle's authority, they soon evolved into independent attempts to define and codify the epic genre in non-Aristotelian terms.[40]

Of major importance in this reorientation in epic theory was the central place given to wonder. Whereas wonder in both tragedy and comedy was usually seen as an incidental effect, subordinate to other emotional effects, wonder in epic was often regarded as the major element in the affective appeal of a work, working its effect severed from other emotions. Thus Torquato Tasso, the chief expounder of epic theory in sixteenth-century Italy, believed that although wonder was involved in all the genres, it was only in epic that it had a distinctive function. As he explains, 'other kinds of poem move wonder in order to move laughter or compassion or some other emotion. But the epic poet … moves compassion in order to move wonder, and in fact moves much more powerfully and more often.'[41]

To some extent, the Renaissance exaltation of wonder in epic poetry drew on Aristotle's statement in *Poetics* 24 that there was greater scope for the marvellous in epic than in tragedy. Thus, in a clear echo of Aristotle, Tasso writes, 'We gladly read in epic about wonders that might be unsuitable on stage, both because they are proper to epic and because the reader allows many liberties which the spectator forbids.'[42] Yet Renaissance critics often went far beyond Aristotle in permitting the inclusion of objects and events that were not merely *alogon* but pure invention, beyond all possibility, involving such things as Chimeras and Cyclops, fairies and sorcerers, men that change into stones or bushes, and ships that turn into nymphs. A major reason for this greater permissiveness was the frequent use of such fantastic inventions not only in the popular romances of the day but also in a classic epic like Virgil's *Aeneid* as well as, though more controversially, in Ariosto's *Orlando Furioso*, where they offered what many saw as sweet and enchanting delights, necessary for the work's overall appeal.

This enlarged scope for the fantastic does not mean, however, that there were not critical voices. Thus Castelvetro speaks contemptuously of poets that achieve their effects by means of obvious impossibilities, since 'they did not come to the more marvellous and the more moving by the gate of verisimilitude, the way of the poet and the true imitator, but by the gate of incredibility, the way of the fool and the ignorant mass of men'. Castelvetro even went so far as to criticise Aristotle for permitting such an improbable incident as the pursuit of Hector in the *Iliad*.[43] Committed to an ideal that required the wondrous and the verisimilar to be properly balanced, he insisted upon a poetic art where the marvellous material was kept firmly within the bounds of credibility, permitting no excursion into the realm of the fabulous. Yet others, showing a more liberal bent than Castelvetro, were willing to accept the inclusion of events that, even if impossible in naturalistic terms, were made rationally meaningful in allegorical terms – as demonstrated by the allegorising tendencies of both Tasso's *Gerusalemme Liberata* and Edmund Spenser's *The Faerie Queene*. Thus, incidents that clearly exceeded natural explanations were deemed acceptable if they could be shown to be the working of supernatural powers and hence causally explicable as miracles – a solution suggested by Tasso when he writes that

> The poet ought to attribute actions that far exceed human power to God, to his angels, to demons, or to those granted power by God or by demons, for example, saints, wizards, and fairies. Such actions, if considered in themselves, will seem marvellous; nay, they are commonly called miracles. But if regarded in terms of their agent's efficacy and power, they will seem verisimilar.[44]

Although this was a solution that accorded with Aristotle's demand for plausible surprises in *Poetics* 9, it clearly contradicted his rejection in *Poetics* 15 of the use of a *deus ex machina* to bring about the denouement. When Italian epic theorists nevertheless chose to ignore Aristotle on this point, it was largely because of the impact of Christian thought, which made them receptive to supernatural explanations – at least when consistent with Christian doctrine. Tasso, in particular, whose aim with *Gerusalemme Liberata* was to write a Christian epic, insisted on the need to include only miracles that were explicable in Christian terms rather than pagan terms, arguing that 'since natural powers cannot effect such miracles, we must resort to supernatural power; and when we resort to the gods of the Gentiles, verisimilitude ends because what our people deem not only false but impossible cannot be verisimilar to them'.[45] Within this Christian parochialism, however, there was a general readiness among Renaissance theorists to liven up epic poetry with marvels that in their inventiveness far transcend anything Aristotle envisioned in the *Poetics*.

In addition to widening epic's scope for the marvellous towards the fantastic, Renaissance theorists also expanded its wondrous range towards the ideal.[46] Drawing on such classic examples as Xenophon's *Cyropaedia* and Virgil's *Aeneid*, they developed a conception of the epic poem as a specifically heroic genre, involving, in Tasso's words, 'an imitation of a noble action, great and perfect, narrated in the loftiest verse, with the purpose of moving the mind to wonder and thus being useful'.[47] Thus, instead of the illustrious but mediocre hero of Aristotelian tragedy and epic, Renaissance epic theory exalted the exemplary hero, commending tales in which the hero's magnificent deeds served to illustrate perfected virtue in ways both pleasant and morally instructive.

At the base of the Renaissance conception of the epic as the projection of idealised or perfected virtue lie the practical concerns of some of its theorists. Notably, the two most prominent sixteenth-century advocates of the heroic poem, Philip Sidney in England and Torquato Tasso in Italy, were themselves practising poets, writing their treatises not only to defend established practice but also to seek a theoretical foundation for their own attempts at heroic composition, Sidney in his revised version of the *Arcadia* and Tasso in *Gerusalemme Liberata*. There was thus an intimate connection between epic theory and epic practice, theory building on practice but also influencing practice.

A further explanation for this preoccupation with heroic idealisation, however, must be sought in philosophical doctrine. As Baxter Hathaway has argued, a number of Renaissance critics, including Tasso and Sidney, tended to interpret Aristotle's contention in *Poetics* 9 that poetry is more universal and hence more philosophical than history in Platonic terms, converting Aristotle's statement that 'the poet's task is to speak not of events that have occurred, but of the kind of events which *could* occur, and are possible by the standards of probability or necessity' (1451a36-9) into the doctrine that the poet's task is to present things as they *should* be or *ought* to be according to some preset moral norm.[48] Although this is a line of interpretation that has some foundation in Aristotle's suggestion in Chapter 25 that the good poet, like the good portrait painter, should improve on the model set before him by painting him 'better' than he actually is (1461b12-13), its main root is first of all the Renaissance tendency to interpret Aristotle's claim for the universal nature of poetry by reference to Platonic ideal forms rather than to considerations of probability or necessity. While Aristotle viewed the poetic universal as a generalised likelihood, or 'the kinds of things which it suits a certain kind of person to say or do in terms of probability or necessity' (1451b8-9), Renaissance theorists, under the influence of Platonic and Neoplatonic thought, tended to see it as an idealised abstraction, embracing the view that poetry is a heightened representation of what should be done rather than what might plausibly be done. This Platonic colouration of Aristotle was quite common among Italian commentators, but it can also be observed in Sidney's formulation that the best kind of poets are those who borrow 'nothing of what is, hath been, or shall be; but range, only reined with learned discretion, into the divine consideration of what may be and should be'.[49] For Sidney, as for the Italians, the superiority of the poet over the historian arose not just from the fact that he could present a world of universal probabilities but also from the fact that he, by the effort of his inventive faculties, could improve on nature, delivering a 'golden' world that far surpasses the 'brazen' world of actual reality.[50]

This emphasis on idealised representation of human conduct was closely linked to the exaltation of the poet as moral teacher. A commonly held view was that the poet was superior to the philosopher in teaching morality, since the philosopher taught merely by precept, the poet by example. As was frequently repeated, mere knowledge of the good – in the form of abstract philosophical doctrine – was not enough to do good. To do good, to translate knowledge into *praxis*, one had to be filled with a love for virtue that could stimulate one's desire to act virtuously. And the best way of inspiring such love was by means of heroic poetry, which by holding up images of exemplary virtue, or what Sidney called a 'perfect picture',[51] could excite in the reader the wish to emulate such virtue and thus attain it in his own life.

To fulfil this aim, however, the exemplary portrait had to be infused with an element of the marvellous and its attendant delights. For this reason, the representation of mediocre or ordinary virtue would not do. Preferably, the hero should be someone of extraordinary stature, or someone who in virtue and courage surpassed the merely normal. Thus, while Aristotle in *Poetics* 13 had argued for a protagonist of middling morality, denying the tragic (and epic) hero the status not only of utter wickedness but also of total perfection, Renaissance theorists developed a peculiar fascination with moral extremes, especially in the form of exceptional virtue. And a major reason for this was that they saw perfected virtue as a special source of wonder, gratifying in itself because of the impression of sublime grandeur it could convey. When Tasso in his definition of the heroic epic singled out wonder as distinctive only to this genre, it was mainly because of its power to bring before the reader's eyes wondrous images of beauty and magnificence. Although conceding that wonder could arise both from 'the laughable' and from 'the graceful', or 'from beautiful' as well as from 'ugly things', he thought that it was 'not equally proper to both', since 'our wonder at ugly things soon disappear as they along with their novelty lose our esteem, while our wonder at the beautiful is more lasting and entails greater esteem. And since the heroic poem is the most beautiful of all kinds, this delight is its very own. It is further its own because the heroic poem is the most magnificent as well.'[52]

As Tasso's words indicate, a special reason for the wondrous quality of the heroic poem is that the wonder it arouses is tinged with admiration, in the combined sense of amazement and reverent esteem. Although in the Renaissance admiration usually was used interchangeably with wonder, the act of admiring being the same as marvelling at or wondering about something, it also began to assume today's more familiar meaning of holding something in high regard. This duality of meaning – of minor importance in our response to tragedy but vital to the epic response – is suggested in an early definition of admiration as 'wonder mingled with reverence, esteem, approbation' (*OED* 2.a). This particular meaning began to be registered precisely at this time, and it is frequently found in Renaissance poetic texts, especially in connection with descriptions of virtue. Sidney, for example, in his revised *Arcadia*, makes an interesting distinction between 'the virtues that get admiration, as depth of wisdom, height of courage and largeness of magnificence' and 'those which stir affection, as truth of word, meekness, courtesy, mercifulness, and liberality'.[53] To admire or marvel at the heroic is consequently not just a question of being astonished by the unexpected or unusual but of being hit by a feeling of awed reverence when witnessing spectacles of moral grace and grandeur – a feeling that in time also came to involve an aesthetic element of 'pleased and gratified contemplation' (*OED* 2.a).

But for a heroic portrait to arouse such admiring wonder in a morally efficacious way, conducive to the desired end of inspiring virtue, it also had (like the fabulous inventions) to be restrained by verisimilitude. The representation of heroic exploits that were merely fantastic rather than 'icastic' (probable) was usually – if not always – rejected for being too far-fetched to have any utilitarian value. To effectively move the reader to virtue, the heroic representation had to strike the right balance between the incredible and the credible – in accordance with Aristotelian prescription. In part, such balance could be achieved by moderating the heroic subject matter. Thus, as argued by critics like Orazio Lombardelli and Paolo Beni, instead of telling fables about heroes performing superhuman deeds, such as the slaying of dragons or fighting whole armies single-handedly so typical of the romance tradition, the epic poet could make his heroes more believable by restricting himself to a mere heightening of desirable moral traits. In this way he remained sufficiently close to human normality to permit reader identification and hence reader emulation.[54]

The right balance between the heroic wondrous and the heroic verisimilar was, however, not merely a question of moderating the subject matter; it was also a question of stylistic manipulation. Of special importance here was the poet's skills in giving the heroic material the appearance of truth by means of vivid elaborations – as suggested by Tasso when he notes that it is not enough for the poet to persuade the readers 'that the things he has written is true. He must also suggest them to their senses in such a way that they do not believe that they are reading but, rather, that they are present and they see and hear them.'[55] Tasso is here invoking the rhetorical quality of *enargeia* so important in Renaissance stylistics, or the ability to depict a scene with a sensuous immediacy that would enable the reader to envision the events as if they were taking place before his very eyes. Not only did such *enargeia* heighten the impression of verisimilitude, but it would simultaneously heighten the effect of wonder, making the heroic representation more striking emotionally and hence more moving morally. According to Sidney, the reason for the poet's superiority over the philosopher as a moral teacher was precisely his opportunity to paint an image of virtue with such vivid colours that it would, as he put it, 'strike, pierce' and 'possess the sight of the soul'.[56] Although Sidney does not here mention the term wonder, his choice of words captures the emotional impact generally associated with wonder – a wonder achieving its striking effect from the visual force of the virtuous image.

In addition to relying on the visual vividness of his representation, the poet could also enhance the wondrous impact of his heroic projections by structural means, especially through his ability to invent unexpected turns in the plot. In this regard, both epic and romance offered, because of their greater magnitude, more opportunities for startling twists in the plot than did tragedy, giving the poets ample scope for going both from happiness to misery and from misery to happiness in the course of one work. Tasso even claimed that a double reversal where 'some characters pass from prosperity to adversity and others the reverse'[57] was distinctive to the heroic poem. As in tragedy, however, there was a special fondness for reversals combined with an *anagnôrisis*, especially when it prevents an unhappy outcome. Yet it is difficult to trace any serious concern with the deeper cognitive or philosophical values of such structurally induced wonders peculiar to the epic and its larger generic aim. Generally, the emphasis seems to be on the pleasures they produce, both through the intrinsic delightfulness of such unexpected happy turns and through the admiration they excite for the poet's artistic skill and ingenuity in inventing them.[58] For a more profound type of wonder in heroic poetry, we must go to methods of representation designed to enhance and beautify but also to complicate the impact of the heroic image.

Of special note here is the use of sudden changes in moral character from apparent bad to good, with virtue appearing unexpectedly and so astonishingly in someone whose character at first is thought to be lacking in virtue. As in the case of tragic metamorphosis, it is hard to find any theoretical reference to this more positive type of metamorphosis. But it can be observed in poetic practice, most notably in Shakespeare's *Henry V*, where the young and apparently undisciplined prince Hal is suddenly metamorphosed into the virtuous king Henry, eliciting these eulogising comments from the Archbishop of Canterbury:

> Hear him but reason in divinity,
> And, all-admiring, with an inward wish
> You would desire the king were made a prelate.
> ... when he speaks,
> The air, a charter'd libertine, is still,
> And the mute wonder lurketh in men's ears,
> To steal his sweet and honey'd sentences;
> So that the art and practic part of life
> Must be the mistress to his theoric:
> Which is a wonder how his grace should glean it,
> Since his addiction was to courses vain;   (I.1.38-54)

The interesting thing about this speech is that the wonder induced by Henry's moral change is not merely a literary device directed at the audience; it is also a device exploited by Henry himself in his heroic self-projection, constituting a response he deliberately aims at as part of his princely strategy – as suggested by Canterbury's later comment 'And so the prince obscur'd his contemplation / Under the veil of wildness' (I.1.63-4). The Archbishop is here obviously referring to the courtier practice of *sprezzatura*, or the habit of hiding one's efforts under an appearance of ease and effortlessness. But Henry's sudden change can also be seen to reflect the strategic appeal to wonder through self-projecting devices that, according to T.G. Bishop, was quite common in Renaissance power-politics. As Bishop writes,

> The emotional energies of wonder were particularly trained on the recurrent Renaissance preoccupation with the figure of the hero, both in life and art. It was especially here that power-politics sought to co-opt wonder and to mobilise its intimations of force to practical ends. By staging the ruler, whether Prince, Emperor, or Pope, as a being utterly outside of common experience, endowed beyond the range of the ordinary yet prepared to condescend, the magicians of Renaissance diplomacy invested their masters with an aura of untouchability and transcendence.[59]

Shakespeare thus exploits for dramatic effect what was a political ploy to induce admiration – a ploy that in its turn may owe its method to the art of epic and dramatic poetry. In the figure of Henry, he has created a hero who in his theatrical self-presentation knows how to exploit poetic wonder for political aggrandisement, thus turning him into an object of wonder not just for the audience watching the play but also for the audience that occupies the world of the play. In so doing, however, Shakespeare also invests his hero with an element of ambiguity that complicates our response to his heroic stature.

Another example of such ambiguously coloured self-projection can be observed in Christopher Marlowe's presentation of Tamburlaine in his epic play *Tamburlaine the Great*. Like Shakespeare's hero, Tamburlaine (described in the play as a 'wondrous man') arouses in other characters in the play world feelings of astonished wonder and admiration, but of a more terrifying kind, generated by the cruelty but also apparent invincibility of his military exploits as well as the superhuman quality of his personal demeanour. Precisely in its excess, however, his is a heroic self-projection that makes the theatrical audience alert to its ambiguous nature, bringing them to a recognition of the thin dividing line between the divine and the monstrous in the classical warrior ideal.

In the cases of both Henry and Tamburlaine, then, admiration in the dual sense of reverent regard and pleased amazement is destabilised by doubt. Instead of arousing a wonder that thrills and excites, commanding cognitive assent, the heroes arouse a wonder that, fed by a sense of cognitive uncertainty, invites questioning and moral resistance. As a result, they excite a type of wondrous response that, although far removed from Aristotle's notion of wonder as a reinforcing element of tragic catharsis, returns us to the Aristotelian emphasis on wonder as an incentive to thought and learning.

Notes

1. See Bernard Weinberg, *A History of Literary Criticism in the Italian Renaissance*, 2 vols. (Chicago, 1961), I, 625.

2. Quoted in Weinberg, II, 783.

3. Daniel Javitch, 'The assimilation of Aristotle's *Poetics* in sixteenth-century Italy', in *Cambridge History of Literary Criticism*, vol. 3: *The Renaissance*, ed. Glyn P. Norton (Cambridge, 1999), 58-9.

4. On this point, see Stephen Halliwell, *Aristotle's Poetics* (London and Chapel Hill, NC, 1986), ch. 6, esp. 74-7.

5. I use John Henry Freese's translation of the *Rhetoric* in the Loeb Classical Library series (London and Cambridge, MA, 1994).

6. Unless otherwise noted, I use Stephen Halliwell's translation of the *Poetics* in *The Poetics of Aristotle* (London, 1987).

7. The translation I use here and in the next citation is that of Hippocrates G. Apostle, Elizabeth A. Dobbs, and Morris A. Parslow (Grinnell, IA, 1990).

8. T.G. Bishop, in *Shakespeare and the Theatre of Wonder* (Cambridge, 1996), 30-1, usefully points out the difference between the two terms by reference to their etymological roots, noting that while *thauma* 'seems to involve spectacle', pointing to an 'object or event which is gazed upon by a beholder, 'the thrust of *ekplexis* ... is of a blow, an act of violence'.

9. D.W. Lucas, *Aristotle: Poetics* (Oxford, 1968), 172.

10. I use Arthur S. Way's translation in the Loeb Classical Library series (London, 1916). Elizabeth Belfiore discusses the same point in 'Aristotle and Iphigenia', in *Essays on Aristotle's Poetics*, ed. Amélie Oksenberg Rorty (Princeton, 1992), 372.

11. See Baxter Hathaway, *Marvels and Commonplaces: Renaissance Literary Criticism* (New York, 1968), ch. 2.

12. Torquato Tasso, *Discourses on the Heroic Poem* (1594), trans. Mariella Cavalchini and Irene Samuel (Oxford, 1973), 15.

13. Lodovico Castelvetro, *Poetica d'Aristotele* (1570, 1576), trans. Andrew Bongiorno, in his *Castelvetro on the Art of Poetry* (Binghamton, NY, 1984), 110.

14. Sir Philip Sidney, *The Countess of Pembroke's Arcadia*, ed. Maurice Evans (Harmondsworth, 1977), 528.

15. On wonder and the complex plot in Robortello, see Terence Cave, *Recognitions: A Study in Poetics* (Oxford, 1990), 58.

16. Sir Philip Sidney, *An Apology for Poetry*, ed. Geoffrey Shepherd (Manchester, 1973), 118/1f.

17. For a study of the role of wonder in Shakespeare's tragedies, see J.V. Cunningham, *Woe or Wonder: The Emotional Effect of Shakespearean Tragedy* (Chicago, 1951).

18. The same combination is also found in John Dryden (1684), who quotes Aristotle as saying that the end of tragedy is 'to beget admiration, compassion, or concernment'. See James T. Boulton (ed.), *Dryden: Of Dramatick Poesie* (London, 1964), 65.

19. *Poetica d'Aristotele*, in Bongiorno, 254.

20. *Poetica d'Aristotele*, in Bongiorno, 113-14.

21. *Apology*, 103/30.

22. Quoted in Weinberg, I, 317.

23. Antonio Minturno, *L'Arte Poetica* (1564), in Allan H. Gilbert, *Literary Criticism: Plato to Dryden* (New York, 1940), 289.

24. For interpretations of catharsis as a mode of learning that take into account the joint operation of cognition and emotion, see Stephen Halliwell, *Aristotle's Poetics*, ch. 6, esp. 194-201, and Martha C. Nussbaum, 'Tragedy and self-sufficiency,' in Rorty, 280-3.

25. Giovambattista Giraldi Cinthio, *On the Composition of Comedies and Tragedies* (1543), in Gilbert, 255.

26. *Apology*, 118/1 note.

27. *Apology*, 118/7ff.

28. See *Poetica d'Aristotele*, in Bongiorno, 110-12.

29. *Poetica d'Aristotele*, in Bongiorno, 112.

30. *Poetica d'Aristotele*, in Bongiorno, 162.

31. *L'Arte Poetica*, in Gilbert, 292.

32. On problems relating to this point, see Stephen Halliwell, *The Poetics of Aristotle*, 111-12, 174-6.

33. *On the Composition of Comedies and Tragedies*, in Gilbert, 255-6.

34. The point has been noted by Daniel Javitch in 'The assimilation of Aristotle's *Poetics* in sixteenth-century Italy', in Norton, 62-4.

35. Martha C. Nussbaum has dubbed this type of tragic fall 'the tragedy of eroded character', holding up Euripides' *Hecuba* as the paradigm. See 'Tragedy and self-sufficiency,' in Rorty, 284.

36. Jonathan Bate, *Shakespeare and Ovid* (Oxford, 1993), 181.

37. *Discourses on the Heroic Poem*, 15.

38. On the marvellous in comedy, see Hathaway, *Marvels and Commonplaces*, 72, 164.

39. Weinberg, I, 587.

40. On the development of epic theory in the Renaissance, see Daniel Javitch, 'Italian epic theory', in Norton, 205-15.

41. See *Discourses on the Heroic Poem*, 17, 172-3.

42. *Discourses on the Heroic Poem*, 16-17.

43. See *Poetica d'Aristotele*, in Bongiorno, 288-9.

44. *Discourses on the Heroic Poem*, 38.

45. Torquato Tasso, *Discourses on the Art of Poetry* (1587), trans. Lawrence F. Rhu, in his *The Genesis of Tasso's Narrative Theory* (Detroit, 1993), 102.

46. On the concern with idealisation in Renaissance epic theory, see Baxter Hathaway, *The Age of Criticism: The Late Renaissance in Italy* (Ithaca, NY, 1962), chs. 8 and 9, and *Marvels and Commonplaces*, ch. 3.

47. *Discourses on the Heroic Poem*, 17.

48. See Hathaway, *The Age of Criticism*, 138-43, and *Marvels and Commonplaces*, 88-97.

49. *Apology*, 102/35ff.

50. See *Apology*, 100/21ff.

51. *Apology*, 107/10f.

52. *Discourses on the Heroic Poem*, 172-3.

53. *The Countess of Pembroke's Arcadia*, 76.

54. See Hathaway, *Marvels and Commonplaces*, 125-8.

55. *Discourses on the Art of Poetry*, in Rhu, 101.

56. *Apology,* 107/15f.

57. *Discourses on the Art of Poetry,* in Rhu, 17-18.

58. On wonder as pleasure in the poet's artistic skills, see Hathaway, *Marvels and Commonplaces,* 154-66, and Cave, *Recognitions,* 58-9.

59. *Shakespeare and the Theatre of Wonder,* 37.

Aristotle, Rapin, Brecht

M.S. Silk

'Aristotle, Rapin, Brecht.' Such schemata have a familiar sound: 'Western representational art, from Giotto to Matisse'; 'the jazz trumpet, from Joe Oliver to Wynton Marsalis'. But 'Aristotle to Brecht' is different, different in kind. In the jazz schema, there is no improbable implication that Marsalis specifically looks back to King Oliver, nor, in the art schema, that Matisse specifically looks back to Giotto – that the link is immediate or immanent. Yet in the field of theorisings of tragedy and other serious drama, the improbable is the fact. Here Aristotle is both the acknowledged beginning *and* the common point of reference – for the Marxist Bertolt Brecht in the twentieth century, as for the Jesuit René Rapin in the seventeenth, as indeed for virtually all theorists from the Renaissance to our own time.

In their reference back to Aristotle, such different theorists reinterpret Aristotle's theory and, inevitably, reinterpret it differently. Yet here too there is a common feature, and a remarkable one: the reinterpretations of Aristotle's theory tend to invest it with more coherence than it would seem, in itself, to possess.

If I say that Aristotle's theory of tragedy lacks coherence, I mean relatively to other theories: say, Hegel's. I do not mean that Aristotle's theory, nor even its incoherences, is (are) decreative: one could indeed argue that the peculiar power and productiveness of the *Poetics* is apparent from, or even implicit in, the very range of its readings. Nor do I mean that Aristotle's theory is predominantly incoherent; nor that it is necessarily untenable in any one of its unrelated aspects; nor that, when incoherent, it is self-contradictory – even if there are, indeed, a few well-known contradictions of a limited kind, like the 'curious fact that the best kind of scene cannot be got into the best kind of play'.[1] The point, however, is not that Aristotle's treatise is fragmentary (though no doubt it is).[2] Nor that, within the scope of his theory in the *Poetics*, there are gaps, in the sense of taboo subjects, though of course there are: notably the connection of Attic tragedy with the polis and its rituals;[3] and the role of lyric poetry within Greek tragedy;[4] and, above all, the metaphysics of the tragic genre – the omni-relevance or omni-immanence of gods and the divine – which is so completely elided that a

173

reader of the *Poetics* who knew nothing else of Greek drama would hardly suspect the existence, let alone the importance, of this dimension.[5]

The grounds for ascribing incoherence to Aristotle's theory are quite different. First, there are important aspects of the theory whose relationship to the whole – variously explicable as it may be – is left unexplained. Secondly, the theory as a whole embodies significant tensions or ambivalences which are never resolved.

The most obvious example of an unexplained connection is the relation of Aristotle's *katharsis* to 'pity and fear' and indeed to his theory overall. The single most remarkable thing about *katharsis*, no doubt, is that it should be part of the formal definition of tragedy in *Poetics* VI – and then be dropped. It is no answer to say that the Aristotle of *Politics* VIII, who expounds a version of *katharsis*, cross-refers to the *Poetics* as part of his exposition (that famous cross-reference famously raises its own intractable questions),[6] nor that 'the answer' was in the second Book of the *Poetics* (which was not even, apparently, centred on tragedy).[7] Heretical question: as far as Aristotle's tragic theory – the theory as a whole – is concerned, does it actually matter quite what *katharsis* is? If it wasn't for its place in the famous definition, would we miss it? The variety of interpretations of *katharsis* offered over the centuries[8] is testimony, perhaps, to a conviction, or prejudice, that there must be, or must have been, a coherent answer. That is the kind of conviction or prejudice (I suggest) that animates not only Aristotle's scholarly interpreters, but also those many post-Aristotelian theorists for whom Aristotle is the first point of reference.

Under the heading of unresolved tensions, the prime example (I would suppose) is the tension, which I have discussed elsewhere, between theory and compositional handbook, visible in the very first sentence of *Poetics* I (1447a8 ff.),

peri poiêtikês autês te kai tôn eidôn autês, hên tina dunamin hekaston ekhei, kai pôs dei sunhistasthai tous muthous ei mellei kalôs hexein hê poiêsis

Our concern is the art of poetry and its kinds <and specifically> (a) what potential each kind has, (b) how plots should be structured if a composition is to work properly[9]

and visible again, for instance, in the list of tragedy's six 'elements' (*merê*) in *Poetics* VI, where some of the six are apparently compositional products (like *muthos*, 'plot' or dramatic 'structure') and at least one is transparently the compositional process (*melopoiia*: 'song-*writing*').[10]

Other loose ends we might point to, under one or other heading,

174

include an intriguing oscillation between a *contextual* and a *textual* identification of tragedy.[11] Contextually, everything called, and performed as, *tragôidia* is equally a tragedy: some such works have (for instance) unhappy endings, some don't (etc.). Textually, some kinds of tragedy, by virtue of their properties (e.g. their unhappy endings), are, it seems, more tragic than others – and one playwright, Euripides, by virtue of his practices (specifically, his penchant for such endings), is even the *most* tragic (*tragikôtatos*).[12] Over the *Poetics* as a whole, the contextual identification clearly predominates – but then that predominance, in turn, engenders new incoherences, because Aristotle, notoriously, is prepared to downplay and marginalise performative context in *other* connections: from *Poetics* XIV, in particular, we learn that the *muthos* should be so structured that even without performance it should convey its tragic effect (1453b3-6).

Rather differently, there is some intriguing shiftiness at the heart of Aristotle's technical vocabulary. What is the goal, the *telos*, of tragedy? In *Poetics* VI (1450a22-3) it is the 'events' and the 'plot' (*ta pragmata kai ho muthos telos tês tragôidias*); in XXV (1460b23ff.), however, the *telos* of poetry in general, and therefore necessarily of tragedy in particular, seems to be its emotional effect:

> *adunata pepoiêtai, hêmartêtai: all' orthôs ekhei, ei tunkhanei tou telous tou hautês (to gar telos eirêtai), ei houtôs ekplêktikôteron ê auto ê allo poiei meros.*

Suppose a composition contains impossibilities: that is a fault. Nevertheless, it is acceptable, provided that <thereby> the work achieves its goal (which has been stated) – i.e. if thereby this or some other part of the work is made more exciting.[13]

And, again, what of the *muthos*, the 'plot', itself? The *muthos* is the first and foremost of the six *merê* of tragedy – but what actually does *muthos* mean? According to the formal definition of the word, in *Poetics* VI, the *muthos* is the organisation of events (*sunthesis tôn pragmatôn*: 1450a4), or the structure, or structuring, of the events (*sustasis tôn pragmatôn*: 1450a15). In ordinary Greek the word *muthos* means 'story', including the famous stories we call 'myths'. According to Aristotle's definition, the *muthos* is what we would tend to see as a *formal* entity, or else – more accurately, perhaps – an entity intermediate between content and form (to use the vulgar, but almost inescapable, distinction).[14] The ordinary meaning of the word, on the other hand, is much closer to *content*: *muthos* (in the ordinary sense) is what (in the ordinary sense) the play is about, its material, the object (in the ordinary sense) of the playwright's mimetic activity, whereas in Aristotle's special sense *muthos* is the way the playwright organises or reorganises that material. And yet the *muthos* is also one of the three *merê* which are, seemingly, described as objects of *mimêsis* (*ha mimountai*: VI, 1450a9-12), which surely brings *muthos* close to 'content'. So indeed does the association of *ho muthos* with *ta pragmata* – the 'plot' with the 'events' – at 1450a22 (discussed in the previous paragraph).[15] In VI at 1450a4 the *muthos* is 'the *mimêsis* of the action' (*tês praxeôs hê mimêsis*); seven lines later, at 1450a11, it is the object of that same *mimêsis* (*ha mimountai*). This ambivalence, certainly, is never resolved.[16]

For any one, or even for all, of these loose ends, an interpreter may have 'an answer': perhaps the 'answer' of privileging one passage and playing down another; perhaps the 'answer' of reconciling passages by reference to some other passage or some other element of Aristotelian thinking beyond the *Poetics*, or in a (supposed) lost part of the *Poetics*. Any or all of these 'answers' may in a given sense be Aristotelian: it does not follow that any (let alone all) should be called Aristotle's.[17]

Aristotle's theory (indeed, his treatise as a whole), nevertheless, enjoys the reputation of a coherent argument, and not merely a series of brilliant, but loosely connected, *aperçus*. What is responsible for this? The answer, I suggest, is not the findings of Aristotle's scholarly interpreters (whose very public disagreements about this, that and the other point of doctrine tell their own story), but rather the constructive – or constructional – use made of Aristotle in post-Aristotelian theories of tragedy (and/or other serious drama), for which Aristotle's theory of tragedy is a given, and for which it is characteristically constructed as a *coherent* given. Of these theories I wish to look at two: the theories of Rapin (briefly) and (in more detail) Brecht.[18]

Rapin's treatise, *Réflexions sur la Poétique d'Aristote*, was published in 1674 and in the same year translated into English by Thomas Rymer (whose translations I quote, in the 1694 revised version).[19] Rapin's status as critic at this time can be gauged from the fact that within twenty years of his death (in 1687) his complete criticism had been translated into English (in 1706) – and likewise from a tribute by his great English contemporary, John Dryden, that 'were all the other critics lost', Rapin, on his own, would be 'sufficient to teach anew the rules of writing'.[20]

Among much else, Rapin's 'reflections' presuppose: intensive scholarly study of the *Poetics* for the best part of 200 years (along with other critical works from antiquity, most notably Horace's *Ars Poetica*); likewise, a climate which Michael Moriarty has characterised with the phrase 'taste and ideology'[21] (with much of the taste, and the ideology too, articulated as conflicts or mediations between Greco-Roman norms and modern practices); and certain specific developments in the general understanding of 'tragedy' over the centuries. These developments include identification of, and emphasis on, the 'tragic hero', along with a tendency to locate the basis of tragic drama not in structure, but in story (*fabula*) – with which, indeed, Aristotle's *muthos* is now generally equated, so that *muthos* in effect reverts to the meaning the word had before Aristotle himself redefined it.[22]

Rapin's treatise ranges far and wide. Among other topics, he confronts the question of the goal, the *telos*, of poetry:

> It is not easily decided what the nature and what precisely is the end of this art: the interpreters of Aristotle differ in their opinions. Some will have the end to be delight, and that 'tis on this account it labours to move the passions, all whose motions are delightful, because nothing is more sweet to the soul than agitation; it pleases itself in changing the objects to satisfy the immensity of its desires. 'Tis true, delight is the end poetry aims at, but not the principal end, as others pretend. In effect, poetry, being an art, ought to be profitable by the quality of its own nature and by the essential subordination that all arts should have to polity, whose end in general is the public good. This is the judgement of Aristotle and of Horace, his chief interpreter.[23]

This is not, of course, 'the judgement of Aristotle', and certainly not in the *Poetics*. It is (more or less) the judgement of Horace, with a few nudges from Aristotelian philosophy elsewhere; *inter alia* Rapin has put the 'polity', which Aristotle left out of the *Poetics*, back into it. In offering, as he does, a synthesis of Horace and Aristotle, Rapin is doing what generations of classicisers had done before him;[24] and like many others, he offers it in the guise of Aristotelian theory.

Characteristic of his age is one particular constructive reading, or misreading, that Rapin's synthesis involves at this and other points: Aristotle's theory is moralised (witness 'profitable' and 'the public good'). As far as tragedy is concerned, the distinctive implications of this moralising become apparent as Rapin's discussion proceeds:

> Tragedy, of all parts of poesy, is that which Aristotle has most discussed, and where he appears most exact. He alleges that tragedy is a public lecture, without comparison more instructive than philosophy [*sic*], because it teaches the mind by the sense, and rectifies the passions by the passions themselves, in calming by their emotion the troubles they excite in the heart. The philosopher had observed two important faults in man to be regulated, pride and hardness of heart, and he found for both vices a cure in tragedy [*sic*]. For it makes man modest by representing the great

masters of the earth humbled; and it makes him tender and merciful by showing him on the theatre the strange accidents of life and the unforeseen disgraces to which the most important persons are subject. But because man is naturally timorous and compassionate, he may fall into another extreme, to be either too fearful or too full of pity; the too much fear may shake the constancy of mind, and the too great compassion may enfeeble the equity. 'Tis the business of tragedy to regulate these two weaknesses; it prepares and arms him against disgraces by shewing them so frequent in the most considerable persons, and he shall cease to fear ordinary accidents when he sees such extraordinary happen to the highest part of mankind. But as the end of tragedy is to teach men not to fear too weakly the common misfortunes, and manage their fear, it makes account also to teach them to spare their compassion for objects that deserve it. For there is an injustice in being moved at the afflictions of those who deserve to be miserable. One may see without pity Clytemnestra slain by her son Orestes in Aeschylus, because she had cut the throat of Agamemnon, her husband, and one cannot see Hippolytus die by the plot of his stepmother Phaedra in Euripides without compassion, because he died not but for being chaste and virtuous. This to me seems, in short, the design of tragedy according to the system of Aristotle [*sic*], which to me appears admirable, but which has not been explained as it ought by his interpreters; they have not, it may seem, sufficiently understood the mystery to unfold it well.[25]

The fall of the tragic hero and its (essentially) moral effects .... Some of this remarkable mixture (one might say) is authentic Aristotle; some is more or less Aristotelian; some is not Aristotelian at all. What in particular the mixture does is synthesise Aristotle's position about tragic 'pity and fear' with the well-known Horatian formula that poetry does, or should, aim at instruction as well as pleasure, at the *utile* as well as the *dulce*.[26] This formula is attached to 'Aristotle' notably by the undeniably Aristotelian pegs of *katharsis* and the 'philosophical' affinities of poetic universalisation (*Poetics* VI, 1449b28, and IX, 1451a36-b11), drastic though Rapin's reinterpretation of both of these notions may be.

In reinterpreting Aristotle in this way, Rapin is not merely adjusting details in Aristotle's theory; he is also bringing seemingly unrelated, or only elusively related, aspects of Aristotle's theory into a coherent relationship. In particular, any loose ends concerning Aristotle's theory of the tragic effect are now neatly joined up. The effect is now a moral one, and this effect is the *telos* of tragedy; the emphasis is shifted from the structural logic of the drama to its desired effect on the audience.

Meanwhile, Horace is invoked not simply as a supplement to Aristotle, but as a more explicit framer of rules for the writer to follow. The Aristotelian mixture of theory and practical advice now becomes a coherent set of rules *tout court*:

> Aristotle drew the platform of these rules from the poems of Homer, and other poets of his time, by the reflections he had a long time made on their works. I pretend not by a long discourse to justify the necessity, the justness, and the truth of these rules, nor to make an history of Aristotle's treatise of poesy, or examine whether it is complete, which many others have done; all these things I suppose. Only I affirm that these rules well considered, one shall find them made only to reduce nature into method, to trace it step by step, and not suffer the least mark of it to escape us. 'Tis only by these rules that the verisimility in fictions is maintained which is the soul of poesy. For unless there be the unity of place, of time, and of the action in the great poems, there can be no verisimility. In fine, 'tis by these rules that all becomes just, proportionate, and natural, for they are founded upon good sense and sound reason rather than on authority and example. Horace's book *Of Poesy*, which is but an interpretation of that of Aristotle, discovers sufficiently the necessity of being subject to rules by the ridiculous absurdities one is apt to fall into who follows only his fancy; for though poesy be the effect of fancy, yet if this fancy be not regulated, 'tis a mere caprice, not capable of producing anything reasonable.[27]

The supposed Aristotelian *rules* are equated with their neo-classical developments, including the infamous three unities (corresponding to Aristotle's single principle of unity of action), while Aristotle's emphasis on action is itself attenuated by the conversion of *muthos* to *fabula*, structure to content. Thus Rapin is prepared to call *muthos* both 'le sujet et le dessein' ('the subject and design', in Rymer's English version) and simply 'la fable, qui sert d'argument au poème' ('the fable, which serves for argument to a poem').[28]

Aristotle's *muthos* is in any case subjected to a further reinterpretation, in respect of the hierarchy of six 'elements': *muthos, êthos, dianoia, lexis, melopoiia, opsis* (plot-structure, character, 'reasoning', verbalisation, song [composition], 'spectacle' or visual design).[29] Rapin's equivalent is a shorter list of four (he ignores the musical sound and the look), and his positive contribution clearly reflects the inclination to invest Aristotle with coherence. The author of the *Poetics* had listed his

179

six *merê* in apparent order of importance, beginning with *muthos* and ending with *opsis* (VI: 1450a15-b20). He offers arguments in favour of the primacy of *muthos* (1) over *êthos* (2) (1450a15-b4), and he also seeks to justify the bottom place for *opsis* (6) (1450b16-20). The rest of Aristotle's order is unargued, nor is there any suggestion of interrelation of the different *merê*, except for the dependence of *êthos* on *muthos*.

For Rapin, this is (it would seem) less than satisfactory. Quietly converting Aristotle's rational-argumentative principle of *dianoia* into 'thoughts or sentiments' ('la pensée où ... les sentimens') and Aristotle's *lexis* (verbalisation) into 'expression' ('l'expression'), 'language' ('la diction') or simply 'words' ('les paroles'), he offers something more organised and systematic. The 'design' or 'fable' comes first, 'because it is the first production of the wit' ('la première production du génie'). Second, more or less as in Aristotle, comes *êthos*, rendered as 'manners' ('les moeurs'); but then 'the third part consists in the thoughts or sentiments which are properly the expressions of the manners' ('les expressions des moeurs'); and the fourth part consists in 'the words' ('les paroles'), because 'words are the expressions of the thoughts' ('les expressions des sentimens').[30] In all this, needless to say, Aristotle's oscillation between compositional process and literary product has given way to a more even stress on product.

Along with other theorists of his age, Rapin offers a remarkable version of neo-Aristotelian theorising in which a quota of non-Aristotelian coherence seems almost to accrue by stealth. Among these theorists, deviations from Aristotle are occasionally acknowledged, but usually only if some other theorist is responsible. 'Rapin' (says Dryden, with evident surprise) 'attributes more to the *dictio*, that is, to the words and discourses of a tragedy, than Aristotle had done.'[31] 'As for the unity of place' (says Corneille) 'I find no such rule in either Aristotle or Horace.'[32] More commonly, deviations are passed off as Aristotelian by implication, as part of the general neo-Aristotelian synthesis; or else notions that are specifically un-Aristotelian are specifically attributed to the *Poetics*. What was it that Aristotle said in *Poetics* IX? – that poetry is more philosophical than history, though, needless to say, not as philosophical as philosophy itself. And what was it Rapin said? – that 'Aristotle alleges that tragedy is a public lecture ... more instructive than philosophy.'[33] Here indeed endeth a lesson.[34]

*

To switch from Rapin to Brecht, from the world of Cardinal Richelieu and the *Académie française* to the ferment of twentieth-century experimental drama, exile from Nazi Germany, and an evasive espousal of its communist successor – such a switch involves more of a culture shock,

180

arguably, than the jump from Aristotle to his neo-classical disciples two thousand years on. On the face of it, the author of *Die Dreigroschenoper* and *Mutter Courage* might seem to inhabit a planet in a different solar system altogether. Remarkably enough, though, the theorist Brecht, albeit hardly revolving around the same Aristotelian sun, continues to take his bearings from it – as is obvious even from the title of his best-known theoretical work, the *Kleines Organon für das Theater* (1948), his 'miniature *organum*', whose name looks back to Bacon's anti-Aristotelian *Novum Organum* of 1620, which in turn looks back, polemically, to Aristotle's masterpieces of logic, the original *Organon* itself. We are, accordingly, less than surprised to find, in the first few sections of Brecht's *Organon*, a discussion of Aristotle and the Aristotelian *katharsis* and *hêdonê*.[35]

Quite unlike Aristotle, or Rapin, or most theorists, Brecht is of course a man of the theatre. From the mid-1920s, furthermore, he is a leading player in a radical-political movement striving to create a new kind of theatre, distinct from the long tradition of European serious drama. It is to be in every sense a revolutionary theatre, in which the Marxist goal of changing society is uppermost. Hand in hand with his developing dramatic practice goes a developing dramaturgical theory; and just as the practice is opposed, specifically, to traditional drama, so the theory which defends, articulates and helps to develop the practice opposes itself to the theoretical tradition which Brecht, correctly, sees as stemming ultimately from Aristotelian theory.

More precisely, Brecht defines a traditional drama which he categorises in terms derived from a range of pre-twentieth-century theory, and the new composite he calls 'dramatic theatre' or 'Aristotelian theatre', in precise contrast to what at first he calls 'epic theatre' and, from about 1930, also 'non-Aristotelian drama' – and phrases like 'nicht-aristotelische Dramatik' now become characteristic of his theoretical vocabulary.[36]

If any one word might be said to sum up the new project, in all its distinctiveness, that word would be *Verfremdung*, 'estrangement': a term with a composite provenance (part Marxian, part Hegelian, part Russian Formalist);[37] a term with multiple applications (though most straightforwardly applied to the stage figures); and a term whose thrust is indicated most conveniently, if we oppose it, as Brecht does, to *Einfühlung*, 'empathy', which Brecht ascribes to Aristotle.[38] The argument in favour of estrangement is conducted in unequivocally Marxian terms. Epic theatre (he writes around 1936) must concentrate on 'the great themes of our time, as, for example, the building up of a mammoth industry, the conflict of classes, war, the fight against disease ...'.[39] Rather in the way that Aristotle's version of tragedy is supposed to reveal patterns of causality (*Poetics* IX: 1451a36-b9), epic theatre seeks

181

to 'expose the laws of cause and effect' – but for Brecht (unlike Aristotle) these causal 'laws' are seen to be operative within the historical specificities of wars, or class conflicts, or the other 'great themes of our time'. It follows that the new theatre is designed to make its audience think – but not only *think*. It is 'an affair for philosophers – but only such philosophers as wish not just to explain the world, but also to change it'.[40]

And how is the audience to be encouraged to think, to think critically and actively, to grasp, within the thinking, the imperative for activity? The answer is: by being confronted with experience in the new, estranged perspective. Looking back, in the mid-1930s, to his own earlier theatrical work, Brecht comments:

The spectator was no longer ... allowed to submit to an experience uncritically (and without practical consequences) by means of simple empathy with the characters in a play. The production took the subject-matter and the incidents shown and put them through a process of estrangement: the estrangement that is necessary to all understanding. When something seems 'the most obvious thing in the world', it means that any attempt to understand the world has been given up.

What is 'natural' must have the force of what is startling. This is the only way to expose the laws of cause and effect. People's activity must simultaneously be so, and be capable of being different. It was all a great change.

The dramatic theatre's spectator says: Yes, I've felt like that too – Just like me – It's only natural – It'll never change – The sufferings of this man appal me, because they're inescapable – That's great art; it all seems the most obvious thing in the world – I weep when they weep, I laugh when they laugh.

The epic theatre's spectator says: I'd never have thought it – That's not the way – That's extraordinary, hardly credible – It's got to stop – The sufferings of this man appal me, because they're unnecessary – That's great art: nothing obvious in it – I laugh when they weep, I weep when they laugh.[41]

It is entirely characteristic that Brecht's thinking is articulated in polarities: his 'non'-Aristotelian' project thus implies its 'Aristotelian' converse. Why, for instance, is the new drama called 'epic theatre'? Brecht answers with reference to Aristotle:

Many people suppose the term 'epic theatre' is self-contradictory, because the epic and dramatic ways of telling a story are assumed – following Aristotle – to be basically distinct ... [But actually

there is a] 'dramatic element' in epic works and [an] 'epic element'
in the dramatic. The bourgeois novel in the [nineteenth] ... century developed much that was 'dramatic', by which was meant the
strong centralisation of the story, a momentum that drew the
separate parts into a common relationship ... The epic writer
Döblin came up with an excellent characterisation, when he said
that with an epic, as opposed to a dramatic work, you can, as it
were, take a pair of scissors and cut it into individual pieces, which
remain fully capable of life.[42]

Evidently, Brecht is appealing partly to *Poetics* XXVI, where Aristotle
contrasts epic and tragedy and argues that epic is less unified: any one
epic supplies the material for several tragedies.[43] One gathers both that
epic theatre is to be segmental and disunified and also that tragedy is
the central instance of traditional drama (though, interestingly, Brecht
tends to avoid use of the word 'tragedy' itself).[44] One question suggests
itself, however: why should estrangement call for disunity? In this
particular discussion, Brecht does not supply an answer. A brief, ten-
dentious, but suggestive answer would be: because their opposites,
empathy and unity, belong together in Brecht's version of Aristotle. The
answer will receive its corroboration in due course.[45]

It might seem surprising, meanwhile, that with so rich and varied a
tradition of German theorising about tragedy to draw on (or to attack)
– from Lessing to Goethe, from Hegel to Nietzsche – Brecht, nevertheless, looks mostly not to his German predecessors, but to Aristotle. This
omission becomes less surprising when one observes that the Aristotle
that Brecht confronts is a distinctly Germanised Aristotle: that is, an
Aristotle incorporating certain striking features of nineteenth-century
theory. In particular, Brecht's Aristotle is somewhat Romanticised and
then Nietzscheanised. This becomes most apparent when Brecht discusses the dramatic effect:

The drama of our time still follows Aristotle's recipe for achieving
what he calls *katharsis* (the spiritual cleansing of the spectator).
In Aristotelian drama the plot leads the hero into situations where
he reveals his innermost being. All the incidents shown have the
object of driving the hero into spiritual conflicts. It is a possibly
blasphemous but quite useful comparison if one turns one's mind
to the burlesque shows on Broadway, where the public, with yells
of 'Take it off!', forces the girls to go further and further in exposing
their bodies. The individual whose innermost being is thus driven
into the open then of course comes to stand for Man with a capital
M. Everyone (including every spectator) is then carried away by
the momentum of the events portrayed, so that in a performance

of *Oedipus* one has for all practical purposes an auditorium full of little Oedipuses, an auditorium full of Emperor Joneses for a performance of *The Emperor Jones*. Non-Aristotelian drama would at all costs avoid bundling together the events portrayed and presenting them as an inexorable fate, to which the human being is handed over helpless despite the beauty and significance of his reactions; on the contrary, it is precisely this fate that it would study closely, showing it up as of human contriving.[46]

It should not be too controversial to point out that Aristotle's theory says nothing about 'inexorable fate' or 'Man with a capital M', nothing about the hero 'revealing his innermost being' or his 'spiritual conflicts'.[47] In part, these phrases recall (say) the Romantic idealism of Schelling, who indeed agonises about 'unavoidable fate' and who identifies as 'the essence of tragedy' a 'conflict between freedom in the subject and necessity'.[48] Then again, there is an unmistakable Nietzschean ring to some of Brecht's formulations, derived (or caricatured) from Nietzsche's classic (or anti-classic) theory in *Die Geburt der Tragödie* (1872), where the representative suffering of the individual hero is massively asserted on a metaphysical-existential level and definitively associated with the Greek paradigm, so that (for instance) with ' ... Sophocles' heroes ... we immediately have the feeling that we are looking into the innermost ground of their being ...' – witness 'that most sorrowful figure of the Greek stage, the wretched Oedipus'.[49]

Brecht is suspicious of *katharsis* (*whatever* it may mean ...) and of all emotional effects – or rather, in epic theatre, 'emotions are only clarified ... steering clear of subconscious origins and not carrying anyone away'.[50] Aristotle, however, says nothing about subsconscious origins (even if, conceivably, they could be read back into *katharsis* theory via *Politics* VIII).[51] By contrast, Nietzsche's concept of the primal Dionysiac is all about subconscious origination. And despite Brecht's appeal to Aristotle, the polarity between epic and drama likewise points, not to the *Poetics*, but again to *The Birth of Tragedy*. For Aristotle, epic poetry and tragic drama are different, but not opposites; indeed, epic is in a sense the spiritual prototype of tragedy as we know it (*Poetics* IV: 1448b24ff.). For Nietzsche, on the other hand, epic is the sphere of Apollo, tragedy (primarily) of Dionysus (and the Dionysiac 'carrying away'), and the two are indeed (in Nietzsche's own words) 'separated by a tremendous chasm'.[52]

Tragic drama, for Nietzsche, involves transformation and, in part, audience identification, whereas epic involves an external narrative without any identification.[53] When Brecht derides a performance of Oedipus, in which the audience become 'little Oedipuses', this is a caricature of the prototypical Nietzschean audience, who are 'magically transformed' as 'unconscious actors' into the visionary figures outside them.[54] The original (and ideal) Nietzschean audience is therefore all one: 'the most immediate effect of ... tragedy [is] that the ... gulfs between man and man give way to an overwhelming feeling of unity.'[55] Brecht is in no way disposed to deny this. It is simply that he requires precisely the opposite kind of audience:

> In calling for a direct impact, the aesthetics of the day calls for an impact that flattens out all social and other distinctions between individuals. Plays of the Aristotelian type still manage to flatten out class conflicts in this way, even though the individuals themselves are becoming increasingly aware of class differences. The same result is achieved, even when class conflicts are the subject of such plays, and even in cases where they take sides for a particular class. A collective entity is created in the auditorium for the duration of the entertainment, on the basis of the 'common humanity' shared by all spectators alike. Non-Aristotelian drama ... is not interested in the establishment of such an entity. It divides its audience.[56]

Brecht is fond of insisting that his dramaturgical practice

> ... does not make use of the identification of the spectator with the play, as the Aristotelian does ... *Katharsis* is not [its] main object ... It does not ... wish to make the spectator the victim, so to speak, of a hypnotic experience in the theatre. In fact, its purpose is to teach the spectator a certain quite practical attitude ... a critical attitude, as opposed to a subjective attitude of being completely 'entangled' in what's going on.[57]

Notwithstanding Nietzsche's vision of the 'magical transformation' of the primitive audience, however, this 'complete entanglement' is not actually Nietzschean, nor is it Aristotelian either. Nietzsche discusses such entanglement, but negatively, with reference, for instance, to Goethe's famous avoidance of 'pathological involvement'.[58] Nietzsche's own proposal, elaborately worked out, is that tragedy in its known embodiments (from Aeschylus to Wagner) calls for an 'aesthetic' response, compounding Dionysiac oneness *and also* Apolline distance.[59] Aristotle's – not so much worked out as implied – is seemingly that, though playwrights (and actors?) must feel their characters' emotions if they are to be convincing to an audience, the audience's own response (the famous 'pity and fear') follows the trajectory of (let us say) the hero's sufferings, but neither the trajectory nor, above all, the specific disposition of the hero's feelings: Oedipus spends much of his play feeling either confident or exasperated or distraught, but himself only briefly experiences fear (for himself, before the dénouement) or pity (for his people at the start, for his daughters at the finish).[60] Broadly, the demand for full identification is neo-classical. One finds it, for instance, in Rapin:

> But 'tis not enough that tragedy be furnished with all the most moving and terrible adventures that history can afford, to stir in the heart those motions it pretends, to the end it may cure the mind of those vain fears that may annoy it, and those childish compassions that may soften it. 'Tis also necessary, says the philosopher, that every poet employ these great objects of terror and pity as the two most powerful springs in art to produce that pleasure which tragedy may yield. And this pleasure, which is properly of the mind, consists in the agitation of the soul moved by the passions. Tragedy cannot be delightful to the spectator unless he become sensible to all that is represented; he must enter into all the different thoughts of the actors; interest himself in their adventures; fear, hope, afflict himself, and rejoice with them.[61]

And if, on occasion, Brecht's 'Aristotelian' categories have a neo-classical point of reference, their tolerance is such that they can also refer back to the classicism of Weimar. The antithesis between epic and dramatic, for instance, looks back partly to a famous correspondence between Goethe and Schiller in 1797, which Brecht certainly knew.[62] Clearly, then, his so-called 'Aristotelian drama' is, genetically speaking, a rich hybrid, although it still is – or should be – a given that Brecht's Aristotle speaks with a markedly nineteenth-century, part-Nietzschean, accent;[63] and in this context it is a supreme irony that his own prescription for his 'critical' audience (and 'criticism … is ultimately revolution')[64] is virtually spelled out by Nietzsche himself, who ascribes it, damagingly, to Euripides. For Nietzsche, Euripides is the 'spectator' with an 'extraordinary fund of critical talent' who rejects the traditional basis of tragedy and attempts to create (what else but?) 'a dramatised epic'.[65]

The various Brechtian oppositions are summarised and definitively schematised by Brecht himself in a famous discussion from 1930:[66]

Das moderne Theater ist das epische Theater. Folgendes Schema zeigt einige Gewichtsverschiebungen vom dramatischen zum epischen Theater.

Dramatische Form des Theaters	Epische Form des Theaters
handelnd	erzählend
verwickelt den Zuschauer in eine Bühnenaktion	macht den Zuschauer zum Betrachter, aber
verbraucht seine Aktivität	weckt seine Aktivität

ermöglicht ihm Gefühle	erzwingt von ihm Entscheidungen
Erlebnis	Weltbild
Der Zuschauer wird in etwas hineinversetzt	er wird gegenübergesetzt
Suggestion	Argument
Die Empfindungen werden konserviert	bis zu Erkenntnissen getrieben
Der Zuschauer steht mittendrin miterlebt	Der Zuschauer steht gegenüber studiert
Der Mensch als bekannt vorausgesetzt	Der Mensch ist Gegenstand der Untersuchung
Der unveränderliche Mensch	Der veränderliche und verändernde Mensch
Spannung auf den Ausgang	Spannung auf den Gang
Eine Szene für die andere	Jede Szene für sich
Wachstum	Montage
Geschehen linear	in Kurven
evolutionäre Zwangsläufigkeit	Sprünge
Der Mensch als Fixum	Der Mensch als Prozeß
Das Denken bestimmt das Sein	Das gesellschaftliche Sein bestimmt das Denken
Gefühl	Ratio

The modern theatre is the epic theatre. The following table shows certain changes of emphasis as between the dramatic and the epic theatre.

Dramatic theatre	*Epic theatre*
plot	narrative
implicates the spectator in a stage situation	turns the spectator into an observer, but
wears down his capacity for action	rouses his capacity for action
provides him with sensations	forces him to take decisions
experience	view of the world
the spectator is involved in something	he is made to face something
suggestion	argument
instinctive feelings are preserved	brought to the point of recognition
the spectator is in the thick of it, shares the experience	the spectator stands outside, studies
the human being is taken for granted	the human being is an object of investigation
the human being is unalterable	the human being is alterable and able to alter
eyes on the finish	eyes on the course
one scene makes another	each scene for itself
growth	montage
linear development	in curves
evolutionary inevitability	jumps
man as a fixed point	man as a process
thought determines being	social being determines thought
feeling	reason

187

There is a good deal that could be said about this schema (not least, a significant qualification offered by Brecht to indicate that the opposed terms do not necessarily hold good in all particulars; rather the oppositions are, so to speak, *this way round*).[67] What immediately concerns us here is the way the 'dramatic' list unites what are Aristotle's specific emphases – like 'plot' and 'organic unity' (implicit in 'one scene makes another') – with emphases that are compatible with Aristotle, without actually being Aristotle's emphases (like the empathetic implication of 'the spectator shares the experience'), and emphases that are, on any interpretation, remote from the Aristotelian tradition as Aristotle himself knew it ('thought determines being'). Especially intriguing are the comments on musical drama that follow the schema, comments which, by comparison with the schema itself, are often ignored:[68]

Der Einbruch der Methoden des epischen Theaters in die Oper führt hauptsächlich zu einer radikalen *Trennung der Elemente*. Der große Primatkampf zwischen Wort, Musik und Darstellung (wobei immer die Frage gestellt wird, wer wessen Anlaß sein soll – die Musik der Anlaß des Bühnenvorgangs, oder der Bühnenvorgang der Anlaß der Musik usw.) kann einfach beigelegt werden durch die radikale Trennung der Elemente. Solange 'Gesamtkunstwerk' bedeutet, daß das Gesamte ein Aufwaschen ist, solange also Künste 'verschmelzt' werden sollen, müssen die einzelnen Elemente alle gleichermaßen degradiert werden, indem jedes nur Stichwortbringer für das andere sein kann. Der Schmelzprozeß erfaßt den Zuschauer, der ebenfalls eingeschmolzen wird und einen passiven (leidenden) Teil des Gesamtkunstwerks darstellt. Solche Magie ist natürlich zu bekämpfen. Alles, was Hypnotisierversuche darstellen soll, unwürdige Räusche erzeugen muß, benebelt, muß aufgegeben werden.

Music, Wort und Bild mußten mehr Selbständigkeit erhalten.

When the epic theatre's methods begin to penetrate the opera, the first result is a radical *separation of the elements*. The great struggle for supremacy between words, music and production – which always raises the question, 'which is the pretext for which?': is the music the pretext for the events on stage, or are these the pretext for the music? etc. – can simply be by-passed by radically separating the elements. So long as a 'Gesamtkunstwerk' ('integrated work of art') means that the integration is a muddle, so long as the arts are supposed to be 'fused' together, the various elements will all be equally degraded, and each will act as a mere feed to the rest. The process of fusion extends to the spectator, who gets thrown into the melting pot too and becomes a passive (suffering) part of the total work of art. Witchcraft of this sort must of course be fought against. Whatever is intended to produce hypnosis, is likely to induce sordid intoxication, or creates fog, has got to be given up.

    Music, words and setting must become more independent of one another.

As this sequence indicates, Brecht's many theoretical opponents include Richard Wagner. For Brecht, the Wagnerian *Gesamtkunstwerk* epitomises the total antithesis of estrangement and critical distance; here, instead of *Verfremdung*, everything, even the spectator, 'fuses' into a single undifferentiated *Verschmelzung*. This account of the *Gesamtkunst*, no doubt, involves a considerable distortion of Wagner's aims, albeit, arguably (as the later Nietzsche, for one, would have agreed), a plausible caricature of Wagner's actual practice.[69]

    In any event, it is clear why Brecht should oppose such 'fusion' and why he should, *per contra*, appeal to the 'separation of elements', words, music and visual presentation. At this point, it is also clear – though we may well register the fact with some surprise – that we are back in Aristotelian territory, and specifically the discussion conducted in *Poetics* VI, where we have the list of six *merê*, from *muthos* to *opsis*. Unlike Aristotle, Brecht, seemingly, insists on the equality of the elements; there is to be no hierarchy, no 'struggle for supremacy'. For once like Aristotle, however, he insists also, and above all, on the need to keep the elements separate. Aristotle (albeit for quite different reasons) would have had no problem with that. After all, in the *Poetics* you can apparently have *muthos* without *êthos*; *opsis* is evidently an optional extra; and Aristotle's very terminology for his 'elements' – *merê*, 'parts' – suggests detachability.[70]

    Remarkably, then, faced with another enemy, notionally within the 'Aristotelian' camp, but considerably more threatening than the original Aristotle himself, Brecht is even prepared to make common cause with that Aristotle – though, needless to say, he says not a word about any of this. If indeed we look ahead to Brecht's later, postwar, thinking (in the *Kleines Organon* and elsewhere), we can find much more, and this time quite explicit, evidence of a compromise with the *Poetics*, as part of a series of shifts in Brecht's overall theoretical position. One has to report, however, that the relative tolerance and restraint of the later compromise seems unimpressive in comparison to the verve and the intellectual edge of the earlier formulations.[71]

    Irrespective of these shifts in position and other complications, the essential point stands: in the 1930 schema, and elsewhere, Brecht combines notions that belonged to Aristotle (more or less) with notions that belonged to others (more or less), like Nietzsche. In doing this, Brecht is doing something strikingly similar to what Rapin does when he glosses the *Poetics* with Horace. Furthermore, in his novel definition of dramatic-Aristotelian theatre, Brecht again is doing what his neo-classical predecessors had done: investing the theory with a coherence that is not a *donnée* of Aristotle's own work. Brecht does this, again, by constructing relationships between separate aspects of Aristotle's position (imagined or actual) – between, for instance, the principles of organic unity and audience empathy and *katharsis*. Empathy-*katharsis* precludes a critical response. It therefore militates against the spectator's capacity for action ('verbraucht seine Aktivität') – and this capacity is likewise undermined by the unified, organic structure which makes everything seem 'natural' and inevitable, determined and unalterable. By contrast, the Brechtian spectator needs to be estranged into a state of critical consciousness in which altering the world is as possible as it is an immediate imperative.

Implicit here, then, is another reinterpetation of 'Aristotle', another creative reconstitution of 'Aristotle', another new and sublimely un-Aristotelian coherence.

Notes

1. Lucas on *Poetics* 1454a8 (commenting on *Poetics* XIII-XIV). Cf. S.A. White, 'Aristotle's favourite tragedies', in *Essays on Aristotle's Poetics*, ed. A.O. Rorty (Princeton, 1992), 221-40.

2. See e.g. the discussions of 'the rough state of the text' in S. Halliwell, *Aristotle's Poetics* (London, 1986), 27-37, and of 'the lost second book' in R. Janko, *Aristotle on Comedy* (London, 1984), 63-6.

3. See E. Hall, 'Is there a polis in Aristotle's *Poetics*?', in *Tragedy and the Tragic*, ed. M.S. Silk (Oxford, 1996), 295-309 – as against S. Salkever, 'Tragedy and the education of the demos', in *Greek Tragedy and Political Theory*, ed. J.P. Euben (Berkeley, 1986), 274-303.

4. As also outside tragedy: cf. Halliwell (n. 2 above), 238-52, 276-85.

5. Adequate consideration of this issue would call for discussion of the point made by Stephen Halliwell (this volume, p. 103) that (notwithstanding plausible misinterpretations of *Poetics* IX) Aristotle does not allow for any immutable human condition. I content myself here with adding that, if he is capable of saying 'we grant that the gods can see everything' (*Poetics* XV: 1454b5-6), it is not apparent why he cannot make some allowance for the pervasive status of the gods in tragedy.

6. See e.g. Halliwell (n. 2 above), 190-4.

7. See, broadly, Janko (n. 2 above), 63-6, but (regarding the implausibility of the supposition that the second Book 'explained' *katharsis*) also Halliwell (n. 2 above), 190-1.

8. Beginning, maybe, with the murky post-Aristotelian theorising in *Pap. Herc.* 1581, on which see M.L. Nardelli, 'La catarsi poetica nel *PHerc.* 1581', *Cronache Ercolanesi* 8 (1978), 96-103.

9. See M.S. Silk, 'The "six parts of tragedy" in Aristotle's *Poetics*', *Proceedings of the Cambridge Philological Society* 40 (1994), 108-15, whose translation of the passage (ibid. 108) I follow here. It is worth adding that, in its tone and phrasing, this opening sentence – and, more generally, *Poetics* I-II – does read like the beginning of a coherent treatise and that, accordingly, it is partly the opening of the *Poetics* that creates readerly expectations which are subsequently frustrated. I owe the thought to Alan Griffiths.

10. *Poetics* 1450a4ff.: see Silk (n. 9 above). Implicit in the processive sequence is a possible compositional order (Silk, ibid.). The implication was grasped in the neoclassical age by (for instance) Dryden in 'Preface of the Translator, with a Parallel of Poetry and Painting' (1695): John Dryden, *Of Dramatic Poesy and Other Critical Essays*, ed. G. Watson (London, 1962), vol. 2, 186 ('... the first business of the poet ... After this he begins to think of ...').

11. With the remarks that follow, cf. my editorial comments in *Tragedy and the Tragic* (n. 3 above), 5-9.

12. *Poetics* XIII: 1453a23-30. The discrepancy between this view of Euripides and the common modern preoccupation with his plays of mixed mode ('romantic', 'melodramatic', etc.) is another matter.

13. This emphasis on 'excitement' (*ekplêxis*), of course, in any case sits awkwardly with the general preoccupation with 'pity and fear'.

14. Notwithstanding the fact that 'a distinction between form and content is difficult in Aristotelian terms': S. Halliwell, 'Aristotle on form and unity', in *Encyclopedia of Aesthetics*, ed. M. Kelly (New York, 1998), vol. 1, 101-4 at 103.

15. Cf. the conjunction of *muthos* and *praxis* at *Poetics* XI: 1452a37.

16. Other candidates for ambivalence would include the way that in *Poetics* VIII, in particular, Aristotle makes a powerful case for a unified structure which does not require a single central 'hero' (*peri hena*: 1451a16-35; cf. XIV: 1453b14-22), whereas in XIII the well-known discussion of *hamartia* strongly implies a predisposition towards just such a focal figure (1453a7-12).

17. Cf. J. Lear, 'Katharsis', in Rorty (n. 1 above), 315-40 at 319. Of the contributions to the present volume, Malcolm Heath's strikes me as a particularly good example of an Aristotelian resolution of some of the paradoxes associated with the *Poetics*, which is not necessarily Aristotle's.

18. On any reckoning the *Poetics* as a whole does contain brilliant *aperçus* – on metaphor, on poetry and history, on unity, on complication and dénouement. In the hope of avoiding possible misunderstandings, let me add three points here. First, I do not exactly claim that modern *Aristotelian scholars* derive their notion of the coherence of Aristotle's theory from the likes of Rapin and Brecht, or (more generally) from the continuum to which they belong, but that such a notion predominates in educated discussion among those interested in modern literature and thought, and that *this* derives from the continuum. To deny, however, that this notion has, in turn, exercised any influence on the scholarly world of Aristotelian studies would be folly. Secondly, in case anyone wishes to deny that the theory is (relatively) incoherent, it is no 'answer' to point to the (relative) incoherence of other Aristotelian theories in other works: their loose-endedness (or whatever) cannot somehow make the loose-endedness (or whatever) of *this* theory less what it is: two wrongs never make a right. And thirdly, I do not suppose that the likes of Rapin and Brecht *set out* to find coherence in Aristotle's theory: they take it as a given (and unwittingly reconstitute it, of course, for their different purposes).

19. Rapin's treatise was republished in 1675 under a modified title (*Réflexions sur la poétique de ce temps et sur les ouvrages des poètes anciens et modernes*): quoted here from the edition by E.T. Dubois (Geneva, 1970). Rymer's translation (London, 1694) was entitled *Monsieur Rapin's Reflections on Aristotle's Treatise of Poesie*; in the quotations that follow I have semi-modernised the English spelling and punctuation.

20. See 'The Author's Apology for Heroic Poetry and Poetic Licence' (1677), in Watson (n. 10 above), vol. 1, 199. Rapin is said, conversely, to have learnt English specifically to read Dryden, on the testimony of Dryden's friend Charles Blount: J. and H. Kinsley (eds.), *Dryden: The Critical Heritage* (London, 1971), 160. The comprehensive English translation was by Basil Kennet 'and others', and was entitled *The Whole Critical Works of Monsieur Rapin, In Two Volumes* (London, 1706).

21. M. Moriarty, *Taste and Ideology in Seventeenth-Century France* (Cambridge, 1988).

22. These developments are already implicit in, for instance, Chaucer's famous formula: 'Tragedie is to seyn a certeyn storie | ... Of him that stood in greet prosperitee, | And is yfallen ...' ('The Monk's Prologue').

23. Rapin, *Réflexions* I.vii (Dubois, 19-20): 'Il n'est pas aisé de décider en quoy consiste la nature de cet art que nous examinons, et quelle est précisément sa fin ... Car la poésie, estant un art, doit estre utile par la qualité de sa nature, et par la subordination essentielle, que tout art doit avoir à la politique, dont la fin générale est le bien public. C'est le sentiment d'Aristote, et d'Horace son premier interprète.' Trans. Rymer, 9-10.

24. See e.g.: M. Herrick, *The Fusion of Horatian and Aristotelian Literary Criticism 1531-1555* (Urbana, 1946); A. Garcia Berrio, *Formacion de la teoria literaria moderna: la topica horaciana en Europa* (Madrid, 1977-80).

25. Rapin, *Réflexions* II.xvii (Dubois, 97-8): Rymer, 109-11.

26. *Poetics* VI-XIV (and cf. e.g. Halliwell (n. 2 above), 168-83) and Horace, *Ars Poetica* 343.

27. Rapin, *Réflexions* I.xii (Dubois, 25-6): Rymer, 17-18.

28. Rapin, *Réflexions* I.xix and xxi (Dubois, 32, 37): Rymer, 26, 32. In effect, Aristotle's *muthos* and *lexis* have become Horace's *res* and *verba* (as at *Ars Poetica* 309-11): verbalisation of action has made way for versification of a subject.

29. On the interpetation of the six items, see Silk (n. 9 above), 109-11.

30. Rapin, *Réflexions* I.xxvi, xxvii, xxvi, xix, xxv, xxvi (Dubois, 44, 46, 44, 32, 42, 44): Rymer, 42, 44, 42, 26, 38, 42.

31. Dryden, 'Heads of an Answer to Rymer' (1677), in Watson (n. 10 above), vol. 1, 219.

32. 'Quant à l'unité de lieu, je n'en trouve aucun précepte, ni dans Aristote, ni dans Horace', Corneille, *Discours des trois unités, d'action, de jour, et de lieu* (1660): Corneille, *Oeuvres complètes*, vol. 3, ed. G. Couton (Paris, 1987), 187.

33. Above, p. 177.

34. Although it is undeniable that, in Renaissance and neo-classical thought, 'Aristotle' may be as much an instigation to think as a body of identifiable doctrine, the pregnant contrast between these Dryden-Corneille and Rapin quotations (above), and equally the affinity between Rapin's use of Aristotle and Brecht's (below), conclusively show that one needs more than a historical explanation of the conceptual acrobatics under discussion. I am grateful to Daniel Javitch for helpful conversation on this topic.

35. *Kleines Organon* 4; on the *Organon* cf. p. 189 with n. 71 below.

36. The expressions 'epic theatre'/'epic drama' were first used by Brecht in 1926, but he was not their inventor. That honour apparently goes to Döblin and Piscator who seem to have introduced them around 1924: see e.g. K.A. Dickson, *Towards Utopia: A Study of Brecht* (Oxford, 1978), 229. In Brecht's writings, 'Aristotelian theatre' is often given further alternative designations, like 'bourgeois theatre' or 'theatre as we know it' ('das bürgerliche Theater' / 'das Theater, wie wir es vorfinden'): see e.g. Bertolt Brecht, *Gesammelte Werke in acht Bänden* (Frankfurt a/M, 1967), vol. 7, 628 and 676). (Citations from Brecht's *Gesammelte Werke*, vol. 7, are hereafter abbreviated as Brecht, *GW*.)

37. See e.g. the succinct discussion by R. Grimm, 'Alienation in context', in *A Bertolt Brecht Reference Companion*, ed. S. Mews (Westport, CT, 1997), 41-4. H. Flashar, 'Aristoteles und Brecht', in id., *Eidola* (Amsterdam, 1989), 179-99, at 192-5, tries, interestingly but implausibly, to relate *Verfremdung* to Aristotle's *xenikon*. If Brecht's term recalls anything in Aristotle (which is doubtful), it would be the principle of plausible surprise on the level of plot structure (*Poetics* IX: 1452a3-4).

38. In any strict sense of the word 'empathy', and certainly if we mean it with reference to the effect of a work of art on its audience, the notion is alien to the *Poetics* – albeit some have misread it into *katharsis* and others into *Poetics* XVII (1455a22ff.), which deals with the composer's rapport with his composition. Cf. Flashar (n. 37 above), 195-7, and see further above, pp. 185-6, with nn. 60-1.

39. Brecht, *GW* 236. Translations from Brecht here and elsewhere are based on those by J. Willett, *Brecht on Theatre* (New York, 1964), with or without minor changes. (Among much else, Willett translates *Verfremdung* not as 'estrangement', but as 'alienation'.)

40. Brecht, *GW* 265 ('die Gesetze von Ursache und Wirkung'), 236, 266 ('solcher Philosophen, die die Welt nicht nur zu erklären, sondern auch zu ändern wünschten'). The allusion in the final quotation is to Marx's *Theses on Feuerbach*, no. 11.

41. Brecht, *GW* 265.

42. Brecht, *GW* 263. 'Fully capable of life' ('durchaus lebensfähig'): like the segments of a worm ...?

43. 1462b3ff. Rather surprisingly, Flashar (n. 37 above) 187-190 argues that Brecht's epic/dramatic antithesis is not based on Aristotle at all.

44. Especially in his earlier writings; on his later practice, cf. Dickson (n. 36 above), 250 and n. 71 below.

45. See above, p. 190.

46. *Brecht, GW* 475-6. 'His innermost being': 'sein innerstes Wesen'. 'Spiritual conflicts': 'seelische Konflikte'. 'Man with a capital M': 'der Mensch schlechthin'. 'Inexorable fate': 'unentrinnbares Schicksal'.

47. It would, for instance, be specious to claim any kinship between this 'fate' and Aristotle's 'necessity' (*to anankaion: Poetics* VII, 1451a12, etc.).

48. 'Ein unvermeidliches Verhängnis', 'Das Wesentliche der Tragödie ist also ein wirklicher Streit der Freiheit im Subjekt und der Nothwendigkeit': *Philosophie der Kunst* (1802-5), in *Schellings Werke*, ed. M. Schröter, supp. vol. 3 (Munich, 1959), 346, 344.

49. *Die Geburt der Tragödie* (hereafter *GT*), IX: '... der sophokleischen

Helden ... wir sofort bis in den innersten Grund ihres Wesens zu blicken
wähnen ...', 'die leidvollste Gestalt der griechischen Bühne, der unglückselige
Ödipus.' Translations from *GT* follow the version by W. Kaufmann – Friedrich
Nietzsche, *The Birth of Tragedy* (New York, 1967) – with or without minor
modifications. On Nietzsche and Oedipus, cf. n. 54 below. On the notion (though
not quite the phraseology) of 'Man with a Capital M', cf. *GT* VII (n. 55 below).

50. Brecht, *GW* 479: ' ... vermeiden als Quelle das Unterbewußtsein und
haben nichts mit Rausch zu tun.' On 'Rausch' cf. n. 52 below.

51. I.e. via the association with orgiastic music which Aristotle touches on at
Politics 1341b32-1342a18.

52. *GT* VIII: 'durch eine ungeheure Kluft ... abgeschieden'. On Nietzsche's
view of tragedy as *primarily* Dionysiac, see e.g. *GT* XXI and M.S. Silk and J.P.
Stern, *Nietzsche on Tragedy* (Cambridge, 1981), 265-7; the Dionysiac, in turn,
is primarily the sphere of 'Rausch' (*GT* I and *passim*; cf. n. 50 above). It should
be borne in mind that in *GT* Nietzsche hardly discusses *drama* as such, except
as *tragic* drama (in *GT* VII-X), and that tragic drama interests him primarily
because it is tragic, not because it is dramatic: Silk and Stern, ibid., 239-82.

53. *GT* VIII, XXII. Contrast Plato, *Ion* 533-6.

54. *GT* VIII: '... Verzauberten ... Verwandelten ... unbewußten Schauspiel-
ern ...' Sophocles' *OT* is a special play for Nietzsche (*GT* III-IV, IX-X), as also
for Aristotle (*Poetics* XI, XIII-XVI, XXVI: cf. Silk and Stern (n. 52 above), 227),
and as also, of course, for Freud, who is perhaps an additional target here. One
should note that in *GT* VIII Nietzsche is concerned specifically with the
audience at the notional *birth* of tragedy; the audience for Aeschylus, and/or
Wagner, is different: see *GT* XXII-XXIV and cf. Silk and Stern (n. 52 above),
268-71 and p. 185 below.

55. *GT* VII: 'die nächste Wirkung der ... Tragödie, daß ... die Klüfte zwischen
Mensch und Mensch einem übermächtigen Einheitsgefühle weichen.' This
effect depends on (ibid.) the capacity of the chorus (originally a satyr-chorus) to
represent 'natural beings who live ineradicably, as it were, behind all civilisa-
tion and remain eternally the same, despite the changes of generations and
the history of nations': 'Naturwesen, die gleichsam hinter aller Zivilisation
unvertilgbar leben und trotz allem Wechsel der Generationen und der Völker-
geschichte ewig dieselben bleiben.'

56. Brecht, *GW* 1062-3: '... In jedem Fall entsteht im Zuschauerraum auf der
Basis des allen Zuhörern gemeinsamen "allgemein Menschlichen" *für die
Dauer des Kunstgenusses* ein Kollektivum. An der Herstellung dieses Kollekti-
vums ist die nichtaristotelische Dramatik ... nicht interessiert. Sie spaltet ihr
Publikum.'

57. An extract from a piece published in English in the *Left Review*, July
1936, and reprinted in Willett (n. 39 above), 78.

58. *GT* XXII; Goethe's own phrase (quoted there) was 'ein lebhaftes patholo-
gisches Interesse'. See Silk and Stern (n. 52 above), 277, 281, 421 nn. 88, 108.

59. *GT* XXI-XXIV (e.g. 'eine ästhetische Tätigkeit der Zuhörer', XXII).

60. Playwrights: *Poetics* XVII (1455a22ff.). Pity and fear: e.g. *Poetics* XIII
(1452b28ff.). Sophocles, *OT* 738ff., 974ff. (fear), 13, 58ff., 1462ff. (pity).

61. Rapin, *Réflexions* II.xviii (Dubois, 98-9): Rymer, 111. Before Aristotle,
the notion of full 'identification' is anticipated by Plato in the *Ion* (n. 53 above)
and, partly, by Gorgias (*Encomium of Helen* IX). Horace's famous 'si vis me
flere' (*Ars Poetica* 102ff.), though (like *Poetics* XVII) primarily centred on the

composer, takes us closer to audience identification ('ut ridentibus arrident', 101) and helps to engender the neoclassical position. Compare and contrast Flashar (n. 37 above), 195-7.

62. Goethe, *Gedenkausgabe der Werke, Briefe und Gespräche* (Zurich, 1949), vol. 20 (*Briefwechsel mit Friedrich Schiller*), 470ff.; Schiller, *Über die tragische Kunst*, in *Schillers Werke* (Nationalausgabe), ed. L. Blumenthal and B. von Wiese, vol. 20 (Weimar, 1962), 148-70, esp. 164-5; Brecht, *GW* 684, 1213.

63. Commentators on Brecht, however, tend to overplay (e.g.) the Goethe connection at the expense of the rest: F. Jameson, *Brecht and Method* (London, 1998), 52, is representative here ('the replacement [sc. re-placement?] of Brechtian theatre in such a classical tradition also offers a useful estrangement, and lends an interesting ambiguity, to his own modernities'). Alternatively, they simply concentrate on the accuracy, as opposed to the provenance, of Brecht's version of 'Aristotle' (so Flashar, n. 37 above). Contrast e.g. W. Mittenzwei, *Brechts Verhältnis zur Tradition* (Berlin, 1972), 98.

64. On 'eine kritische Haltung des Zuschauers' see e.g. Brecht, *GW* 347; 'criticism and revolution', *GW* 378.

65. *GT* XI, 'Von diesen beiden Zuschauern ist der eine – Euripides selbst', 'die außerordentliche Fülle seines kritischen Talentes'; *GT* XII, 'das dramatisierte Epos'. On Nietzsche's Euripides and Brecht, cf. Silk and Stern (n. 52 above), 359-60.

66. From 'Ammerkungen zur Oper "Aufstieg und Fall der Stadt Mahagonny" ': Bertolt Brecht, *Werke*, ed. W. Hecht et al., vol. 24 (Frankfurt a/M, 1991), 78-9. The text is often quoted in a later (1938) revised form: ibid. 85 (= Brecht, *GW* 1009-10).

67. After the opening heading ('... epischen Theater' / '... epic theatre'), Brecht has a pertinent note (*Werke* 78 = *GW* 1009): 'Dieses Schema zeigt nicht absolute Gegensätze, sondern lediglich Akzentverschiebungen. So kann innerhalb eines Mitteilungsvorgangs das gefühlsmäßig Suggestive oder das rein rationell Überredende bevorzugt werden.' ('This table does not show absolute antitheses but mere shifts of accent. In a communication of fact, for instance, we may choose whether to stress the element of emotional suggestion or that of plain rational argument.')

68. Brecht, *Werke* 79 = *GW* 1010-11.

69. See, in general, H.M. Brown, *Leitmotiv and Drama: Wagner, Brecht, and the Limits of Epic Theatre* (Oxford, 1991). 'Das Gesamtkunstwerk [ist] negativer Fixpunkt des Brechtischen Denkens': M. Voigts, *Brechts Theaterkonzeptionen* (Munich, 1977), 101.

70. *Muthos* without *êthos*: *Poetics* VI, 1450a23-9. *Opsis* optional: VI, 1450b16-20, XIV, 1453b1-8. *Merê*: VI, 1450a8 etc.

71. For the compromises, see notably *Kleines Organon* 4 and 12. The analysis of Brecht's relationship with Aristotle offered by Flashar (n. 37 above) seems to me unduly weighted towards the later, compromising Brecht.

The Afterlife of the *Poetics*

Terence Cave

At the end of such a wide-ranging book on the *Poetics* and its reception, it seems important to consider once again the phenomenon of the treatise's survival – not merely its continued presence in the European canon, but its authority, its infiltration into so many of the ways in which literature is talked about, despite the radical transformations which poetics has undergone even in the last two hundred years.[1] That issue will be addressed in the first part of this chapter, following a schematic survey of the various scholarly and critical methodologies according to which the *Poetics* has been and continues to be read. The second part consists of a brief post-Aristotelian case-study which picks up certain of the themes of part one in fictional mode and is meant to provide a quasi-symbolic epilogue for the volume as a whole.

Aristotle's afterlife

I shall begin, then, by reviewing some of the different ways in which the *Poetics* may be read and interpreted within a historical or critical framework; most if not all of them are illustrated by the various chapters in this volume. The categories I have chosen are crude, but they will provide a starting-point:

1. philological and contextual readings, in which the *Poetics* becomes an object of study for specialists of ancient Greek literary and philosophical culture;
2. reception history: a study of the different texts that the *Poetics* becomes, the different meanings its terms acquire in the course of its passage through European cultural history, especially in the early modern period, the golden age of its *Nachleben*;
3. hermeneutics in the manner of Gadamer: an endless dialogue between what the terms and concepts of the *Poetics* mean or might signify for us and the historical and philological evidence of their meaning in the past; this could include a hypothetical 'new historicist' reading of the *Poetics* and its reception, although new

historicists have not been much concerned with poetics in the formal
sense;
4. the post-modern reading: the *Poetics* as the big bang, the emergence
of a new critical universe in the shape of an extremely small, highly
unstable text which subsequently explodes, scattering fragments in
all directions; such a reading would make it pointless to speak of
Aristotelian poetics as in any sense a coherent body of materials or
'tradition', and would allow any use or definition of Aristotelian
terms that seemed helpful to the user.

Of the chapters in this volume, one might assign those by Heath,
Belfiore, Janko, Halliwell and Fantham to category 1, those by Javitch
and Minsaas to category 2, and Fossheim's to category 3. Silk's paper
shows signs of an affinity with category 4, but he might well prefer to
be placed in either or both of the first two categories, since the fourth is
meant to represent a limit-case at the opposite end of the spectrum from
the more or less orthodox historicism of category 1. My point here, at all
events, is that it is a *necessary* category, expressing in an extreme form
the difficulties that even the most conservative scholar is obliged to
grapple with in handling the *Poetics*.

We need to note already, as this example suggests, that these categories are not rigidly distinct. The first and second are clearly
compatible, and it could be plausibly argued that even the specialists of
category 1 are in fact unavoidably engaging in a dialogue between their
own mental world and that to which the *Poetics* belonged, rather than
neutrally recovering a supposedly original sense.

A further group consists of what one might call essentialist or
transcendentalist readings. The word 'reading' is liable to be misleading
here, since the focus is shifting from textual interpretation as such
towards intellectual systems that conscript Aristotelian terms and
concepts for their own purposes. I propose just three examples, although others are easily imaginable:

5. anthropological, cross-cultural or comparative;
6. psycholoanalytic;
7. cognitive.

All three assume the existence of deep and enduring structures in
human behaviour, in the psyche, or the brain, for which the terms of
Aristotle's analysis provide an approximate equivalent at the surface
level. For Northrop Frye, his predecessors and his successors, these
terms refer to rituals and ceremonies which are intrinsic to ancient
cultures in the way suggested by Frazer; they also point towards
'archetypes' of a broadly Jungian nature, the archetype being by defini-

tion a deep structure. A Freudian poetics would of course focus on the unconscious, on the repressed and its return, and on a therapeutic release corresponding to 'catharsis'; Peter Brooks' analysis of fictional plots in terms of psychic energies is a well-known recent representative of this category,[2] but various twentieth-century commentators on the *Poetics* itself exhibit Freudian leanings.

A cognitive reading would equally presuppose that Aristotle succeeded in reaching through to enduring human responses, but now at the level of more accessible mechanisms of learning, processing and response, those mechanisms being presumed to be 'hard-wired' in the brain, as in Chomskian theories of language. Certain recent varieties of narratology, in particular perhaps Paul Ricœur's, could be regarded as illustrating this category, even though Ricœur does not himself flaunt the word 'cognitive'.[3] I shall return later to the question of a cognitive poetics.

Meanwhile, I want to revert to a derivative of category 4, the post-Aristotelian fall-out.[4] Instead of considering the *Poetics* or any of its rewritings as an integral system, one is here looking primarily at different uses of Aristotelian *terms*, removed from their original context, in the European lexicon. Again, three categories suggest themselves:

8. terms which have become current in academic literary criticism (mimesis, catharsis, hamartia, peripeteia); these of course always carry traces of particular definitions according to the cultural strand from which they emerge;
9. *translations* of Aristotle's terms which have become durable lexical items in modern European languages, as for example the notion of a tragic 'flaw', or of 'recognition' or 'discovery': this last pair shows how the choice of a particular translation can immediately set up divergent views of the feature in question, and how the assimilation of an Aristotelian term to a pre-existing common-language word may broaden the potential sense of the term;
10. terms which have entered European languages as common-language words: French *péripétie* is an obvious case; in English, 'cathartic' is now in general use in sentences such as 'Throwing out all my old love-letters was a really cathartic experience for me.'

Category 10 may be set aside here as a standard instance of the 'cascading' of learned vocabulary into everyday speech, irritating as it may be to hard-line Aristotelian scholars. Categories 8 and 9 may be equally tiresome at times: the apparently ineradicable habit among literary critics of evoking Aristotle whenever tragedy is at issue makes one wish sometimes that, far from recovering the lost book of the

Poetics, we could lose the one we have. Putting it more neutrally, these categories together illustrate the tenacious survival of Aristotelian terms, even if survival often seems to come at the price of dilution. Their continuing use as operative concepts in literary criticism and even in other domains, in professional and non-professional circles, in students' papers and media chat-shows, suggests that they have entered the European languages in much the same way that, for example, the word 'metaphor' has. Their usefulness is in direct proportion to their success-ful assimilation into a *different* culture: in other words, to their *devia-tion* from some originary sense. They are not so much terms pre-defined by reference to an original authentic Aristotelian meaning, but rather heuristic concepts seeking a precise definition within the cultural con-text where they are now being used.

I wish to emphasise once again at this point that the foregoing review of different ways of reading, approaching and using the *Poetics* is only approximate, and is not meant to be exhaustive. I have, for example, omitted the category which would have seemed most obvious to early modern commentators, namely the *prescriptive*: although in modern times no creative writer is likely to regard Aristotelian poetics as providing a set of rules guaranteeing the correct composition of drama and narrative, it might not be difficult to find cases where the writer's imagination has been in some degree shaped or influenced by a knowledge of the *Poetics*. The object of the classification exercise, at all events, is to mark out the terrain within which the participants in a conference like this one take their various stands, and to raise two key questions. Both are implicit in the way specialists of various persuasions engage with Aristotle and with each other; both are also likely to surface explicitly from time to time in the conference papers and debates.

The first question is this: does the philological or contextual approach (specialist Aristotelian scholarship) provide a necessary grounding for all the others – or, if not a grounding, at least a limiting frame in the case of the more centrifugal approaches? More particularly, do we need to assume an 'authentic' meaning for Aristotelian terms or *loci* which will serve as a point of reference for given historical interpretations?

In practical terms, we can certainly say that some readings of the *Poetics* – for example, certain of the interpretations advanced by neo-Aristotelian theorists of the early modern period – are 'wrong', in the sense that they are incompatible with the linguistic, cultural and intellectual world to which Aristotle and his treatise belonged. Modern classical scholars are undoubtedly in a strong position to arbitrate on such questions: they have, for example, a larger body of textual materi-als to work from, and they of course also have the advantage of hundreds of years of scholarly hindsight.

Yet a certain unease begins to creep in at the point where we find earlier interpretations being dismissed on the assumption that scholarship, like technology, gets better and better all the time. One cannot help remarking that there has been a notorious lack of consensus among modern scholars on the interpretation of the *Poetics*: one could even say that readings are more plural, more centrifugal nowadays than they were, say, in the sixteenth century. And the history of modern readings of the *Poetics* shows that what one generation confidently asserts and believes to be historically authentic will be rejected, or at least challenged, by succeeding generations. If a volume like this had been published fifty years ago, the focal points and areas of consensus would have been quite different; they will certainly also be different again in 2050.

It follows that one should at least let the reception history of the *Poetics* have its full and independent value, rather than congratulating its approximations to what current scholarship regards as correct while deploring or mocking its aberrations and deformations. We obviously can't set aside, whether consciously or not, our knowledge of modern readings that may seem to us more plausible. But it is important to resist the temptation to use them as a reliable criterion for judging particular historical interpretations; otherwise we run the risk of undermining the cultural identity of those interpretations.

Let us take two examples from the early modern period. Pierre Corneille understood catharsis in a Christian perspective as the moral improvement that flows from seeing vice punished and virtue rewarded. Clearly that is not what Aristotle meant by catharsis, even if we are not sure what he really did mean. But it is more helpful to compare Corneille's reading with others available in his day, and to understand it as a coherent element in an ethical view of drama derived in part, for example, from Jesuit teaching, than to regard it as hopelessly naive. This example may have less force, however, to the extent that Corneille was in any case trying to distance himself from Aristotle. He was not unduly concerned whether his readings were cavalier, since he saw himself as a 'modern' in the seventeenth-century sense, writing for modern audiences. He was himself aware, in other words, of the cultural changes which produce successive revisionist readings.

This is not the case with my second example, which I borrow from a recent paper by María-José Vega.[5] It concerns the way in which sixteenth-century commentators read Aristotle's reference to the story of Mitys at the end of *Poetics* 9 (1452a1-10). Renaissance commentators regard this passage as central to Aristotle's whole account of tragedy, and in this respect at least they have a modern supporter in Stephen Halliwell.[6] They accept that he excludes pure unmotivated chance from tragedy: tragic outcomes have the greatest impact when they defy expectations but at the same time prove to be, or at least are taken to be, the consequence of a chain of cause and effect. However, they read the loose and fragmentary syntax of the passage very differently from most modern commentators. Several of them – Robortello and Vittori, for example – interpret the last clause ('therefore such plots as these must necessarily be the best') as referring to the example of the statue of Mitys which immediately precedes it. Far from representing the lowest step in the hierarchy of tragic actions, the case of Mitys in their view gives priority to the notion of an overriding fate or providence. The best plots thus become the ones in which human understanding of cause and effect is baffled, but where a marvellous congruity between human action and the unexpected event is retrospectively discerned. Other commentators, like Castelvetro, at least place the Mitys case on a footing with other ways in which tragic *maraviglia* may be elicited.[7]

Modern commentators and translators, by contrast, regard the final clause of the chapter as referring back to plots in which outcomes are unexpected yet the result of a rationally analysable cause-and-effect sequence. The story of Mitys is bracketed out and considered as at best providing material for an *a fortiori* argument ('if purely accidental cases which seem to happen by design generate a sense of wonder, how much greater will the effect be when the unexpected outcome is shown to be the result of a rational sequence'). The modern consensus is almost certainly bound up, I would suggest, with a secular imagination according to which rational and verifiable causality is necessarily superior to some concept of fate or divine providence. Perhaps we are right to say that Aristotle shared that preference with us, and that early modern commentators were misled by their Christian world-view; perhaps, if we could ask Aristotle about it, his answer would surprise us. However that may be, the case can only be decided in terms of probabilities rather than certainties; the only certainty is that one generation's *doxa* will be different from another's.

In deciding how to judge such matters, it is essential to distinguish between two different issues. Most specialists of Aristotelian poetics, whatever their particular area of interest, might without too much difficulty be persuaded that it is unhelpful to use modern scholarship as a criterion leading to negative value-judgements about interpretations advanced in other periods, and that the cultural integrity of each period ought to be respected. But this leaves open the more intractable question whether, when talking about the reception of the *Poetics*, one ought simply to forget about Aristotle's work as a text belonging to ancient Greek culture and focus exclusively on its rewriting in a given reception culture. This move is easily justified in theory; in practice, it is hard to apply, given what we already know, and arguably even counter-productive. In the first place, one needs to admit what one does know in order to avoid that knowledge exercising its influence surreptitiously. And secondly, familiarity with a series of rewritings of the *Poetics* over time makes it much easier to read the shifts and deviations of which that historical sequence is composed. Such a relativisation of the *Poetics* and its meanings along a historical axis would of course be in every respect analogous to a study of the transformations of ancient philosophies – the Platonist tradition, the Stoic tradition, and indeed the Aristotelian tradition in its broadest sense – in later European culture.

This is the kind of answer to our first question which will inevitably be given by a historian of ideas, although philosophers might take a different view. It is essentially a way of reconciling historical positivism with a relativism less radical than that suggested by my fourth category of possible approaches to the *Poetics*. We need now, however, to move beyond questions of scholarly style or preference (which are equally applicable to many other canonic texts) to the problem that underpins them. We thus come to the second of the two questions mentioned at the outset. Why is the *Poetics* so powerful, so apparently unavoidable still in any account of European drama? Why do we keep returning to this obscure, incomplete little text from two and a half millennia ago?

One of the answers proposed in the course of the Oslo symposium focuses precisely on the brevity and (arguably) lacunary character of the text. Passing remarks made even by scholars seeking to establish a single authentic sense pointed in this direction: 'We've got to do the best we can with the little we've got'; 'Aristotle's statements are neither easy to interpret nor obviously consistent with one another.'[8] Such an explanation is by its nature relativising, even potentially 'postmodern'; it accords with the view that readers compose the texts they read, *a fortiori* where the text fails so visibly to provide all the requisite information. It is certainly part of the answer to the enigma of the *Poetics*, but is not ultimately satisfying on its own.

Another possible answer flows from the normative role that the *Poetics* seems to have acquired as it were of its own momentum, its persistent presence in all kinds of discourse on the nature of dramatic and narrative fiction. That role appears to be a long-term after-effect of the *authority* of Aristotle, that is to say of the way in which the power of his discourse became embedded in the European cultural tradition. The corpus of principles and practices broadly known as neoclassical doctrine is the most obvious embodiment of this authority. However, it is helpful to remember that the phenomenon of neoclassicism, with its progressive evolution towards the establishment of a set of prescriptive 'rules', was itself the outgrowth of the centuries-old ascendancy of Aristotelian thought as the underpinning for scholastic philosophy and theology, to which one should no doubt add the revisionist Aristotelian-

203

ism of the Paduan school that formed the immediate context for the mid-sixteenth-century revival of the *Poetics*. The moment when the 'rules' were beginning to be established in France – the moment, for example, of the founding of the Académie Française and of the first acrimonious debates over what was and was not acceptable dramatic practice – was also the moment when the scholastic establishment, in the name of Aristotelian science, was repudiating experiments demonstrating the existence of a vacuum and evidence for the heliocentric structure of the universe. It is hard to imagine that the *Poetics* could have achieved its unique status without that profound political and even theological backing. The result, at all events, was that neo-Aristotelian terms and concepts were naturalised in the languages of Western Europe and remained there as points of reference long after neoclassical poetics itself – let alone its scholastic godfather – had been superseded or discredited.

Once again, however, this explanation cannot be complete, if only because Aristotelian poetics, having reached its peak in the seventeenth and eighteenth centuries, then went into relative abeyance as alternative ways of reading tragedy began to be explored. Two other possibilities then present themselves, both separately and as a connected pair.

The first is that the *Poetics* attached itself from the outset and by its nature to an extraordinarily powerful body of existing texts, some of which have become the founding texts of the European canon. In its later rewritings, it continued to refer to those texts, but it also harnessed itself to new canonic texts – Shakespeare, Racine – from which it drew new energies and a potent mode of survival, rather like a virus adapting itself to the changing physiology of its hosts.

The second is that, as his neoclassical admirers claimed,[9] Aristotle succeeded in the *Poetics* in giving expression to deep and relatively invariant structures of human experience. Or, putting it another way, one might say that the persistence of Aristotelian concepts, their ability to remain useful through many transformations of meaning and context, suggests a transhistorical community of experience. When a modern audience sees *King Lear*, its responses will be in all kinds of ways different from the responses of ancient Greek audiences to, say, the *Oedipus* plays; yet one is tempted to believe that certain loosely-defined parameters of those experiences are analogous. That is the insight on which Freud built his famous analysis of the *Oedipus*: his mistake was to think that his way of defining the common element was not itself strictly determined by the epistemology and culture of his own day. If that argument is accepted, it is not difficult to see why the term 'catharsis' functions so well as a loose umbrella concept for the various ways in which a tragedy may occasion some kind of emotional or psychic shift in the spectator, or 'hamartia' as a flexible category designating in general terms what one might call the primary skid, the malfunction in human behaviour or perception where catastrophe originates.

This kind of argument would lead us back, then, from the brink of a radical scepticism about the value of such terms towards a more moderate view, still relativistic, still rejecting the possibility of any single objective viewpoint from which these phenomena can be evaluated, yet accepting the probable existence of recurring patterns of human experience. In that view, the formulations of Aristotle's *Poetics* would still be shaped in most respects by the culture within which they arose; but they could also be seen as achieving an unusual degree of penetration to the ways in which *homo sapiens* tries to make sense of the world. I must stress here that this is not an argument for an uncompromisingly essentialist view: it goes no farther than the well-known paradigm of translatability between languages (although no proposition is perfectly translatable from one language to another, any proposition in any language can be meaningfully translated into any other language).

This move would have various consequences. It would substitute a 'layered', archaeological model of cultural variation for a linear, transformative model on the one hand, or a universalist one on the other.[10] It would suggest that various different interpretations of the *Poetics*, even incompatible ones and discredited ones, have an enduring and cumulative value. And it would also authorise an approach to poetics focusing on the cognitive functions and properties of literary texts rather than, say, on their purely formal properties or their ethical status or their aesthetic effects: we return here, then, to category 7. Such an approach would be in accord with the work which is now being done on human cognitive evolution, including of course the evolution of language skills, but also, by extension, of other ways of comprehending and modelling the world: what one might call cultural skills. Several contributors to this volume refer to the cognitive aspects of Aristotelian poetics, which are also foregrounded in Halliwell's *Aristotle's Poetics*, and it seems indeed that there has been a shift in the last decade or so among Aristotelian scholars towards that kind of perspective.

Following that line, Aristotle's *Poetics*, with its emphasis on learning and mimesis, on the distinction between historical truth and probable fictions, and on the modalities of narrative logic, would emerge as a powerful early attempt to understand fiction as a way of thinking and as a model for experiencing the world; in the cognitive archaeology, it would therefore occupy a critical layer (although of course not an *authoritative* one). The enduring value of the *Poetics* as a model, however it may have been hijacked by successive cultures, then becomes a less arbitrary phenomenon, less of a mere historical accident.

Incidentally, the same argument might also support the proposition that anagnorisis, far from being the poor relation that it has tended to be in modern poetics at least, is central *both* to Aristotle's *Poetics and* to poetics in general. Might one not argue, for example, that the passage on mimesis and identification of represented likenesses in chapter 4 (1448b4-19), which Halliwell's chapter in this volume discusses so pertinently, is connected with the role Aristotle assigns to anagnorisis in his discussion of plot in chapters 10 and 11?[11] As I suggested in *Recognitions*, the plot of anagnorisis, far from being a spurious and discredited stratagem for engineering an artificial closure, is the paradigm of the way story-telling (in which I include dramatic performance) has helped humans to make sense of their experience, to understand the sequential relations between events, to come to terms with surprising and unexpected sequences, with chance and with its other face, which is logic. Anagnorisis ought to have its day, since it has a particular value in displaying the cognitive structures inherent in works of dramatic and narrative fiction. We have surely had enough, for the time being at least, of the emotive-psychological-psychoanalytic readings surrounding 'catharsis'.

The word 'incidentally' at the beginning of the last paragraph is of course not innocent. This shift to the theme of recognition plots is designed to bring to a close my discussion of the special critical phenomenon constituted by the afterlife of the *Poetics* and to provide a bridge to the second section of this chapter, in which a particular recognition plot will be the focus of attention. Meanwhile, it is perhaps necessary to add a qualification to the points made above in favour of a 'cognitive' approach. I hope it will be clear that it is not my intention to suggest that such an approach, or any other, will yield the essential truth about Aristotle's text, still less about literary poetics as a whole. Future generations may well see it as an irrelevant or even misguided product of a late twentieth-century obsession with media and information technology. Each generation, however, needs its readings, needs its obsessions even, and this one looks as if it still has some way to run.

Mignon's afterlife

I turn now from generalities and abstractions to a particular story – the story of Mignon – which is neither an 'example' nor a direct continuation of the argument sketched out so far; it is meant rather to complement that argument. It takes the form of a recognition story, the type of plot for which Aristotle uses the term of art 'anagnorisis', and we may immediately note that the recognition scene is itself an ancient and potent narrative core, capable of virtually infinite transformation into new and surprising forms – a 'deep structure', in the sense already indicated.

The story of Mignon begins with Goethe's *Wilhelm Meisters Lehr-jahre*, first published in 1796.[12] It thus belongs to a critical moment in the history of poetics, perhaps to a critical layer in the archaeology of poetics. The later eighteenth century represents the last phase in the transmission and assimilation of the *Poetics* as a key point of reference for dramatic theory and practice. It continues to be cited, its concepts are still being deployed and reinvested, but the aesthetic and cultural contexts of its reception are now changing rapidly: Lessing's *Hamburg-ische Dramaturgie* is an obvious example, or the dramatic poetics of Schiller,[13] not to mention Schlegel. At the same time, the balance between the genres is changing decisively: the novel is evolving rapidly and the poetics of the novel is moving towards centre stage.

In order to evoke this particular moment and Goethe's place in relation to it, I shall first consider a connection between the explicit poetics of *Wilhelm Meisters Lehrjahre* (henceforward *WML*) and its implied poetics.

At various points in the novel, there are extensive discussions – usually dialogues between Wilhelm himself and other characters – about questions of poetics or questions bearing on poetics. One of these concerns the relative merits of tragedy and the novel (Book V, ch. 7); another sequence concerns the dramatic unity, or lack of unity, of *Hamlet* (IV.15, V.4); yet another is about fate and chance – the supposed logic of events (I.17, II.9, VII.9).[14] The key discussion of this last series takes place between Wilhelm and a mysterious stranger he meets at the beginning of the novel; it is echoed, briefly but with an explicit reference to its importance, in the initiation scene of Book VII. Ostensibly, what they are talking about is actual human experience, not causality in fictional plots. However, when such dialogues occur in a novel in which there are a large number of unexpected incidents and events that appear to occur purely by chance, the reader is likely to transpose the question of causality discussed by Wilhelm and the stranger to the level of fictional plots, or rather to consider the way in which fictions repre-sent the perceived cause and effect relations of the world. This is confirmed by the fact that Wilhelm's second dialogue with the stranger is part of the crucial sequence in which Wilhelm discovers that the apparently random series of events which he had experienced up to this point in his life may be retrospectively organised and transformed into a structure, a logic. Given that the dialogue about the distinctive features of the novel and of drama turns largely on this same question of chance and fate, it is clear that the theme is meant to provide a central thread, or meta-thread, in the complex weave of *WML*.

What emerges from these discussions and from the way in which the novel itself is plotted is a model of novelistic form which explicitly takes into account the fading away of metaphysical guarantees and outcomes.[14] This is of course an issue which is raised contemporaneously in several European literatures. *Tristram Shandy* and *Jacques le Fataliste* are the most obvious cases, and there happens to be a crucial connection between *Jacques le fataliste* and *Wilhelm Meister* which has, as far as I know, never been pointed out. When Wilhelm is finally admitted to the quasi-Masonic mysteries of Lothario's castle, he discovers his own story in the form of a *Rolle* or scroll: the narrative of his life has already been written out for him (VII.9). The word *Rolle* is the exact etymological equivalent of the French word *rouleau* which, in *Jacques le Fataliste*, designates the script of fate: 'ce qui était écrit là-haut'. Jacques's story, too, is already written on a scroll, and in both novels, it is impossible not to read this device as an ironic comment on the supposed 'fatality' governing many fictional stories as well as human life itself. It draws attention to the fact that it is the writer in each case who creates the 'fatality' of his characters; the two novels are themselves the scroll on which their lives are written.

In this way, the late eighteenth century reworks the questions raised at the end of chapter 9 of the *Poetics*. It is at least likely that Goethe and Diderot were aware of the Aristotelian precedent; but it seems pointless to ask whether their interest in these matters was prompted by that *locus* and similar ones, since by this time the issue of causality had permeated the whole intellectual frame of reference of Western Europe, thanks to the calling in question of religious belief and authority, the rise of experimental science and technology, and no doubt many other historical factors.

At all events, anagnorisis begins, for Wilhelm Meister, with a reading of the 'Rolle' entitled *Wilhelm Meisters Lehrjahre*. As a *Bildungsroman*, Goethe's novel could hardly be a more complete paradigm of novelistic structure as cognitive structure. Wilhelm's life begins with an error – his obsession with the theatre and his ambition to become an actor and a playwright – which is repeated over and over again throughout the first five books. In the final stages of the novel, he emerges from error (the theme is quite explicit) and readjusts his perceptions and goals, even if some issues remain unresolved (an even longer novel, *Wilhelm Meisters Wanderjahre*, still lies ahead of him). Wilhelm's love-affair with the theatre, and with women who variously represent theatre, is an allegory, recalling earlier Neoplatonist allegories of progress through illusion towards the truth. In its overt mediation of knowledge, allegory is also a markedly cognitive narrative mode, and as I have just shown, *Wilhelm Meister* explicitly, *reflexively*, enacts a cognitive process. It unmasks the error of confusing life with art (whether as tragedy or as heroic novel), and thus becomes a key text in the sequence which runs approximately from Cervantes to Flaubert.

So is Goethe's work a product then of a rationalising culture, even of a narrative move into 'Enlightenment'? The answer to that question is complicated by the fact that this explicit cognitive structure serves as a scaffolding for one of the most extravagant – and no doubt implausible – multiple recognition sequences in world literature: Books 7 and especially 8 of *WML* rival the virtuoso recognition sequences even of the *Æthiopica* and of *Cymbeline*. In these last two books, a large number of previously mysterious or anonymous characters are identified (Mignon, the Harpist, Natalie, the Countess, Lothario, Jarno, the Abbé, Felix, Friedrich); and in particular, whole life-histories are provided for Mignon and the Harpist in the mode of the romance recognition plot: incest, severance, abduction, abjection, wanderings, and eventual recovery of origins. In accordance with the critical-reflexive turn of the novel as a whole, this romance plot is ultimately sidelined: since Mignon and her father belong to the world of illusion, they are doomed to be extinguished without having enjoyed even a brief moment of mutual recognition and happiness (we shall return to that point shortly). But the prominent presence of such a plot and its denouement in the cognitive structure of the *Bildungsroman* provides us with a very clear example of the archaeology of poetics: an ancient story, coming from everywhere and nowhere, finds itself imbricated into a rationalising discourse on the structures of fiction, much as the *Oedipus* and the *Odyssey* find themselves connected with an analytic discourse in the *Poetics*, although of course in *Wilhelm Meister* the poetics is itself framed within a narrative structure.

I have already spoken of the generic relation between tragedy and the novel in *WML*. But another genre is involved here, too, one which falls, it would seem, outside the ambit of Aristotelian poetics, although the famous passage on music at *Politics* VIII.5 would no doubt give it a conceptual home.[16] The Mignon strand of the story is also a lyric strand, since Mignon, and the Harpist, who belongs to the same strand, are singers who accompany themselves on a stringed instrument (the harp or zither). It seems likely that Goethe meant the reader to perceive this instrument as the equivalent of the ancient lyre, so that these figures become virtually allegorical representations of the lyric.[17]

This lyric strand, considered in relation to the plot as a whole, appears to carry another facet of Wilhelm's trajectory through illusion: Mignon's songs are a representation of his ill-defined yearning towards the unattainable; he must eventually grow beyond them. In fact, he frequently neglects Mignon and her feelings for him, and towards the end of the novel he leaves her behind when he sets off for Lothario's allegorical château. She reappears, but only to die; the Harpist dies too, rather summarily, after an apparently miraculous recovery. They are both finally marginalised by Wilhelm's progress towards integration into the moral and practical life. Lyric poetry, like theatre, must not, it seems, be confused with life.

However, although Mignon's role in the novel is marginalised, her songs are crucial to and participate in her recognition story.[18] From the beginning, these songs, with their motif of knowledge (*'Kennst* du das Land', 'Nur wer die Sehnsucht *kennt')*, suggest enigmas or at least leave questions unanswered. Within the lyric form, these questions are connotative or expressive rather than diegetic. But since they are all finally answered in the denouement of the novel, the lyrics form one of the primary vehicles of the recognition plot. They are embryonic narratives, embryos of the narrative. Nicholas Boyle speaks of the violence which is in consequence done to Goethe's wonderfully suggestive lyrics:[19] lyrics are supposed to remain in some sense immature, unfulfilled, pubescent, like Mignon herself. I would say rather that we have here an exceptional form of lyric agnoia, a fusion of lyric and narrative which leaves a space open for anagnorisis.[20]

Let us consider one specific example, which again shows how Wilhelm's narrative strand exploits and colonises Mignon's lyric strand. In the second Mignon song, 'Nur wer die Sehnsucht kennt', there appear to be few narrative implications. It shares with the earlier song 'Kennst du das Land?' the theme of yearning for a lost place, but in this instance there is also a lost *person* ('der mich liebt und kennt / Ist in der Weite'). Most later readers of the poem will assume that the person in question is a lover: indeed, this will become one of the great love-songs of the nineteenth century. But in the novel, there is nothing to suggest that Mignon has had a lover. She is extremely young, almost a child, and her spontaneous love for Wilhelm makes it unlikely that she has a lover hidden away somewhere. In fact, the song is sung by both Mignon and the Harpist as a duet, so that the words, with their yearning for a lost home and a lost loved one, should presumably be attributed to both characters, not just to Mignon. Both of them are indeed lonely and exiled, both are distressed, both voice their distress in song: they are united through music. This affinity is likely to lead the reader to guess that there is some further connection, and such eventually proves to be the case. Although they are not aware of it and never will be, they are father and daughter. In the light of that information, which we are only given towards the end of the novel, the unknown person of lines 7-8 has a precise identity: for Mignon, it is her lost father; for the Harpist, it is his lost daughter. Interpreted in that context, the song has a tragic irony: the very person each singer longs for is actually present, singing the same song. In this way, despite its primarily lyric character, the song is deeply connected to the narrative of the novel as a whole.

However, the local narrative context of the song gives it a quite different function. It is introduced at the end of a chapter (IV.11) where Wilhelm is recovering from a bullet-wound he had received in an encounter with robbers. The chapter describes his daydreams about a beautiful but unknown woman who had appeared and given him aid while he lay wounded, then disappeared. He feels an intense yearning for her: the text tells us that 'He fell into a dreamy state of yearning' ('Er verfiel in eine träumende Sehnsucht'), and at that very moment he hears Mignon and the Harpist singing the song with great feeling. In other words, the *Sehnsucht* expressed by the song is also narrativised as a function of Wilhelm's perceptions, and of Wilhelm's strand of the plot: the unknown woman will continue to haunt his imagination, and she reappears towards the end of the novel. So the song is connected with two *different* recognition stories, one in which Wilhelm plays a central role, one concerning Mignon and the Harpist, and it is Wilhelm's which will in the end become dominant, to the point of appropriating the lyric strand.[21]

As a novel of the hero's *Bildung*, WML will be highly influential, prefiguring many nineteenth-century novels of lost illusions and sentimental education with male heroes. But the Mignon strand will also have a highly successful afterlife in its own right: innumerable composers, including Beethoven, Schubert, Schumann, Liszt, Tchaikovsky and Wolf provide settings for her songs, making her a kind of Romantic heroine of drawing-room recitals. In 1866, an opera called *Mignon* by the French composer Ambroise Thomas was first performed; it was an instant success, and remained at the top of the charts for some twenty years. Mignon is not only revived in this version, she takes centre stage, returning finally with Wilhelm to Italy, where she recognises her lost home and father, and where Wilhelm declares his love for her. The opera thus culminates in a dazzling operatic anagnorisis which takes the words and melody of Mignon's first-act aria based on 'Kennst du das Land?' and turns it into an ecstatic final trio affirming home-coming and amorous union.

The settings of Mignon's poems as *Lieder*, together with the opera, give her the freedom to become many different kinds of woman and to undergo many types of feeling. They demonstrate the power residing in the lyric nuclei with which Goethe had strewn his plot. At the same time, they also demonstrate the power of the oldest archaeological layer of *Wilhelm Meister*, Mignon's story of incest and abduction. Whatever the importance of Wilhelm's story as the founding text of the German *Bildungsroman*, it is Mignon and *her* story which will achieve celebrity throughout Europe for a hundred years, in a series of extraordinarily productive rewritings.[22] She becomes a myth – more specifically, a recognition myth. She is Iphigenia and Perdita, a figure *from* recogni-

211

tion; and she is also the figure of a reconceived poetics, a genetic variant or mutation in the history of poetics. It is true that the explicitly cognitive frame of reference is stripped away in the later musical versions, yet this *is* the embryo from which cognition and recognition came and continue to come.

One might say, then, that the example of *WML* provides a model of the way in which profound cultural changes – the emergence of new generic types and new approaches to poetics – may carry with them vestiges of ancient structures, of deeper cultural layers. And one might argue analogously that the terms of Aristotelian poetics are persistent and powerful, first because they seem to be connected to the most powerful and persistent elements in fictional plots, and secondly because they are flexible, capable of change. Like Mignon, they can escape from the structure that originally contained them and create new openings, new stories, and new ways of thinking about stories.

Notes

1. It will thus be evident that I shall not be seeking here to sketch the *Nachleben* of the *Poetics*. For such a sketch, consult Stephen Halliwell, *Aristotle's Poetics* (London and Chapel Hill, 1986), ch. 10. In his 'Epilogue: the *Poetics* and its interpreters', in *Essays on Aristotle's Poetics*, ed. Amélie Oksenberg Rorty (Princeton, 1992), Halliwell presents a methodologically revised version of this outline, in the course of which he raises the kinds of issue I shall revert to in this chapter. It is for that reason above all that I have used the phrase 'once again' in my opening sentence: I am conscious of treading on ground already covered, although I approach it from a rather different angle. Rather than making specific allusion to Halliwell's arguments in what follows, I would like here to acknowledge my debt in general terms. For a much more extensive discussion of the problems posed by the afterlife of one particular Aristotelian term (anagnorisis), see my book *Recognitions: A Study in Poetics* (Oxford, 1988).

2. See in particular Brooks, *Reading for the Plot: Design and Intention in Narrative* (New York and Oxford, 1984).

3. See Ricœur's critical trilogy *Temps et récit* (Paris, 1983, 1984, 1985).

4. See also Halliwell, *Aristotle's Poetics*, 317-18, on the 'critical fragmentation' of the *Poetics*.

5. 'El azar y la maravilla en la teoría neoaristotélica de la tragedia: la estatua de Mitis en el Renacimento', in *Theatralia III: Tragedia, Comedia y Canon*, ed. Jesús G. Maestro (Vigo, 2000), 123-59.

6. See *Aristotle's Poetics*, ch. 7, especially 209. For another discussion in a sixteenth-century perspective, see Kirsti Minsaas' chapter in this volume.

7. One may remark here that the scene in *The Winter's Tale* where Hermione's statue comes to life is remarkably similar to the Mitys example as a scene generating wonder through its apparently supernatural character, which is indeed referred to by the characters themselves. The consonance between these two cruxes, regardless of any putative reading of the *Poetics* by Shakespeare, may help us to understand the sense of both in a culture for which 'wonder' was a critical and complex category (see once again Kirsti Minsaas' chapter).

8. These remarks (the first by Malcolm Heath, the second by Elizabeth Belfiore) were noted by hand at the time and may not exactly represent the intention of the speaker or their respective contexts. See also Michael Silk's chapter in this volume.

9. See for example the passage from Rapin's *Réflexions sur la Poétique d'Aristote*, I.xii, quoted by Silk, above, p. 179.

10. My use of the archaeological analogy here and elsewhere in this chapter is not meant to have a specifically Foucauldian sense.

11. The principal objection to this argument would be that, in chapter 4, Aristotle is speaking of the spectator's recognition, whereas in chapter 11 it is the character who recognises. However, the whole point of speaking about the spectator's recognition is to bring out the process by which the spectator makes sense of a dramatic 'imitation', so the link seems to be entailed in the nature of the discussion. Much bolder connections are routinely made by Aristotelian scholars in elucidating passages from the *Poetics* in the context of the treatise itself, let alone other Aristotelian texts or other ancient Greek texts.

12. Or, more strictly, with Goethe's unfinished novel *Wilhelm Meisters theatralische Sendung*, out of which the *Lehrjahre* grew. What follows here is only a preliminary sketch of a subject to which I hope eventually to devote a full-length study. Since its role in the present argument is largely symbolic, detailed bibliographical and scholarly reference will be omitted here. References to the text of *Wilhelm Meisters Lehrjahre* will be given in the form of book- and chapter-numbers.

13. Schiller's *Über die tragische Kunst* (1792), for example, discusses issues similar to those addressed by Aristotle, but in a different language and without direct engagement with the *Poetics*.

14. The same theme is discussed also in V.7 in relation to the differences between the drama and the novel: chance is allowed in the novel, whereas the characters of drama must be driven forward by their destiny ('destiny' here representing a higher sphere of causation).

15. This process is thematised in relation to Christian belief in Book VI, the *Bekenntnisse einer schönen Seele*.

16. On this question in Aristotle, see Stephen Halliwell, 'Music and the limits of mimesis', *Colloquium philosophicum* IV (1997-8) (Florence, 1999), 9-30.

17. The first appearance of the Harpist in II.11 prompts some remarks from Wilhelm on the superiority of song over music alone, an attitude that Goethe himself is known to have adopted.

18. Mignon's songs, in the order in which they appear in the novel, are as follows: 'Kennst du das Land?', 'Nur wer die Sehnsucht kennt', 'Heiss mich nicht reden; heiss mich schweigen', 'So lasst mich scheinen, bis ich werde'.

19. Nicholas Boyle, *Goethe: The Poet and the Age*, vol. 2, *Revolution and Renunciation, 1790-1803* (Oxford, 2000), 387-8.

20. It is also relevant here that the Harpist is connected not only with lyric song but also with the tragic, both through the character of his songs and through his encounters with madness and death – he at times resembles a Lear, a Leontes or perhaps a Pericles. He is a figure from tragedy assigned to the lyric margins, able only to sing about his sorrows.

21. This happens in an even more striking way with 'Kennst du das Land?', which is appropriated for Wilhelm's story in Book VII.

22. I omit here the extensive and fascinating English strand of this story, which involves George Eliot as well as a whole series of minor English novelists of the late nineteenth century.

Select Bibliography

Armstrong, J., 'Aristotle on the philosophical nature of poetry', *Classical Quarterly* 48 (1998), 447-55.

Barnes, J., 'Roman Aristotle', in J. Barnes and Miriam Griffin (eds.), *Philosophia togata II: Plato and Aristotle at Rome* (Oxford, 1997), 1-70.

Belfiore, E., 'Pleasure, tragedy and Aristotelian psychology', *Classical Quarterly* 35 (1985), 349-61.

—— *Tragic Pleasures: Aristotle on Plot and Emotion* (Princeton, 1992).

—— 'Aristotle and Iphigenia', in Rorty, 358-78.

Bignami, E., *La Poetica di Aristotele e il concetto dell' arte presso gli antichi* (Florence, 1932).

Bishop, T.G., *Shakespeare and the Theatre of Wonder* (Cambridge, 1996).

Cave, T., *Recognitions: A Study in Poetics* (Oxford, 1990).

Cooper, J.M., *Reason and Emotion* (Princeton, 1999).

Crane, R.S. (ed.), *Critics and Criticism: Ancient and Modern* (Chicago, 1952).

Cunningham, J.V., *Woe or Wonder: The Emotional Effect of Shakespearean Tragedy* (Chicago, 1951).

Eden, K., *Poetic and Legal Fiction in the Aristotelian Tradition* (Princeton, 1986).

Else, G.F., *Aristotle's Poetics: The Argument* (Cambridge, MA, 1957).

Feagin, S.L., 'The pleasures of tragedy', *American Philosophical Quarterly* 20 (1983), 95-104.

Ferrari, G.R.F., 'Aristotle's literary aesthetics', *Phronesis* 44 (1999), 181-98.

Flashar, H., 'Aristoteles und Brecht', in id., *Eidola* (Amsterdam, 1989), 179-99.

Fortenbaugh, W.W., *Aristotle on Emotion* (London, 1975).

—— and P. Steinmetz (eds.), *Cicero's Knowledge of the Peripatos* (Rutgers University Studies in Classical Humanities, New Brunswick, NJ, 1989).

Gallop, D., 'Animals in the *Poetics*', *Oxford Studies in Ancient Philosophy* 8 (1990), 145-71.

Golden, L., 'Aristotle and the audience for tragedy', *Mnemosyne* 29 (1976), 351-9.

—— 'Comic pleasure', *Hermes* 115 (1987), 165-74.

—— 'Aristotle on the pleasure of comedy', in Rorty, 379-86.

—— *Aristotle on Tragic and Comic Mimesis* (Atlanta, 1992).

Goldschmidt, V., *Temps physique et temps tragique chez Aristote* (Paris, 1982).

Hall, E., 'Is there a polis in Aristotle's *Poetics?*', in *Tragedy and the Tragic*, ed. M.S. Silk (Oxford, 1996), 295-309.

Halliwell, S., *Aristotle's Poetics* (London and Chapel Hill, NC, 1986, repr. with new Introduction, 1998).

—— 'Pleasure, understanding and emotion in Aristotle's *Poetics*', in Rorty, 241-60.

215

—— 'Aristotle on form and unity', in *Encyclopaedia of Aesthetics*, ed. M. Kelly, vol. I (New York and Oxford, 1998), 101-4.

—— 'Music and the limits of mimesis', *Colloquium philosophicum* 4 (1997-8 [1999]), 9-30.

—— *The Aesthetics of Mimesis: Ancient Texts and Modern Problems* (Princeton, 2001).

Hathaway, B., *The Age of Criticism: The Late Renaissance in Italy* (Ithaca, 1962).

—— *Marvels and Commonplaces: Renaissance Literary Criticism* (New York, 1968).

Heath, M., *Unity in Greek Poetics* (Oxford, 1989).

—— 'Aristotelian comedy', *Classical Quarterly* 39 (1989), 344-54.

—— 'The universality of poetry in Aristotle's *Poetics*', *Classical Quarterly* 41 (1991), 389-402.

Herrick, M., *The Fusion of Horatian and Aristotelian Literary Criticism 1531-1555* (Urbana, 1946).

Janko, R., *Aristotle on Comedy: Towards a Reconstruction of Poetics II* (London, Berkeley and Los Angeles. 1984).

—— *Aristotle:* Poetics *I with the* Tractatus Coislinianus (Indianapolis and Cambridge, 1987).

—— 'Philodemus' *On Poems* and Aristotle's *On Poets*', *Cronache Ercolanesi* 21 (1991), 5-64.

—— 'From catharsis to the Aristotelian mean', in Rorty, 341-58.

—— 'Reception of Aristotle in Antiquity', in *Encyclopedia of Aesthetics*, ed. M. Kelly, vol. 1 (New York and Oxford, 1998), 104-7.

Javitch, D., 'The emergence of poetic Genre theory in the sixteenth century', *Modern Language Quarterly* 59 (1998), 139-69.

—— 'The assimilation of Aristotle's *Poetics* in sixteenth-century Italy', in Norton, 53-65.

—— 'Italian epic theory', in Norton, 205-15.

Kosman, A., 'Acting: *drama* as the *mimesis* of *praxis*', in Rorty, 51-72

Kraut, R., *Aristotle Politics Books VII and VIII* (Oxford, 1997).

Lear, J., 'Katharsis', *Phronesis* 33 (1988), 297-326, repr. in *Open Minded: Working out the Logic of the Soul* (Cambridge, MA, 1998).

—— 'Katharsis', in Rorty, 315-40.

Lord, C., *Education and Culture in the Political Thought of Aristotle* (Ithaca, 1982).

Lucas, D.W., *Aristotle:* Poetics (Oxford 1968).

Nardelli, M.L., 'La catarsi poetica nel *Pherc.* 1581', *Cronache Ercolanesi* 8 (1978), 96-103.

Norton, G.P. (ed.), *Cambridge History of Literary Criticism*, vol. 3: *The Renaissance* (Cambridge, 1999).

Nussbaum, M., 'Tragedy and self-sufficiency: Plato and Aristotle on fear and pity', in Rorty, 261-90.

—— 'Aristotle on human nature and the foundations of ethics', in *World, Mind, and Ethics: Essays on the Ethical Philosophy of Bernard Williams*, ed. J.E.J. Altham and R. Harrison (Cambridge, 1995), 86-131.

Packer, M., 'Dissolving the paradox of tragedy', *Journal of Aesthetics and Art Criticism* 47 (1989), 211-19.

Reiss, T., 'Renaissance theatre and the theory of tragedy', in Norton, 229-47.

Bibliography

Roberts, D.H., 'Outside the drama: the limits of tragedy in Aristotle's *Poetics*', in Rorty, 133-54.

Rorty, A.O. (ed.), *Essays on Aristotle's Poetics* (Princeton, 1992).

Savile, A., *The Test of Time: An Essay in Philosophical Aesthetics* (Oxford, 1982).

Schrier, O.J., *The Poetics of Aristotle and the Tractatus Coislinianus: A Bibliography from about 900 till 1996* (Leiden, 1998).

Sherman, N., *Aristotle's Theory of Moral Education* (Diss. Harvard University, 1982).

Sifakis, G.M., 'Learning from art and pleasure in learning: an interpretation of Aristotle *Poetics* 4 1448b8-19', in *Studies in Honour of T.B.L. Webster*, ed. J.H. Betts, J.T. Hooker and J.R. Green (Bristol, 1986), vol. 1, 211-22.

Silk, M.S., 'The "six parts of tragedy" in Aristotle's *Poetics*', *Proceedings of the Cambridge Philological Society* 40 (1994), 108-15.

Solmsen, F., 'The origins and methods of Aristotle's *Poetics*', *Classical Quarterly* 29 (1935), 192-201, repr. in *Kleine Schriften*, vol. 2 (Hildesheim, 1968), 119-28.

———— 'Aristotle and Cicero on the Orator's playing upon the feelings', *Classical Philology* 33 (1938), 390-404, repr. in *Kleine Schriften*, vol. 2 (Hildesheim, 1968), 216-30.

———— 'The Aristotelian tradition in ancient rhetoric', *American Journal of Philology* 62 (1941), 35-50 and 169-60, repr. in *Kleine Schriften*, vol. 2 (Hildesheim, 1968), 178-215.

Sutton, D., *The Catharsis of Comedy* (Lanham, 1994).

Tigerstedt, E.N., 'Observations on the reception of Aristotle's *Poetics* in the Latin West', *Studies in the Renaissance* 15 (1968), 7-24.

Too, Y.L., *The Idea of Ancient Literary Criticism* (Oxford, 1999).

Urban, R.T., 'All or nothing at all: another look at the unity of time in Aristotle', *Classical Journal* 61 (1966), 262-4.

Verdenius, W.J., '*Katharsis tôn pathêmatôn*', in *Autour d'Aristote: Recueil d'Études de philosophie ancienne et médiévale offert à Monseigneur A. Mansion* (Louvain, 1955), 367-73.

von Fritz, K., 'Die Bedeutung des Aristoteles für die Geschichtsschreibung', in *Histoire et Historiens dans l'Antiquité* (Fondation Hardt, Entretiens 4 (Geneva, 1956), 85-128.

Walton, K.L., *Mimesis as Make-Believe* (Cambridge, MA, 1990).

Weinberg, B., *A History of Literary Criticism in the Italian Renaissance*, 2 vols. (Chicago, 1961).

White, S. A., 'Aristotle's favorite tragedies', in Rorty, 221-40.

Index Locorum

This index is to the works of Aristotle only.

Poetics

1447a8ff.: 174
1447a19-20: 21
1448a1-6: 58
1448a2: 11
1448a19-28: 35, 37
1448a21: 37
1448a22: 37
1448a23: 37, 41
1448a25-8: 59
1448a25-9: 54
1448a26-7: 11
1448b4-5: 20
1448b4-9: 84
1448b4-19: 88, 206
1448b5-20: 20
1448b8-9: 88
1448b9: 90
1448b9-10: 89
1448b10-12: 10
1448b11: 92, 104
1448b14-15: 21
1448b16-17: 95
1448b17: 90, 91, 104
1448b17-18: 105
1448b17-19: 9, 90
1448b20-1: 9
1448b20-2: 20-1
1448b23-1449a6: 105
1448b24f.: 85
1448b24ff.: 184
1449a1-3: 85
1449a19: 26, 47
1449a20-1: 56, 58
1449a21: 26
1449a31-3: 61
1449a32-3: 55
1449a32-7: 53, 59

1449b9: 28
1449b9-10: 161
1449b9-20: 58
1449b10: 11
1449b11: 161
1449b12: 45
1449b12-14: 26
1449b12-13: 26, 44
1449b12-16: 44, 45
1449b14: 27
1449b15-16: 47
1449b24: 9, 11
1449b24-5: 25
1449b24-8: 65
1449b25: 9
1449b26: 37
1449b27-8: 12
1449b28: 178
1449b28-9: 9
1449b31-3: 35, 38
1450a3-4: 9
1450a3-5: 98, 99
1450a4: 175, 176
1450a4ff.: 191
1450a8: 195
1450a9-12: 176
1450a10-11: 20
1450a11: 176
1450a15: 175
1450a15-17: 98
1450a15-b4: 180
1450a15-b20: 180
1450a16-17: 99
1450a17: 73
1450a22: 176
1450a22-3: 175
1450a23-9: 195
1450a29-b4: 20
1450a36: 104

219

1450b3-4: 98
1450b5-7: 105
1450b12: 100
1450b15-20: 180
1450b16-17: 9
1450b16-20: 195
1450b25: 44
1450b26: 44
1450b36: 44
1450b36-9: 26
1450b37: 26, 44
1450b37: 25
1450b38-9: 36
1451a4: 36, 44
1451a5: 26, 36
1451a6: 26, 39
1451a6-7: 26, 35
1451a9-10: 35
1451a9-15: 61
1451a11: 44
1451a11-15: 26
1451a12: 44, 193
1451a13: 27, 38
1451a15: 44
1451a16-35: 191
1451a24: 21
1451a28: 36
1451a36-9: 163
1451a36-b5: 181
1451a36-b11: 178
1451a37-8: 101
1451b7: 97
1451b8-9: 86, 98, 164
1451b9-10: 97
1451b14-15: 105
1451b38-1452a1: 38
1452a1-10: 148, 201
1452a1-11: 34
1452a3-4: 193
1452a16: 46
1452a23: 27, 46
1452a24: 124
1452a31: 27
1452b28ff.: 194
1452b30-2: 61
1452b35-8: 156
1452b35-1453a3: 137
1453a1-6: 149
1453a7-11: 156
1453a7-12: 191

1453a8-17: 61
1453a18-22: 124
1453a23-30: 191
1453a30-9: 12
1453a33-4: 12
1453a34: 18
1453b1-8: 195
1453b1-14: 9
1453b3-6: 9, 175
1453b3-7: 46
1453b3-10: 38
1453b10-13: 7
1453b14-15: 20
1453b14-22: 191
1453b22: 113
1454a2-4: 149
1454a6-7: 149
1454a8: 190
1454a10-11: 21
1454b2: 190
1455a16-21: 149
1455a22ff.: 98, 193, 194
1455a34-b2: 86
1455a35ff.: 107
1455b17: 43
1455b17-23: 43
1455b29: 27, 46
1455b30: 41
1456a19-23: 153
1456a19-25: 148
1456b1: 65
1457b22-5: 30
1459a17: 37
1459a17-20: 42
1459a19: 36
1459a20: 37
1459a23: 38
1459a27-8: 38
1459a33: 36
1459b2-3: 43
1459b2-7: 37
1459b17: 26, 161
1459b17-31: 25
1459b18: 26
1459b18-20: 38
1459b19: 36
1459b20-2: 37
1459b21-2: 26
1459b22-3: 25
1459b22-8: 27

1459b23: 26
1459b24-5: 38
1459b24-6: 38
1459b26: 37
1459b26-27: 41
1459b29: 26
1460a7: 37
1460a7-8: 96
1460a11-18: 150
1460a26: 150
1460b23ff.: 175
1460b25: 151
1460b36: 105
1461a11: 105
1461b2: 105
1461b11: 150
1461b12-13: 164
1461b18: 105
1462a11-12: 20
1462a12: 46
1462a16: 9
1462a18-b2: 27
1462a18-b1: 42
1462a18-b11: 25
1462b1-3: 25
1462b3ff.: 193
1462b7: 46
1462b8-9: 37
1462b10-11: 37
1462b12-15: 42
1462b19: 68
ch. 4: 9, 10, 21
ch. 7: 26, 33, 38
ch. 9: 190
ch. 10: 206
ch. 11: 206
ch. 13: 12, 113, 116
ch. 14: 113, 116
ch. 23: 38
ch. 26: 12, 16, 27, 37, 183
fr. II Kassel: 56, 66

Rhetoric

1342a10-11: 12
1342a11-15: 12
1356b2-6: 107
1360a35-7: 106
1370b1-7: 22
1370b10-15: 8
1370b25-9: 8

1370b30-2: 8
1371a31-4: 147
1371a31-b10: 89, 91, 94
1371b4-10: 9
1371b9: 90
1371b10-12: 148
1371b27-8: 147
1378a30-b10: 8
1382a21: 7
1385b13: 7
1393a26-7: 107
1394a21-8: 107
1394a22-3: 106
1406b6-8: 55, 58
1410b10-11: 9
1410b10-26: 104
1410b17-20: 91
1410b19: 90
1412a19-22: 59
1414a8-12: 105
1417a12-16: 47
1419b3-9: 56, 66

Politics

1253b8: 94
1291a28: 105
1332a29: 85
1333a30-b5: 22
1334b6: 85
1336a28-34: 88
1336a30-2: 82
1336a39-b23: 55
1336b4-7: 82
1336b33f.: 82
1337b27-1338a30: 13
1337b28-9: 13
1337b29-32: 13
1337b35-1338a1: 13
1338a1-6: 13
1338a4-6: 16
1338a13-30: 13
1339a14-b10: 13
1339a41-b4: 14
1339b10-11: 14
1339b15-31: 14
1339b31-42: 14
1339b32-33: 14
1339b42: 15
1339b42-1340b19: 14
1339b42-1340a27: 69

1340 a12-13: 15
1340a14-18: 107
1340a23-8: 21
1340a36-8: 58
1340b13: 15
1340b20ff.: 14
1341b32-1342a18: 194
1342a1-15: 63
1342a11-13: 65
1342a11-15: 21
7.17: 65
8.5: 86, 209

Nicomachean Ethics

1095b4-9: 82
1099a7-20: 16
1099a31-3: 17
1101a32ff.: 47
1101a32-3: 41
1103a19-24: 77
1103a24-26: 77
1103b7-30: 81
1104a1-7: 99
1104b11-13: 78
1104b30-1105a1: 73
1105b28-1106a6: 22
1107a28-32: 106
1109b20-3: 106
1110b18-22: 86
1115b12: 86
1116a12f.: 79
1116a18-20: 79
1116a27: 79
1116a28: 86
1116a30-b2: 79
1116a31: 79
1116b2-3: 86
1117a29-b22: 17
1117a32-5: 22
1117b9: 86
1119b16: 86
1120a12: 86
1122b6: 86
1123a24: 86
1126a31: 66
1126b11-1128b9: 66
1127a18: 66
1128a3-16: 55
1128a22-32: 55
1128a25: 57

1128a25-32: 56
1128b4-9: 66
1135b1-25: 69
1136b22: 86
1137b13-27: 99
1139a20-b7: 76
1139b25-36: 105
1140b31-2: 106
1141a9: 104
1141b14-15: 99
1143a4-18: 92
1143a25-35: 105
1143a28-b5: 100
1144a24-9: 84
1144b1: 84
1153b12: 86
1153b14-21: 17
1154b33: 94
1169b33-5: 22
1172a22: 78
1172a23-26: 78
1173b24-31: 81
1174b20-3: 11
1174b33: 86
1175b24-8: 80
1176a17f.: 81
1176b27-a11: 22
1177a9-11: 16
1177b4-5: 22
1179b11: 79
1180b20-3: 106
1181b10-12: 105
4.6-7: 66

Eudemian Ethics

1249a18-21: 16

Parts of Animals

644a25-6: 106
645a7-15: 89
645a7-17: 21
645a10: 21

Metaphysics

980b21-5: 107
981b19-20: 22
982b12: 147
1038b12: 106
1038b22: 106

1077b23-4: 94
12.8: 45

Physics

218b21: 46
218b21-3: 32
219a3-4: 32
219a14-19: 32
219a22-b2: 32, 33
219b1-2: 32
220b15-32: 27, 31, 34
223b12-224a2: 45
265b8-11: 45
8.8-9 (e.g. 265b8-11): 45

Memory and Recollection

450a9-10: 32

Topics

108b1: 94
142b3: 45

On the Heavens

2.8: 45

On the Soul

413b23f.: 85
414b3: 85
415a16: 94
434a17-18: 107

Problems

956a11-14: 104
30.6: 88

History of Animals

597b23-6: 104
609b16: 104
631b9: 104

Posterior Analytics

71a1-b8: 105

General Index

act division 134
admiratio, admiration 152, 155, 160, 165, 167, 168
Aeschylus 30, 113, 132, 178, 185
aischrologia (obscene language) 54, 55
alazoneia (boastfulness) 66
Aldus Manutius 127
allegory 98, 208
Altham, J.E.J. 107
Altheim, F. 109, 113, 115, 116
alogon (contrary to reason) 147, 150, 151, 162
anagnôrisis (recognition) 1, 113, 115, 116, 117, 118, 119, 120, 147, 149, 150, 151, 152, 157, 158, 167, 199, 206, 208, 209, 210, 211
analêpsis (flashback) 38, 39, 41, 42
Anaxagoras 67
Andronicus 110, 122
Anicius 112
anthropological reading 198
anticipation, see *prolêpsis*
Antiphon 30, 31
Antonius 109
Apellicon 109, 110
Apollo 184
Apollodorus 114, 115
aporia 111
archetypes 198
Archilochus 58
Ariosto 162
Aristarchus 47
Aristias 113
Aristonikos 47
Aristophanes 51, 52, 54, 56, 67
Aristotle, authority of 203
Armstrong, J. 98
Arnott, G. 53
Ars Poetica 120, 128, 129, 140, 146, 176

askêsis (training) 77
Astydamas 114
Averroes 127

Bacon, F. 181
Baez, F. 52
Barnes, J. 52, 110
Bate, J. 158, 159
Beerbohm, M. 66
Beethoven, L. van 211
beginning, middle, end 33, 34, 35, 38, 42
Belfiore, E. 10, 11, 16, 46, 113, 169, 198
Ben, N. van der 68
Beni, Paolo 166
Bernays, J. 53, 54, 59, 64
Bignami, A. 26
Bishop, T.G. 168
Blair, H. 18
Bolofin, D. 27, 32, 33
bômolochia (buffoonery) 55, 56, 66
Boyle, N. 210
Brecht, B. 180-90
Bremer, J.M. 52
Brooks, P. 199
Budd, M. 91, 92, 93
Bywater, I. 38

Campagnolo, M. 52, 59
canon 204
Capasso, M. 58
Carneades the Academic 112
Castelvetro, L. 2, 3, 18, 88, 152, 153, 156, 162, 202
catharsis, see *katharsis*
Cato the elder 112
causality 202, 207, 208
character 179
characters 137
chorus 133

225

Cicero 109
citation of Greek tragedy 132
cognitive reading 198, 199, 205, 206, 208, 209
coherence 173, 179, 180, 190; coherent 174, 176, 178, 179, 198, 201
compassion or horror, see *eleos kai phobos*
consistency 129
context 175
Cooper, J.M. 73
Cooper, L. 53
Corneille, P. 180, 201
Cramer, J.A. 52, 59, 68
Crates of Mallos 63, 112
Cratinus 56, 57
Critolaus the Peripatetic 112, 123

D'Anna, G. 113
deception, double 119
decorum 129, 135, 139, 140, 141
Denoras, G. 145, 146, 154
dénouement 67, 163, 186, 210
deus ex machina 162
Diagoras of Melos 67
dianoia (reasoning) 100, 112, 179, 180
Dickie, M. 30
dictio, see *lexis*
Diderot, D. 208
Diogenes Laertius 109
Diogenes the Stoic 112
Diomedes 127
Dionysus 184
discovery 199
disunity 183
Dobbs, E.A. 169
Döblin, A. 193
Donini, P. 91
Dover, K.J. 67
drama: non-Aristotelian 181, 185; traditional 181, 183
Dryden, J. 141, 176, 180
Dupont-Roc, R. 37

earnestness, see *semnon, to*
eikones (images) 89
eikos (probability) 103
Einfühlung 181
eirôneia (understatement) 56, 66

ekplêksis (striking effect) 149, 150; *ekplêktikon, to* 145, 149
elements of tragedy, see *merê*
eleos kai phobos (pity and fear) 7, 8, 10, 11, 12, 16, 17, 20, 112, 119, 120, 137, 139, 140, 145, 149, 150, 152, 154, 155, 156, 157, 174, 178, 185, 186
Else, G. 2, 28, 29, 36, 37, 38, 95
empathy 182, 183
Empedocles 30
emphasis (innuendo) 57
enargeia 98, 166
energeia kat' aretên (virtuous activity) 15, 16
Ennius 112, 120
epic 161-7
episode 34, 36, 42, 43
Ercole II 134, 135
estrangement 182, 183
ethismos (habituation) 73, 74, 77, 78, 85
ethos (habit) 85, 120
êthos (character) 179, 180, 189
Eubulus 52
Eupolis 56
Euripides 30, 54, 58, 113, 121, 132, 135, 175, 178, 186
Euripidean tragedy 158
experience, transhistorical continuity of 204

fabula, see *muthos*
Fantham, E. 198
Faustus 110
Feagin, S.L. 19
Felsch, W. 28
flashback, see *analêpsis*
Fortenbaugh, W.W. 53, 110
fortune, good and bad 42, 43
Fossheim, H. 198
Fränkel, H. 29, 30
Frazer, J.G. 198
Freud, S. 204
Frye, N. 198

Gadamer, H.-G. 3, 197
Gallop, D. 89, 90
geloion, to (the laughable) 53, 55, 56, 58

Gesamtkunst 189; Gesamt-
  kunstwerk 188, 189
Giotto 173
Giraldi Cinzio, G.B. 127, 129, 130,
  131, 132, 133, 134, 135, 136, 138,
  139, 141, 154, 155, 157
gnômai (maxims) 101
gods 135, 173
Goethe, J.W. von 185, 186, 207, 208,
  209
Golden, L. 53, 65
Gomme, A.W. 67
Gomperz, T. 57
Gorgias 7
gravity 132
Gudemann, A. 26, 30, 90

habit, see *hexis*
habituation, see *ethismos*
Hall, E. 103
Halliwell, S. 2, 37, 38, 54, 113, 198,
  201, 205, 206
hamartia (error) 156, 199, 205
Hammerstaedt, J. 58
Hathaway, B. 151, 163
Heath, M. 37, 52, 53, 55, 198
hêdonê (pleasure) 7, 8, 10, 11, 181,
  186; cognitive pleasure 9-12
Hegel, G.W.F. 173, 183
Helitzer, M. 59
Henderson, J. 57
Hermann the German 127
hermeneutics 197
hero, character of 141
hexis (habit) 62, 73
historicism 198
hoia an genoito (what could/might
  happen) 101
Homer 36, 179
Horace 109, 128, 151, 176, 180, 190
Horace and Aristotle, synthesis of
  177
horror and pity, see *eleos kai phobos*
House, H. 65
huparkhein (subsist, underlie) 99
huponoia (innuendo) 55, 57
Hyginus 114, 115, 116, 117, 118, 119

Iamblichus 64, 65
imitation, see *mimêsis*

innuendo, see *huponoia, emphasis*
intrigue 119

Janko, R. 54, 137, 198
Javitch, D. 120, 146, 198
Johnson, S. 29
joke, see *skôptein*
de Jong, I. 42

Kassel, R. 2
katharsis (catharsis) 1, 12, 19, 52,
  53, 54, 57, 60, 61, 63, 64, 65, 139,
  145, 154, 155, 169, 174, 178, 181,
  183, 184, 185, 190, 199, 201, 204,
  206; Christian and didactic conception of 139; cathartic 150, 152
katholou, Aristotle's explanation of
  term, 97, 98
Kosman, A. 33

Lallot, J. 37
Lanza, D. 53, 65
learning 169, 199, 205
Lentulus Spinther 109
Leo, F. 113
Lesbonicus 111
Lessing 183, 207
lexis (verbalisation) 120, 179, 180
Liszt, F. 211
Lodge, D. 66
logos (story) 43, 85; *logoi* and *muthoi*
  88
loidoria (abuse) 57
Lombardelli, O. 166
Lombardi, B. 127
Lord, C. 14, 62
Lucas, D.W. 36, 150
Lucretius 153
Lucullus 110
Lycos 39, 40
lyric form 210
lyric poetry 173, 210
Lysiteles 111

majesty 134
*manthanein kai syllogizesthai ti
  hekaston* (to learn and reason
  what each thing is) 91, 92, 93, 94,
  95
Mariotto, I. 113

Marlowe, C. 168
Marsalis, W. 173
Martelli 133
mathêsis (teaching), *manthanein* 77, 89, 91, 92, 93, 94, 102
Matisse, H. 173
Mazzi, V. 127
Mazzoni, J. 160
megaloprepeia (grandeur) 26, 36
megethos (magnitude) 25, 26, 31, 33, 34, 42, 43
mêkos (length) 25, 26, 31, 33, 43
melopoiia (song-writing) 174, 179
Menander 54
merê (elements) of tragedy 174, 175, 179, 180, 189
messenger speech 39, 40, 41
Mesturini, A.M. 53, 65
metabasis (change) 27, 158
metabolê, *metaballein* (change) 27, 34
metaphor 200
Mette, H.J. 113
miaros (shocking) 156
Milo of Croton 67
mimêsis, mimetic 1, 8, 9, 10, 16, 17, 25, 35, 37, 38, 41, 43, 54, 57, 59, 60, 62, 63, 64, 73, 74, 84, 87, 90, 94, 96, 100, 102, 103, 145, 147, 148, 161, 163, 175, 176, 199, 205, 206; means of 130; objects of 130; modes of 130; anti-mimetic 145
Minsaas, K. 198
Minturno, A. 154, 156, 157
Montaigne, M. 1, 3
moral effects of poetry 151
Moraux, P. 110
Moriarty, M. 176
mousikê (music) 62
Mussato, A. 132
muthos (plot) 9, 10, 26, 27, 31, 34, 35, 36, 37, 42, 56, 67, 98, 99, 101, 111, 112, 113, 120, 129, 130, 133, 134 (plot, divided), 146, 147, 150, 152 (complex), 153, 156, 157, 161 (plot-structure), 166, 174, 175, 176, 177, 179, 180, 187, 188, 189, 202, 206, 207, 209, 210, 211
myth, see *muthos*

Nachleben 197

narrative, narrator 37, 39, 41, 42
necessity 1, 31, 33, 34, 101, 146, 164
neoclassicism 203
Nesselrath, H.-G. 53
new historicism 197
Nietzsche, F. 183, 184, 185, 186, 189, 190
Nünlist, R. 42

Oliver, J. 173
Olson, S.D. 42
opsis (spectacle) 179, 180, 189
order 129
Ovid 136, 158

Pacuvius 109-25
paradeigmata (examples) 101
parts: quantitative 130; qualitative 130
Patrizi, F. 145, 146
Pauson 58
Pazzi, A. 2, 3, 127, 133
peripeteia (reversal) 113, 116, 118, 119, 120, 147, 148, 151, 152, 156, 157, 167, 199
Pfister, M. 29
philanthrôpon (moral sense) 148, 149
Philemon 111
Philodemus 54, 57
phronêsis (practical wisdom), *phronimos* 62, 92, 99, 100
Pigna, G.B. 137, 141
pity and fear, see *eleos kai phobos*
Plato 151
plausibility 148, 156
Plautus 111, 132
pleasure, see *hêdonê*
plot, plot-structure, see *muthos*
Plutarch 109, 155
poetics, Horatian 140
Polybius 112, 123
practical wisdom, see *phrônesis*
Praxiphanes of Mytilene 57
praxis (action) 11, 33, 37, 43, 53, 73, 97, 119, 145, 148, 163, 176, 202; actions, simultaneous 42
probability 1, 31, 33, 34, 101, 146, 156, 164
Proclus 64
prohairêsis (moral decision) 119

prolêpsis (anticipation) 38
prosody 137, 140
protagonist 129, 134, 135, 137, 141
Protagoras 67
psychoanalytic reading 198, 206

Quintilian 132

Racine, J. 204
Rapin, R. 176-80, 186, 190
'reasoning', see *dianoia*
reception 197, 201, 202
recognition, see *anagnôrisis*
recognition and intrigue
   (*mechanema*) 119
Rengakos, A. 39, 41, 42
reversal, see *peripeteia*
rhyme 140
Ribbeck, O. 113
Riccoboni, A. 161
Richelieu, Cardinal 180
Ricoeur, P. 199
rituals 173, 198
Robortello, F. 127, 152, 202
Ross, Sir D. 1
Rucellai, G. 133
rules 200, 203, 204
Rymer, T. 176, 179

Sbordone, F. 57
Scaliger, J.C. 3
Schelling, F. 184
Schenkeveld, D. 53
Schiller, F. 186, 207
Schlegel, A. 207
scholiasts, Homeric 41
Schrier, O. 1, 25
Schubert, F. 211
Schumann, R. 211
Scipio 112
Segni, B. 128
sêmeion (sign) 89
semnon, to (earnestness) 55, 56
Seneca 120, 132, 133
Senecan tragedy 158
Shakespeare, W. 145, 152, 153, 157,
   167, 168, 204
Sharpe, T. 66
Shepherd, G. 155
Sherman, N. 62

Sidney, P. 152, 153, 155, 163, 164,
   165, 166
Sifakis, G.M. 59
Silk, M.S. 198
skôptein (joke) 56
Solmsen, F. 109, 119
song-writing, see *melopoiia*
Sophocles 30, 58, 118, 132, 133, 184
Sottomayor, A. 52
spectacle/ visual design, see *opsis*
Spenser, E. 162
Speroni, S. 130, 133, 136, 137, 138,
   141
Spingarn, J. 131
Spintharos 114
Starkie, W.M. 59
Ste Croix, G.E.M. de, 67
Steiner, G. 3
story, see *logos*
Strabo 109
Suetonius 111
Sulla 109
sullogismos (reasoning) 89
sunesis (discernment) 92, 93, 99, 100
sunthesis tôn pragmatôn (organisa-
   tion of events) 175
sustasis tôn pragmatôn (structure of
   events) 175
Sutton, D. 53, 65

Taplin, O. 28, 112
Tasso 136, 152, 160, 161, 162, 163,
   165, 166
taste and ideology 176
tautology 67
Tchaikovsky, P. 211
teaching, see *mathêsis*
Teichmüller, G. 28
teichoscopic report 39, 40
tekhnê (skill) 93; *graphikê* 89;
   plastikê 89
tekhnitai (theatre companies) 112
telos (end) 175, 177, 179
Terence 132
terms, Aristotelian 199; authentic
   meaning of 200
terror and pity, see *eleos kai phobos*
thauma (wonder) 169; *thaumasmos*
   150; *thaumaston, to* 145-71;
   thaumazein 94, 147

theatre: epic 181, 182, 183; dramatic
  182
Theophrastus 57, 111
Thomas, A. 211
time 42; Aristotle's views of 27
Todd, O.J. 29
Tractatus Coislinianus 51-71
tradition 198
tragic flaw 199
tragic hero 177; middlingly good 137,
  138, 139, 154, 163, 165; exemplary 163; of extraordinary
  stature 164
training, see *askêsis*
Trissino, G.G. 130, 133, 136, 137, 160
Tyrannio 110

unexpected, the 202, 206
unity 36, 129, 183, 188; of action
  141, 179; of place 179; of time 179
universals 95, 96, 98, 99, 100, 101,
  102; mimesis of 96, 97, 98
utile et dulce 146, 153, 178

Valla, G. 2, 3, 127
Valsa, M. 113
Vega, M.J. 201
verbalisation, see *lexis*
Verfremdung 181, 182, 183
verisimilitude, verisimility 141, 162,
  163, 166, 179
Verschmelzung 189
versification 140, 141
Vida, M. 128
Virgil 128, 162, 163
Vittori 202

Wagner, R. 185, 189
Warmington, E.H. 113
Weinberg, B. 131, 146, 161
Wolf, H. 211
wonder 145-71; as an independent
  tragic feeling 152; distinctive function of in epic 161

Xenophon 163

Zielinski, T. 41